T0368653

Waves
Of
News

Carolyn Gerdink Cavolt

An Entertaining News Book

authorHOUSE®

AuthorHouse™
1663 Liberty Drive, Suite 200
Bloomington, IN 47403
www.authorhouse.com
Phone: 1-800-839-8640

©2009 Carolyn Gerdink Cavolt. All rights reserved.

No part of this book may be reproduced, stored in a retrieval system, or transmitted by any means without the written permission of the author.

First published by AuthorHouse 2/5/2009

ISBN: 978-1-4389-5343-4 (sc)

Printed in the United States of America
Bloomington, Indiana

This book is printed on acid-free paper.

Forward

My idea for the book happened because I like to read the morning newspaper. I always found so many interesting articles and I like to share with people. So I decided to rewrite the articles by shortening them, give recognition to the original author and add my thoughts. People are so busy these days, I wanted to share the information in an easy to read book. Hopefully some will use the "Waves of News" for home schooling and to continuously reread the book.

Our country is in a precarious position. People need easily available information quickly. There is so much illegal immigration information that I put it together so readers can find it quickly in this book and keep rereading it. I realize that some people want more and more illegals in our country to gain citizenship. I hope they read the results and then make their decisions.

Also, this book is useful as a gift. Give it to a friend or relative so they'll have a record of what happened in their life during the time of the articles. Combine it with their own photo albums. Their own life in pictures with stories about the country. This is the gift that keeps giving useful information.

Make your own "Waves of News." Subscribe to your local morning paper, cut out the articles you like, put them in a scrapbook to present to your child, grandchild, or keep for yourself.

By doing so you'll also help save daily newspapers because many are closing. I believe we truly need the daily newspaper.

Carolyn Gerdink Cavolt
    (CGC)

    Knick Knacks are little bits of information. They are used throughout this book.

    All the typing and preparations for the printing of this book were done by Paul E. Cavolt. All the pictures in this book, unless otherwise noted, are by Cavolts with the majority by Paul E. Cavolt

CONTENTS

Freedom

Gifts

Government

Words

ANCHOR

BABIES

$6 Billion a Year for Mexican Anchor Babies?

This information is from a special report by Andy Selepak, "Accuracy in Media", June 5 2007. http://www.aim.org/special-report/print/6-billion-a-year-mexican-anchor-babies/

Go to the web site to get the **full report** or go to Accuracy in Media.

Babies born to illegal aliens in the United States get ***AUTOMATIC*** United States Citizenship! This is called birthright citizenship. For illegal aliens birthing a child in the United States becomes the Golden Ticket to staying here in the United States. This child is called an Anchor baby. These children, anchor babies, become eligible to sponsor for legal immigration MOST of their relatives, including their illegal-alien mothers. They can do this when they turn 21 years of age. They then become the U.S. anchor for an extended immigrant family.

Birthright citizenship was never intended to be the law of the land. It is a flawed interpretation of the 14th. Amendment, but it accounts for more than 380,000 children EACH year born to illegal alien mothers. But this figure could be low! The actual number of illegal aliens in the United States could be as high as 20 million! So using this number and 33 births per 1,000 of the foreign born population this would double "FAIR'S" estimate to 574,000 to 726,00 anchor babies born in the United States each year. Having an anchor baby does not prevent the illegal parents from being deported but it rarely happens. The real solution is for the illegal alien parents to return to their native countries with their children to avoid the potential deportation "…is there even one American standing in the way of an alien family leaving intact to return to its Country of origin? Some foreigners would rather be here in the United States illegally than back home preserving their families.

Exploiting America
According to "Numbers USA", thousands of pregnant women who are about to deliver come to the United States each year from South Korea to Mexico so that they can give birth on U.S. soil. They may come on legal travel visas or come illegally. The baby gets a United States birth certificate and a passport and their future link to this country is established and irreversible.

Also these illegals that enter have little or no health insurance. All UNINSURED people, regardless of citizenship receive medical care in hospital emergency rooms under the "Emergency Medical Treatment and Active Labor Act of 1985 (EMTALA). The act requires hospitals to treat any patient that enters an emergency room for "emergency care," a cough to drug addiction to gunshot wound to depression to being HIV-positive. The act requires emergency rooms to treat anyone that comes in, but does not require patients to pay for their care.

2

The costs are passed on to the American taxpayers and those with health insurance through rising premiums. Some hospitals can't afford the care for the illegals. In 2001 the average cost of having a baby in the United States ranged from $6,000 to $8,000 for a normal vaginal delivery and $10,000 to $12,000 for a cesarean birth. If the $8,000 cost is used for 2007 births and all 380,000 babies born to illegal aliens in the United States all had normal deliveries, this would cost hospitals around the country approximately
$3 billion. But if 726,000 anchor babies are born in the United States each year, the cost rises to nearly $6 billion. Check the Dr. Spock website, Marjorie Greenfield, M.D.

If complications occur with the pregnancy or if there is a premature birth and the child needs to be admitted into a Neonatal Intensive Care Unit, the cost rises by tens of thousands of dollars.

Illegal alien mothers are not the only ones benefiting. There are reports that some pregnant Mexicans are entering the United States for the sole purpose of giving birth and having the cost paid for by Americans. A University of California survey found that of new Hispanic mothers in California border hospitals, 15% had crossed the border specifically to give birth.

The 14th. Amendment to the United States Constitution original intent was to give former slaves citizenship after the Civil War. Scholars conclude that the authors of the 14th Amendment did **NOT** want to grant citizenship to every person who happened to be born on United States soil. It is a misinterpretation. Without a ruling by the Supreme Court, OR Congressional action to end the practice, citizenship will continue to be given to everyone born in the United States.

Birthright citizenship has almost ended in the industrial world. In 2004, Ireland ended it. In 1981, the United Kingdom, which has a growing Muslim and Southeast Asian population ended it except, due to immigration pressure, it restricted birthright citizenship to requiring that one parent be a legal resident.

Representative Nathan Deal, Republican-Georgia, introduced H.R. 1940, the Birthright Citizenship Act of 2007. On April 19, 2007 the bill was referred to the House Committee on the Judiciary. The bill has only 46 co-sponsors in the United States House. No reform of the immigration system will be complete without the provision of the Nathan Deal bill becoming law. BUT the media, led by illegal alien-supporting **Washington Post,** will fight any such change every step of the way.

ANIMALS

The Budweiser Clydesdales

The low down on Clydesdales:

1. They stand 6 feet tall.
2. Weigh a ton.
3. A shoe is 20 inches of steel=8 feet per horse.
4. They eat about 50 pounds of hay daily.
5. Eat 20 quarts of grain daily.
6. Drink 30 to 40 gallons of water per day.
7. They were 150-pound babies who needed their mother to produce 55 pounds of milk daily.
8. A team is 8 horses.
9. There are 6 teams of Clydesdales in the country, equals 48 horses.
10. Between exhibitions at an event the horses stay in the barns.
11. Matt Anderson, 25, is part of an 8 man team who takes his group from its Sea World headquarters in San Diego to events throughout California from May through October, 6 months.
12. Matt says the personality of the Clydesdales are like a professional football team. The 2 lead horses are like star quarterbacks or receivers; they're a bit smaller than the others, high strung and egotistical. They know they're at the front of the parade and their personalities reflect the glory. They have attitude, Matt says.
13. The largest horses that do the heavy lifting of starting and stopping the wagon are like linemen in the trenches seeking no fame.
14. Visitors at the California Mid-State Fair in Paso Robles have the opportunity to see the behemoths pulling the Budweiser beer wagon at the midway.

Information from an article in "The Tribune", San Luis Obispo County, California, July 28, 2007, by Bill Moren, bmoren@thetribunenews.com

My thoughts – God knows how to make huge beautiful horses! Maybe some children would like to do Matt's job someday. There are six teams (6 x 8 = 48 horses) of horses who need 8 caretakers for each team. (8 x 6 = 48 caretakers). What an outstanding job that would be for a horse lover!!! I wonder how old they are when they retire. What is their lifespan? We saw them in Pismo Beach in July 2007! They are Showstoppers.

The Budweiser Clydesdales

The Clam Shells around Pismo Beach are painted for
Holidays. This one is ready for Labor Day.

Jaws is Back

Be cautious when taking a dip in local waters of the Pacific Ocean. Shark attacks are extremely rare but remember they are possible. There are fewer than 100 fatal shark attacks reported from around the world in a year.

Three years ago in August a woman was killed by a great white shark while swimming at Avila Beach on the Central Coast. A year later a great white shark took a bite out of a young surfer's board off Pismo Beach. A month later a great white shark was observed cruising off Morro Bay's south jetty. This month, seven otters have been chomped on by a great white. There was a shark sighting at Avila Beach. All these cities are on the Central Coast of California.

Scientists have known for years that at least one great white lives off Point Buchon near Diablo Canyon where the nuclear plant is located. It's an ideal environment, a huge concentration of seals and sea lions. Sharks also cruise beyond their immediate haunts.

To lessen the odds of an attack:
Do not swim with seals or in waters filled with baitfish.
Avoid the water if you are bleeding, even a little bit.
Do not swim at dusk or dawn, a favorite feeding time for sharks.
Stay out of water if a fishing boat is nearby.
Swim in a group.
Do not wear metal or jewelry.

If a shark has an interest in you, "playing dead" will not help.

George Burgess of the International Shark Attack File, an organization that studies sharks, skates and rays, says, "be as aggressive as you are able. Pound the shark in any way possible. Try to claw at the eyes and gill openings, two very sensitive areas."

Information from the Editorial opinion of the Tribune, published August 30, 2006, in "The Tribune", San Luis Obispo County, California.

My thoughts – These few words of caution might save a life. I only know one person who surfs the Central Coast. He isn't fearful. He is Bob Pull. These Central Coast Cities of Pismo Beach, Avila Beach, are about 1½ hours north of Santa Barbara, California and Morro Bay is 2 hours.

A Shark!

According to the International Shark Attack file --- a project at the Florida Museum of Natural History that tracks shark attack statistics --- the odds of being attacked by a shark are 1 in 11.5 million and the likelihood of being killed are less than 1 in 264.1 million.

There have been 4 Central Coast of California shark sightings this year (through September 2007).

Excerpts from and article by Sona Patel, spatel@thetribunenews.com published in "The Tribune", San Luis Obispo county. California, October 1, 2007.

My thoughts – After reading those statistics I guess swimmers and surfers will not be wearing body armor. We had 2 sons who were surfers in high school and one of them swam in oceans of the world during his career of 28 years as a Navy Seal.

The Venerable California Academy of Sciences in San Francisco

On January 7, 2008, this museum will begin transferring its collection on Howard Street in downtown San Francisco into a new $484 million home in Golden Gate Park.

This will be a reference library of life on earth:
   A. 2 million fish preserved in jars of alcohol,
   B. more than 700,000 pin-mounted butter flies and moths,
   C. 3 million dead beetles,
   D. Giant clams, Elephant tusks,
   E. Dinosaur bones,
   F. Meteorites and
   G. Millions of pressed flowers and plants.

"These are treasures. And we are handling them like they are treasures," said John McCosker, senior curator of aquatic biology.

Information from an article in "The Tribune", San Luis Obispo County, California, January 6, 2008, by Tribune wire services.

My thoughts – This must be the place for parents to take their home-schooled children. I hope they take the grandparents also! I want to go! I want to see the giant clams, elephant tusks and meteorites.

A Rogue Sea Lion

In San Francisco, California, a California sea lion has bitten at least 14 people and chased 10 others out of the water at a public park's lagoon in San Francisco.

The area is now closed to swimmers until the testy marine mammal has moved on. Experts say the rogue sea lion could be protecting his harem of mates or might have brain damage from algae! The veterinarian said the sea lion might soon leave the area and go North to Washington State and Oregon.

Associated Press-November 17, 2006
Published in "The Tribune", San Luis Obispo County, California

My thoughts – Is anyone sending a warning to Washington and Oregon? Is this like dumping patients on the streets when the hospital has no address for them, which has happened! Here we come ready or not. How many sea lions in a harem?

06/02/2007

9

Your Pet Pictures

David Sutton's photographic studio is in Evanston, Illinois. Sutton's skills are on display in his 7th annual Dog Days Calendar. He has donated 10,000 copies to 25 local animal welfare organizations to sell to raise funds. A complete list is at www.suttonstudios.com. Here are his suggestions for photographing your pet.

    1. Find a good location, in a home or in a yard. Avoid a cluttered background.

    2. Spend an hour on the photos; take a break after fifteen minutes, which is about as long as animals will cooperate.

    3. Work at the animal's eye level, for a more compelling photo.

    4. Get your pet to look directly at the lens. You have to be interesting which can be a challenge for a dog that lives with you. When you want the dog to look right at the camera, say, "Do you want…." Almost every dog responds to this phrase. Sutton doesn't even have to finish it. That's good for saying at least 2 to 3 times before it wears out. Be ready, have your camera focused and the dog in the viewfinder before you say it.

    5. Turn off the flash if you can and use natural light. You'll find more favorable lighting early in the day or late afternoon.

    6. If you use the flash, try to move it to one side so you're not shooting directly at the animal, which results in big "green saucer eyes." If you're using film, do at least a roll. Digitally, 30 to 50 shots. "Throw most of the film shots away" Sutton says.

Pick one or two you really love, get a really big print made.

Excerpted from an article by William Hageman, Chicago Tribune.
Published in "The Tribune", San Luis Obispo County, California, December 19,2006.

10

A 58-Pound Horse

Thumbelina, a dwarf miniature horse, weighs 58 pounds, is 17 ½ inches tall and is 6 years old. She is considered by the Guinness World Records book to be the world's smallest horse. Her mother lives at the family "Goose Creek Farms" in Missouri.

She travels to 9 states in a custom RV where the walls are padded and she sleeps in the master bedroom. Her legs are slightly crooked so she wears special orthotic hoof covers. She has no other health problems.

She appears at benefits for the nonprofit Equine Alliance, which is a program for kids and teens with special needs and at-risk backgrounds. The Equine Alliance also works with horses that have been rescued from livestock auctions and destined for slaughter. Her prowess as a moneymaker benefits the charities and children's hospitals she visits.

Michael Goessling, her manager, whose parents own Goose Creek Farms in Missouri, is where Thumbelina's mother lives and where the little horse was born. Michael says Thumbelina is fearless, she thinks she's huge.

Information from an article in "the Tribune", San Luis Obispo County, California, by Leah Etling, letling@thetribune.com published August 11, 2007.

My thoughts – Thumbelina is only 6 ½ inches taller than a sheet of 11' paper. She spends her life doing good works for children and other horses through all The money she raises.

Knick - Knack

Bill O'Reilly said on his TV show "The Factor", April 1, 2008 that 34 million Americans have exotic animals for pets.

Ask This Guy!

Smuggled Parrots and Parakeets Deported

"They were caught coming into the United States illegally from Mexico, sedated and hidden under blankets or in duffel bags. 149 parrots and parakeets seized from smugglers were sent home! The neon-green birds had been held in quarantine for up to 18 months on U.S. soil at San Diego Otay Mesa border crossing were handed over in cages to Mexican authorities. If veterinarians determine they cannot survive in the wild they will be kept for breeding purposes, otherwise they will be returned to native habitats in Southern Mexico. Talking parrots – some cawing in Spanish or calling for "Lolita" can be sold for $1,000 each."

"There is a thriving black market for pet birds due to strict quarantine rules, due to outbreaks of exotic Newcastle disease in California," authorities say.

"A woman stopped at San Diego's San Ysidro border crossing faces up to 5 years in prison and $250,000 in fines after pleading guilty to bringing in 47 Amazon parrots and half-moon Conures without permits. Both species are protected by international trade restrictions on endangered animals."

Another man caught transporting 10 baby Amazon parrots faces up to a year in prison if he is convicted of violating wild importation rules.

"Smugglers quiet birds with sedatives to stop them from talking or moving in transit, usually by spiking foods, sometimes with tequila."

This is the Black Market said an assistant special agent in charge of U.S. Immigration and Customs Enforcement in San Diego.

"This is all about money," said Assistant U.S. Attorney Anne Perry, whose prosecution of animal-smuggling cases has earned her the nickname "Bird Lady." "It's all about getting around the quarantine, which can be very expensive."

Information from an article by Allison Hoffman, Associated Press, published in "The Tribune", San Luis Obispo County, California, August 23, 2007.

My thoughts – This is another reason why we must have secured, fenced and patrolled borders. I wonder how many illegal alien parrots and parakeets are living in the United States! Also does the U.S. government charge the Mexican Government for the care and feeding and quarantining for up to 18 months of all these birds? I doubt it, because Americans are simply too generous my dear! Why can't the birds stay here so they can be sold to recover cost of their care, of trying court cases and imprisoning the guilty smugglers!

Lost for 45 Days

After 45 days being on the lam, Chipper, a 3-year-old Nova Scotia duck-tolling retriever, found his way home. The dog's owner said Chipper is normally a good listener but he took off on a walk near Kenai Golf Course on December 12. Chipper, looking the worse for wear, returned home January 29 almost to the disbelief of his family. Only Chipper knows where he was.

Information from the Tribune wire services, February 18, 2007, in "The Tribune", San Luis Obispo County, California.

My thoughts – Chipper had his fling and decided home was where he wanted to be.

Komodo Dragons-Virgin Birth

1. Flora is now the busy mother of five without ever having touched a male dragon.
2. Scientists say the five Komodo dragons are the product of a virgin birth.
3. The shells began cracking; a Komodo dragon emerged between 16 and 18 inches long, weighed between 3 ½ and 4 ½ ounces.
4. They eat crickets and locusts.
5. When they grow up, keep them out of the barnyard. They can grow to be 10 feet long and weigh about 300 pounds.
6. They'll be capable of eating a whole pig or deer at one sitting, hooves and all!
7. About 70 reptile species including snakes and lizards are known to reproduce asexually in a process known as parthenogenesis. Flora's and another Komodo dragon at the London Zoo in April 2006, are the first documented in Komodo dragon births documented as a virginal conception.

Information from an associated Press article Chester, England, published January 25, 2007 in "the Tribune", San Luis Obispo County, California.

My thoughts – Didn't a Komodo dragon bite Sharon Stone's then husband in the foot several years ago while they were visiting a zoo? I believe he was Phil Bronstein, publisher of the San Francisco Chronicle.

13

Tokyo, Japan

Japan's first nursing home for dogs comes with 24 hours monitoring by veterinarians and puppies to play with the aging dogs to help keep them fit, said a pet products company spokesperson.

Owners pay $800 a month to keep their dogs at the Soladi Care Home. The home can accept 20 dogs at a time and will give them specially fortified food.

> Information from an article published in "The Tribune" San Luis Obispo County, California, June 14, 2007, Associated Press.

> My thoughts – Why? I always have my dogs at home while they are growing older. I would rather be at home also while I am aging.

> I think the dogs would die faster being away from home.

Own a Cat – Live Longer

If you don't own a cat you're 30 to 40% more likely to die of cardiovascular disease than those who do. This doesn't seem to be true for dog owners.

Dr. Adnan Quershi, a stroke expert at the University of Minnesota with his team studied a group of 4,435 people who had answered questionnaires about pet ownership. He thinks NOW he will become a cat owner.

> Information from an article by Maura Lerner, Star Tribune, Minneapolis, Minnesota, in "The Tribune", San Luis Obispo county, California, January 22, 2008.

> My thoughts – I believe it! We jointly owned Kitty-Kitty with our son, Steven, for almost 18 years. He lived with Steven in his homes. He lived with us in four houses in California; 1 in Hillsborough, 2 in Pebble Beach, and finally in Roseville, where he died at age18. I held him in my arms in a lounge chair for the last 24 hours of his life. He was one of my Faithful Friends Forever (FFF)! I need him now. He was a big black 18 # cat.

> He let our 6 grand children pick him up and carry him around. Our big Irish Setter thought he was "Big Red" when he chased Kitty-Kitty up a tree, until finally Kitty-Kitty stopped running and stood his ground. It worked!

> We inherited the Irish Setter, Jeremy, when our fourth child, Peter, went to a Pet store one Sunday to buy a bird, something to talk with. He didn't get a talking bird but he came home with a 6 week old little Irish Setter whom we inherited when he married two years later. That's another book length story.

14

Mousers

Los Angeles – Prowlers at police stations scare the enemy. They're doing their jobs keeping the rodents in check. They are feral cats that now have a home and a job. They don't usually kill the rats and mice but leave their scent so the rodents decide to leave. Their reputation as exterminators grew after they were introduced to the parking lot of Wilshire Division almost 6 years ago.

Give thanks to the Los Angeles based animal advocacy and rescue group, "The Working Cats" program of "Voice for the Animals". These feral cats would have faced death in shelters or on the streets.

> Information from an article in "The Tribune", San Luis Obispo County, California, December 31, 2007, "Tribune wire services."

> My thoughts – Someone sure had a bright idea! There's a place for almost every creature on earth!

Uno, the Best in Show, Beagle

New York, N.Y. ------"Uno" became the first Beagle to win "best in show" at the Westminster Kennel Club. Madison Square Garden had a sold-out crowd. "Uno", almost a 3 year old, demonstrated his other title noisiest in show. He drew a standing ovation.

A beagle had never won in the 100 times Westminster picked a winner. The beagle has been consistently listed among America's most popular breeds for nearly 100 years.

Uno beat out 2 perfect poodles, a top Sealyham terrier, a Weimaraner, a Australian Shepard and a Akita.

> Information from an article from the, "Associated Press", in "The Tribune", San Luis Obispo County, California, February 13, 2008.

> MY thoughts – Hooray for the beagle and Snoopy too! Snoopy is one of my favorite comic strips.

Watch Your Cat!

A 2-year old cat named Meatloaf had a 3-week ride from Pompano Beach, Florida to Phoenix, Arizona in a storage container. The owner of Meatloaf was loading the container in Florida for a move to Phoenix. The container was in a Florida warehouse and on a semi-trailer before it was delivered to a Phoenix facility. A worker heard the hungry and thirsty cat meowing inside the container.

Luckily, Meatloaf's owners had posted signs in their neighborhood and when the Humane Society called, the manager remembered the signs. Officials will give Meatloaf time to recover before flying him home.

> Information from an Associated Press article February 22, 2008, in "The Tribune", San Luis Obispo County, California.

> My thoughts – I believe it is a miracle that Meatloaf survived. God gave cats a loud meow for this very reason. So every time you hear a loud meow think of Meatloaf and why he lives today. God knew what he was doing! He also gives babies a loud cry.

Heat Wave May Cost $1 Billion

Fresno, California -16,500 cows died after two weeks of triple digit temperatures in California in July 2006.

California dairy operators asked for federal disaster assistance.

The heat disrupted breeding of animals and cut milk production particularly in the central San Joaquin Valley, CA.

> Information from an article published in "The Tribune", San Luis Obispo County, California, August 1, 2006.

16

World's Largest Animals

Whale watchers seeking a glimpse of the world's largest animals this summer will have the best chances off the coast of Orange and San Diego Counties and Northern Baja, California, according to Marine biologists. Blue whales have in recent years come to favor Southern California waters. Capable of traveling 100 miles a day, the blue whales migrate north each summer from their winter grounds off Central America.

Their worldwide population is estimated at 10,000 but before whaling, scientists say as many as 300,000 swam the world's oceans. In the summer of 2006, a boat Captain sighted and logged 440 blue whales in Southern California. He is the owner of Captain Dave's Dolphin Safari in Dana Point.

> Article in "The Tribune", San Luis Obispo County, California, by Tony Barboza, Los Angels Times, July 29, 2007.

> My thoughts – Now you know where to go to sight the blue whales. Will you be there in the summer of 2009 and will they? Call Captain Dave.

09/09/2007

BUSINESS

Pesos for Pizzas

Pizza Patron, a Dallas based pizza chain is accepting pesos at its 59 stores in Texas, Colorado, Arizona, California and Nevada (5 states). The company's clientele is 60% Hispanic. The company has received thousands of angry e-mails and even death threats.

According to market experts, Fortune 500 Companies spend more than $2 Billion per year on advertising for a shot at nearly $800 Billion in annual Hispanic spending power.

Others worry about the dissolving of our borders and the creation of a free-trade region of America stretching from Alaska to Chile. U.S. Commerce Secretary Carlos Gutierrez, Cuban-born Gutierrez, who earned praise as the youngest CEO in the history of Kellogg Company before joining the Bush Administration in 2005, described a free-trade zone of the America's as "A vision that will one day come to be."

Gutierrez acknowledges that there is something called the "Security and Prosperity Partnership of North America." It involves Canada, the United States and Mexico and the goal is to improve the North American Free Trade Agreement.

According to the Associated Press, many responses read like this: "This is the United States of America, not the United States of Mexico. Quit catering to the damn illegal Mexicans."

The writer of this story, Ruben Navarrette Jr., believes that what bothers those against illegal aliens is the fear that people are no longer catering to him – or those who look like him. That's what drives so much of the debate over illegal immigration. It's cultural displacement, or what the U.S. commerce secretary terms "xenophobic nationalism."

> Information from article by Ruben Navarrette Jr., "The Desert Sun," Southern California Desert Cities, published January 17, 2007.

> My thoughts – Personally I'm against using pesos in the United States of America! We must use the currency of America not of another country, if not, what next? We must object to what is happening in America. If you come to America abide by the laws and rules or leave.

On The Job Wardrobe

Your office threads speak volumes about your personality, says a survey by THELADDERS.com, an online recruiting resource. The Ladders.com surveyed 2,245 executives during August.

The top fashion faux pas: too revealing clothes
flip-flops
jeans
sleeveless shirts

More traditionally dressed employees, the button down types, are perceived as more senior level, said 70% of survey executives.

60% said they are taken more seriously. Button-up employees are considered less creative and less fun than their casually dressed counterparts.

16% said the suit and tie employees come across as rigid.

Information from an article in "The Tribune", San Luis Obispo County, California, Associated Press, September 16, 2006.

My thoughts – I am so happy to hear that revealing clothing, flip-flops, jeans and sleeveless shirts are fashion no-nos! Many Americans dress like they just stepped out of a ragbag. I call this "Ragbag Couture." This is clothing that is ready for the ragbag.

I believe the outfits of people on the streets of America get worse every year. There seems to be a contest – "Who can be the ugliest and sloppiest." There is no pride in appearance.

Rite Aid Corporation, the Nation's 3rd. Largest Drugstore Chain

Harrisburg, Pennsylvania – They will close 28 unprofitable stores in the Las Vegas, Nevada area. Some of the stores were part of the Thrifty Payless chain that Rite Aid acquired in 1997. The company is selling the patient prescription files to Walgreen Company.

Information from an article in "The Tribune", San Luis Obispo County, California, January 5, 2008.

My thoughts – I'm surprised as I thought Las Vegas was such a booming area. Unprofitable stores can happen to anyone so don't feel so bad if your one store closed!

Millionaires

10 million people in the world as of 2007 have at least $1 million in assets. Their average wealth was more than $4 million, the highest it has ever been.

The wealthy ranks are growing fastest in India, China and Brazil.

Information from an Associated Press article in "The Tribune", San Luis Obispo County, California, June 25, 2008.

My thoughts – Why isn't America listed among the fastest growing? Maybe because we buy the products from these countries! It's time America starts producing again! Where are the intelligent, moral people that should be running for elected offices, such as Congress and the President of the United States of America???

We need experienced, smart business people to lead our country and make America # 1 again. We need fearless leaders!

Knick – Knack

Bill Gates is the worlds 3rd richest person. His company, Microsoft, in 2007 employed 957 H1B visa people from other countries. He wants more foreigners in America to work for American companies. The United States Government now issues 65,000 H1B visas.

Heard on TV, March 12, 2008.

My thoughts – What's wrong with American workers working in America, Mr. Gates! Many Americans need jobs! Would you have to pay them a little more money??? You made your money in America, how about letting Americans make some money here also, Mr. Gates!

Pint-Sized Protocol

Diane Diehl, the creator of "Petite Protocol" that teaches children about conduct takes place at the Hotel Bel-Air in Los Angeles.

1. 4 times a year
2. half-day seminar
3. Ages 6 to 12, boys and girls
4. ends with a formal luncheon
5. $250 per child
6. class size is 15
7. 701 Stone Canyon Road
   310-207-5175.

"We're teaching a return to graciousness," says Diane Diehl, the correct telephone etiquette, how to write thank you notes.

The children dress in their best outfits and dine on gourmet French food at the formal luncheon.

> Information from an article by Jennifer Rachel Shapell
> Town and Country magazine-September 2006.

Matchbox Toys

Jack Odell, 87, died July 7, 2007 in London. He was born into a poor family in North London on March 19, 1920. He was a self-trained engineer whose toy invention led to Matchbox Toys.

His daughter's mischievous habit of taking spiders to school in a matchbox prompted him to make her a tiny steamroller as a substitute, which led to Matchbox Toys, maker of 3 billion Lilliputian Vehicles in 12,000 models. The steamroller made of brass and painted shiny red and green satisfied his daughter Anne and so impressed her friends that he raced to meet their demand.

Josh Walsh, his son-in-law, said Odell had had Parkinson's disease.

> Article in "The Tribune" San Luis Obispo County, California, Tribune Wire Service, July 17, 2007
>
> My thoughts – I wish I had known him.

Knick – knack

General Electric does business with Iran. Jeffery Immelt is the CEO of General Electric.

Do not do business with G. E. Iran insurgents have killed United States troops in Iraq.

> Heard on Bill O'Reilly TV show "The Factor" April 17, 2008.

> My thoughts – Say no to General Electric! Do not buy G.E. products. American citizens who love their country must do everything they can to help America.

Knick Knack

Wish you were a CEO?

2 chief executive officers failed to increase their company's share prices but left with severance packages of $200 million or more.

> From an article in "The Tribune", San Luis Obispo County, California, September 29, 2007.

Knick-Knack

Brazil is the world's largest producer of oranges.

> Heard on Fox News, April 13, 2008.

Working From Home Saves Energy

The Consumers Electronic Association released a study that said:

1. Using electronic devices to telecommute saves enough energy to power 1 million United States households for a year.
2. The United States has about 3.9 million telecommuters who **save** about 840 million gallons of gas.
3. They save 14 million tons of carbon dioxide emissions a year.
4. That is equal to taking 2 million vehicles off the road.

Information from an article in "The Tribune", San Luis Obispo County, California, September 25, 2007, by the Washington Post.

My thoughts – This study gives excellent results. Someone should tell Al Gore that some Americans are doing their part to conserve! They also do not fly their own jets to get to appointments or get to work. Well, maybe a few do.

Guard Your Nuts!

A nut-nabbing syndicate is gathering nuts to the tune of $1 million of stolen almonds discovered in a Sacramento, California warehouse. A ringing alarm brought the owner to the warehouse when he saw men loading boxes of almonds into a truck. He called police who arrested 2 men. Investigators suspect the almonds inside the warehouse had been stolen from orchards throughout the Central Valley.

Article in "Northern California", Sacramento, Published in "The Tribune", San Luis Obispo County, California, November 28, 2006

My thoughts – Is this the best time of year to steal nuts? Obviously, if they're worth $1 million.

Americans Will do the Jobs

Arizona made some of their laws stricter consequently some illegal aliens left the state. So surprise, what happened??? More **Americans** applied for the jobs to pick produce than they could hire.

Fox TV News, February 19, 2008.

My thoughts - So there, President Bush and all you other illegal alien sympathizers! Americans will do the jobs!

Knick Knack

Barry Diller made $470 Million dollars in one year. T.V. June 10, 2007.

He was born February 2, 1942 in Beverly Hills, California. The New York Times, October 26, 2006 reported that Diller was the highest paid executive (fiscal year 2005) with a total compensation package in excess of $295 million. This is reported in Wikipedia. He is the CEO of IAC (Inter Active Corp) and holds numerous positions. Check Wikipedia.

In 2001, Diller married fashion designer and longtime friend Diane von Furstenberg.

Farmed Trees

Did you know that trees are farmed like fruits and vegetables for paper production and wood products such as homes.

The trees are planted on managed timberlands. They do not come from public woodlands.

From the column "Ask Marilyn" by Marilyn vos Savant.
Parade, August 13, 2006 – published in "The Tribune", San Luis Obispo County, California.

Home Depot

1. Home Depot has about 1870 stores nationwide.
2. In recent years Home Depot has grown by about 100 stores a year.
3. Home Depot's plan is to create 15,000 new positions nationwide in 2007.
4. The Atlanta-based retailer added about the same number in 2006 and 20,000 in 2005.
5. Also they are hiring about 50,000 people to fill existing jobs that open during the year.
6. Nationally, most of the new jobs will be fulltime, but the total includes part-time and seasonal hiring. The jobs range from sales to night operations and specialty departments.
7. Spring is their key hiring season.

Information is from "Business Wrap", Tribune Wire Services, published in "The Tribune", San Luis Obispo County, California, January 30, 2007.

My thoughts – I wonder what they are doing in 2008.

Starbucks Corp. Seattle, Washington

The world's largest chain of coffee houses posted net earnings for the 13 weeks ending September 30, 2007
> of $158.5 million or
> 21 cents a share
> compared with
> $117.3 million or
> 15 cents a share
for the same period in 2006.

Its fiscal 4th quarter profit jumped 35%, despite a slowdown in store openings and a drop in U. S. traffic.

Information from an Associated Press article in "The Tribune", San Luis Obispo County, California, November 16, 2007.

A Dime Worth $1.9 Million

This dime is an 1894-S dime, and one of only 24 known to have been coined that year in San Francisco.

John Feigenbaum, 38, of Virginia Beach, VA is a rare coin dealer. He picked up the coin from the seller in Oakland, CA and delivered it to the buyer in Manhattan.

> Information from an article in "The Tribune", San Luis Obispo County, California, Tribune Wire Services, July 28, 2007

> My thoughts – I wonder what he charged for delivery!

A $16.2 Million Diamond

Geneva, Switzerland – A D-Color, or finest white diamond, of 84.37-carats which has the highest grading, flawless clarity and its cut, polish and symmetry have all been graded excellent has sold at Sotheby's Auction for just under $16.2 Million on November 14, 2007, purchased by Guess Clothing Company founder, George Marciano.

The all-time auction record for a stone or piece of jewelry is a 100.1-carat diamond that sold for $16.5 Million in 1995 at the same Sotheby's branch in Geneva.

> Information from an article by the Associated Press in "The Tribune", San Luis Obispo County, California, November 15, 2007.

> My thoughts – Instead of buying a diamond I would build a huge house with an ocean view and guest houses for family and friends to gather for parties. I guess I'd better start a clothing company.

"Your Black Muslim Bakery"

Oakland, Northern California. The headquarters of the "Your Black Muslim Bakery" franchise has been placed on the real estate market. They have legal and financial woes. Yusuf Bey founded it nearly 40 years ago.

The goal was to provide support and a haven for Oakland's poor and its growth included a security service, a school and other businesses. The Oakland police raided the bakery's properties in early August 2007 in connection with a number of serious crimes, including the murder of Oakland Post editor Chauncey Bailey.

Information from an article by Tribune Wire Services in "The Tribune", San Luis Obispo County, California, September 9, 2007.

Beware!

Discount stores have plenty of bad deals. Some items are not worth the $1.00 price tag, according to the current issue of Shop Smart magazine, a Consumer Reports publication.

Watch out for the following five items:
1. Vitamins – some multi-vitamins lacked one or more nutrients listed on the label, some failed to dissolve properly.
2. Electrical products – Christmas tree lights, extension cords and fans might have fake labels vouching for their safety.
3. Toys for kids younger than 3 – Toys with small parts or sharp edges must be labeled as unsafe for children under 3 years old. But some imported toys, particularly those manufactured in China might be mislabeled or unlabeled.
4. Fishy brand names – Counterfeit products sometimes have brand names that sound like well-known brands such as Dinacell batteries packaged to look like Duracells.
5. Soft vinyl lunch boxes – Several brands of soft insulated lunchboxes have tested positive for lead, which can seep into unwrapped food. Some states have recalled the lunchboxes, but the products have turned up at dollar stores.

Article in "The Tribune", San Luis Obispo County, California, August 23, 2007, by Associated Press.

My thoughts – Don't trust anyone!

Native American Capitalism

The Seminole Tribe of Florida catapulted itself onto the global entertainment scene with the $965 million purchase of "Hard Rock International". The 3300 Seminoles will now own one of the world's biggest brands and biggest collections of rock'n' roll memorabilia, 70,000 pieces ranging from Madonna's bustier to Eric Clapton's guitar.

The tribe will also take over 68 Hard Rock Cafes in 45 countries and licensing and franchise agreements for 56 other restaurants and five hotels, plus two Hard Rock Live concert venues.

"The days when tribes were considered marginal people with a bingo hall are over," said Eugene M. Christiansen, chief executive of gaming consultancy Christiansen Capital Advisors. "It's a Milestone."

> Article in "Nation Roundup" Miami, Published in "The Tribune", San Luis Obispo County, California, December 8, 2006
>
> My thoughts – Amazing!

A $300,000 Car

Ford Motor Co. may sell Aston Martin Lagonda, whose luxury sports cars were James Bond's preferred ride. The sale would free time and talent to concentrate on the woes affecting the company's core, Ford, Lincoln and Mercury brands.

Aston Martin, which Ford said is profitable, sold about 5,000 cars worldwide last year, including 1,800 in the U.S. Ford's Premier Automotive Group also includes Britain's Jaguar and Land Rover and Sweden's Volvo

Aston Martin cars start in the U.S. at $110,000. The top V12 Vanquish model approaches $300,000 with options.

> Information from an article in "The Tribune", San Luis Obispo County, California, September 1, 2006, by the Los Angeles Times.

116 Brands of Cigarettes

The Massachusetts Department of Public Health requires tobacco companies to measure the nicotine content of cigarettes each year and report the results. 92 of 116 brands tested, had higher nicotine yield in 2004 than in 1998, 52 had increases of more than 10%.

The brands that were most popular with young people and minorities registered the biggest increases and highest nicotine content. Nicotine is addictive. The higher levels theoretically could make new smokers more easily addicted as well as make it harder for established smokers to quit.

> Information from an article published in "The Tribune", San Luis Obispo County, California, August 31, 2006, "Health Roundup"- Washington.

> My thoughts – I had no idea that 116 brands of cigarettes were made. It is disgusting to realize that the higher nicotine yield was targeted for young people and minorities.

Deadly Mine Work

Princeton, Indiana – 3 men being carried in a construction bucket fell out and plunged 500 feet down an air shaft at a coal mine on August 10, 2007 killing them, authorities said. The open-top bucket was somehow upset as it was descending in the mineshaft; the 3 men fell to the bottom. The "sinking bucket" can hold 6 to 10 people, is about 6 feet high.

At the start of the shift, the bucket typically takes about 6 people down to the work area at the bottom of the shaft. The bucket is inspected daily. Frontier-Kemper Constructors Inc. is building the 550-foot vertical ventilation shaft at the Gibson County coal mine in southern Indiana.

> Information from an Associated Press article, August 11, 2007 in "The Tribune", San Luis Obispo County, California.

> My thoughts – Coal Mines are dangerous places to work. Coal is a dirty source of energy. Use nuclear power.

> Coal miners must be given a chance to learn a new trade, one that isn't as dangerous as coal mining. The coal mine owners should be responsible for new training. Burning coal puts too much CO_2 in the air.

Our United States Businesses

Boston, Massachusetts – Talbots Inc. will close its 78 Children's and men's apparel stores. They will focus on their core middle-aged female customers because of disappointing sales amid tough economic conditions. 800 employees are affected. It has 1,157 Talbot stores and the 271 J. Jill locations it bought in a 2006 acquisition.

Information from an article in "The Tribune", San Luis Obispo County, California, January 5, 2008.

My thought – It seems to me from the people I see on the streets, the uniform of the year is a pair of denim pants and a T-shirt top that is frequently white. The same uniform the illegal aliens used when they marched in the streets of America. So who buys clothes other than jeans and tops? Women, men, teens and children have almost the same uniform. It would be terrific if females wore dresses or skirts. I believe that if you are dressed well you are treated better.

Flip Burgers to get a High School Diploma

London-------Complete on-the-job training programs and the government is giving U.S. MacDonald's, a rail company and an airline the right to award credits toward a high school diploma. This is a first. It has already been called "McQualifications". McDonalds will offer it's British course to 7,000 restaurant managers in the country, regardless of their age.

Network rail and low-cost airline Fly be will offer more advanced courses that may count toward vocational diplomas or university degrees.

Information from an article in "The Tribune", San Luis Obispo County, California, January 29, 2008, by Associated Press.

My thoughts – Forward thinking, great idea.

CHINA

Chinese Toy Makers and Lead Paint

Shanghai, China – China reported August 9, 2007 that it had suspended the export licenses of 2 companies that used lead paint in toys made for American companies. This lead paint can poison children who played with the toys.

Here are some of the recalls of products made in China:

1. Tainted pet food ingredients.
2. Poisonous toothpaste.
3. Defective tires.
4. Contaminated seafood.
5. Toys

Last week, Mattel, the world's largest toy maker, said they would spend about $30 million to recall 1.5 million Fisher-Price brand toys, including Sesame Street and Dora the Explorer items, after discovering that the levels of lead violated American and European laws.

In June "RC2", based in Rockport, Illinois recalled 1.5 million "Thomas & Friends" wooden toy railroad sets after discovering that from 2005 to 2007 many of those products were coated with paint that had high levels of lead.

Chinese "Lee Der Industrial", Southern China, produced goods for Mattel. Hansheng Wood Factory, worked for "RC2", and is also in Southern China, near Hong Kong. Lee Der Industrial, a long-time Mattel vendor had used a paint supplier that used a pigment that was falsely described as lead free.

Most of the **world's toys** are now made in China, usually by companies that have contracts with the large toy companies.

Chinese regulators say more than 10,500 toy makers operate in the country, and Mattel alone uses more than 3,000 Chinese companies as contractors or as makers of Mattel-branded items under licensing arrangements.

Two companies were shut down who were involved in selling contaminated ingredients to American pet-food makers. This was one of the largest pet-food recalls in U.S. history. They also closed a chemical maker suspected of selling falsely labeled ingredients to foreign countries.

China has defended its exports; they say most products were safe, and only a small number of companies have sold tainted supplies.

Beijing said those that have shipped bad products will be punished.

33

Excerpted from an article by the New York Times in "The Tribune", San Luis Obispo County, California, August 10, 2007.

My thoughts – I'd rather have my clothes, tires, toys, foods and pet products and everything I buy "Made in America." My husband went to 9 stores today (9-07-07) to find a pair of pajamas made in America. He was unsuccessful!!! With 2 other stores he tried a few days ago, he has been to 11 stores.

Swiping Milk Crates=$80 Million

A new breed of crate rustlers is cashing in by swiping thousands of the containers from loading docks and selling them to shady recyclers.

They are shipped to booming factories in China to be made into a variety of products from pipes to flower pots. In the distant past it was college kids who stole the crates for coffee tables and dorm room shelves. Dairies across the country are losing $80 million a year. Companies in California, the country's largest dairy state, are hiring private detectives and staging sting operations. Who are the thieves? In 2006, 20 million crates were stolen.

An underground recycling network is targeting copper, aluminum bleachers, beer kegs, cemetery vases and nameplates.

Information from an article in "The Tribune", San Luis Obispo County, California, 2007

My thoughts – What's next for thieves to steal?

China is the World's Leading Source of Illegally Copied Goods

Officials from China and the United States said Chinese police have busted 2 criminal organizations and seized pirated software worth half a billion dollars. This is 2 years of work with the FBI.

The gangs pirated Microsoft Corp. and Symantec Corp. software and sold it around the world and in the United States. Chinese police arrested 25 people and seized property worth about $8 million. They confiscated counterfeit software with a retail value of $500 million.

China has long been the world's leading source of illegally copied goods, designer clothes, movies and music. The country has been under pressure to crack down which has been increasing before the start of the 2008 Summer Olympics in Beijing.

Information from an article in "The Tribune", San Luis Obispo County, California, Associated Press, July 25, 2007

My thoughts – It's about time!!!

35

Over $2 Million

In a charity auction a Chinese investment fund manager won the chance to have lunch with billionaire Warren Buffett by bidding $2,110,100 on eBay. He is Zhao Danyang of the Hong Kong based Pureheart China Growth Investment Fund.

Information from an Associated Press article in "The Tribune", San Luis Obispo County, California, June 29, 2008.

My thoughts – Will this bring prestige to Mr. Danyang? How long was lunch? Where did they eat? What was their conversation? Can you imagine someone paying $2 million to have lunch with you?

Warren Buffett
Wikipedia

Tooth Paste From China

Miami – A Florida company issued a nationwide recall of toothpaste it imported from China and distributed to wholesalers, saying that the product may contain a poisonous chemical! Gold City Enterprise LLC said 170,000 recalled "Shir" toothpaste products might contain diethylene glycol, a thickening agent used in antifreeze and as a cheaper substitute for the sweetener glycerin.

Information from an article published in "The Tribune", San Luis Obispo County, California, June 12, 2007, Tribune Wire Services.

My thoughts – Check everything you buy to determine where it was made!!! I want products that are made in the U.S.A.!

Drug Plants Abroad Rarely Inspected

Experts say medicines from China and India pose a risk of being contaminated, counterfeit or simply under strength and ineffective! The past food scandal triggered widespread fears.

In the past 7 years, the United States conducted only about 200 inspections of manufacturing plants in India and China. Only a few were the kinds that U.S. firms face to ensure that the drugs they make are of high quality.

Information from an article published in "The Tribune", San Luis Obispo County, California, June 17, 2007, by the Washington Post.

My thoughts – Does the U.S. government (the politicians) care about us, the taxpayers, the citizens, the people who pay their salaries??? They don't care about our pets either!

If every citizen refused to buy products made in China and India and tell the stores where they shop that they will not buy foreign-made goods then we could reverse the trend of our products being outsourced! Try it. Let's work together for our own wellbeing. My husband bought frozen mixed vegetables and didn't discover until we were ready to eat them that they were made in China. We checked another package of mixed vegetables from another company, which read **"Contains vegetables from China, Ecuador, Guatemala, Thailand, and USA.**
Check everything you buy!

These wild turkeys decided to check out the roof of this new house right after the new owners moved in.

Escape from China

Beijing, China. State media reported on August 10, 2007 that 12 Chinese teenagers tried to sneak into Canada by masquerading as kung fu masters from the famous Shaolin Temple. They were caught.

The official Xinhua News Agency said the 12 had no Martial Arts experience but had joined a team of genuine kung fu performers from a school in Henan province that was leaving for a tour of Canada. The 1,500-year-old temple is also in Henan province.

They had paid up to $90,000 each to a human smuggler (snakehead) and 2 coaches from the Martial Arts school who often accompany students on trips abroad, said the News Agency.

Information from an Associated Press article in "The Tribune", San Luis Obispo County, California, August 11, 2007.

My thoughts – What has happened to them? What were they going to do after they arrived here? Where did they each get $90,000? I believe I know why they wanted to leave China.

They want to try Kite-Surfing at the Dunes in Grover Beach, California.

38

Wal-Mart in Beijing, China

In China Wal-Mart employs 30,000 people at 60 outlets.

Workers in China have formed their first trade union, after demands from the Chinese government that Wal-Mart allow organized labor.

Wal-Mart has long sought to bar unions particularly from its stores in the U. S. Wal-Mart is the world's largest retailer.

Information from an Associated Press article published in "The Tribune", San Luis Obispo County, California, July 31, 2006

My thoughts – On vacation in the 1990's we saw the first store by Sam Walton in Arkansas. You've come a long way Sam!

China is the World's Leading Source of Illegally Copied Goods

Officials from China and the United States said Chinese police have busted 2 criminal organizations and seized pirated software worth half a billion dollars. This is 2 years of work with the FBI.

The gangs pirated Microsoft Corp. and Symantec Corp. software and sold it around the world and in the United States. Chinese police arrested 25 people and seized property worth about $8 million. They confiscated counterfeit software with a retail value of $500 million.

China has long been the world's leading source of illegally copied goods, designer clothes, movies and music. The country has been under pressure to crack down which has been increasing before the start of the 2008 Summer Olympics in Beijing.

Information from an article in "The Tribune", San Luis Obispo County, California, Associated Press, July 25, 2007

My thoughts – It's about time!!!

CHOCOLATE

A Mother

A mother must have the best time of her life while she pursues the art of motherhood.

Enjoy the precious babies, give them every opportunity she can to beautify their lives.

How she raises them determines their life's journey.

Teach them morals, honesty, manners, skills, how to dress, how to choose friends.

Give them lessons in dance, gymnastics, swimming, and public speaking.

Use every opportunity available, trips to art galleries, museums, plays, and political meetings.

Teach them that animals are special and deserve kindness.

Give them a private school education for 16 years and then they choose.

Teach them to love their brothers and sisters, respect and love their parents.

Teach them gratitude, how to write thank you notes, how to say thank you.

Boys show respect by removing a hat indoors.

Teach them to volunteer, to help the poor.

Teach by example; teach them about public service, that it is a duty to work for our country, to run for office.

Ditto for Dad.

Carolyn Gerdink Cavolt
August 16, 2008

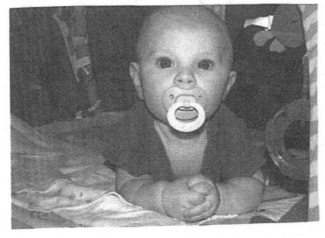

<u>Commercials</u>

I believe all the people who make commercials should be put in the same cell!

Every time a person watches or hears a commercial a little brainpower is lost and the person is driven to stupidity.

The only cute commercial on TV or radio is Geico with the little talking green geeko.

Carolyn Cavolt
September 25, 2008

Time Out

Don't Change the Chocolate!

Mars Inc./ said October 1, 2007 that it will continue to use 100% cocoa butter in its U.S. chocolate products.

A dozen food industry groups want to change long-established federal standards to allow using vegetable fat, up to a level of 5%, instead of the usual 100% cocoa butter. The change would save MONEY for manufacturers and allow more flexibility and innovation so they say.

Manufacturers can already use vegetable fats instead of cocoa butter, BUT they are not allowed by Food and Drug Administration to call it Chocolate.

"Changing the definition of what chocolate is would be a mistake," said Todd Lachman, president of Mars Snackfoods US of Hackettstown, New Jersey. "The bottom line is that we are not going to change our chocolate. Today Mars US chocolate products are pure, authentic chocolate, and they're going to stay that way." He also said the company could have saved millions of dollars by going along with the move, but allowing vegetable oil would have diluted the quality of its chocolate.

Mars' products include:
1. Mars Bars
2. M & M's
3. Dove Chocolate
4. Snickers
5. Milky Way
6. 3 Musketeers
7. Twix
8. Skittle's
9. Starburst

Consumers want genuine chocolate and not a cheaper substitute. The Grocery Manufacturers Association wants revised standards. The European Union has used a 5% ceiling since 2003.

Information from an Associated Press article titled "Mars Inc. to stick with cocoa butter", in "The Tribune", San Luis Obispo County, California, September 18, 2007.

My thoughts – I'm a consumer and I don't want chocolate changed. Manufacturers have a perfect product now – why change the formula so they can make more money! Here is their website if you wish to express your opinion
www.mars.com and Grocery Manufacturers Association www.gmsbrand.com

The Hershey Company

Hershey, Pennsylvania ----- Richard H. Lenny is retiring at the end of 2007 as chairman, president and chief executive officer. He has struggled to preserve the Hershey Company's prominence as the Nation's largest candy maker. Lenny has been Hershey's top executive since 2001. Since then, Hershey has announced:

1. It will close 6 U.S. and Canadian plants
2. Cut more than 3,000 workers in the 2 countries, including up to 900 at its hometown plants.
3. It also plans to shift more production to contractors and a new plant it is building in Monterrey, Mexico.

Information from an article by the Associated Press in "The Tribune" San Luis Obispo County, California, October 2, 2007.

My thoughts – The Hershey Company is celebrating 100 years in business 1907-2007. As a child and as an adult Hershey was my favorite candy. I thought it was great that Hershey didn't advertise until these last few years. They didn't need to spend million of dollars on advertising to get people to buy their candy because it was so delicious! Now to read that they plan to shift more production to contractors and a new plant they are building in Monterrey, Mexico is devastating news to me and probably to many Hershey chocolate lovers!

I hope every Hershey Chocolate lover writes to them and complains. I certainly intend to do so. We want all our foods made in the United States of America!!!

The President, The Hershey Company
Hershey, Pennsylvania 17033-815 – U.S.A.
Or call toll-free weekdays 9 to 4 E.T. 1-800-468-1714
Or www.hershey.com
For gift ideas www.hersheygifts.com

Herb, a man from WW I who enjoyed chocolates   44

CHURCHES

The Latin Mass

Pismo Beach, California – A traditional Latin Mass will soon be said at St. Paul the Apostle Catholic Church in Pismo Beach. The Latin Mass will return to San Ardo, California and at the Old Mission San Juan Bautista in the town of San Juan Bautista, California, off Highway 101 about 2 ½ hours north of Pismo Beach.

The Latin Mass has its own Liturgy, Music and location for the Altar. Pope Benedict XVI told priests last July 2007 to bring back the traditional Latin Mass for members who want it.

After the second Vatican Council, 1962 – 1965, Bishops disliked the Latin Mass. Masses were then celebrated in the languages of the parishioners. The Priests will continue to face the parishioners in the Latin Mass from the Altar.

Before Vatican II the Altar was at the very front of the church and the priest faced away from the people.

> Information from an article by Sally Connell, "The Tribune", San Luis Obispo County, California, September 6, 2007.

> My thoughts – Just like old times!

St Paul The Apostle Catholic Church, Pismo Beach, California

The Los Angeles Catholic Church Clergy Abuse Settlement

The settlement is $660 Million with more than 500 alleged victims of clergy sexual abuse. The scandal first emerged in Boston, Massachusetts in 2002.

Each settlement will depend on how badly the person was abused and how long the abuse lasted.

Lawyers for the plaintiffs will get 33 to 40% of the settlement – anywhere between $218 million and $264 million!

The plaintiffs will get their money by December 1, 2007. Cardinal Roger Mahoney said the archdiocese will sell some of its property, dip into its investment portfolio and borrow money.

Parish churches and schools will not be sold.

In 2002 California legislators rolled back the statute of limitations on sexual abuse for one year. Other states did not pass such a law, so the number of cases in California was much larger-nearly 1,000 claims statewide and more than 500 in Los Angeles alone. Also the archdiocese must release confidential priest personnel files that could show how much church leaders knew and when they knew it.

A judge must review each file before it is released. Attorneys for the priests still living may be able to get the files sealed because they contain private medical and psychological evaluations. Released files may show attempts to cover up abuse and the shuffling of troubled priests between parishes.

> Article in "The Tribune" San Luis Obispo County, California, July 17, 2007
> By Gillian Flaccus, Associated Press.

> My thoughts – What a mess! All the files should be made public. This must never happen again. How many priests were involved? What involvement does Cardinal Mahoney have? Did he shuffle priests? If he did, what is his punishment?

Knick – Knack

Fox TV News reported March 31, 2008:

> 19.2% of people in the world are Muslim.
> 17.4% of people in the world are Catholic.
> 33% of people in the world are Christian.

Massive Settlements for the Catholic Church

The massive settlement approved July 14, 2007 in the archdiocese of Los Angeles, California has pushed the clergy sex abuse for America's Roman Catholic Church beyond $2 Billion nationwide.

Church leaders have found the way to fund the payouts and survive. Several dioceses have sold off property.

Information from an article by Associated Press published in "The Tribune" San Luis Obispo County, California, July 17, 2007.

My thoughts – The question is why wasn't the abuse made public when first discovered and stopped and priests dismissed or jailed. The attorneys get 33 to 40% of the $2 billion! Well, at least it isn't 50%!

Speaking in Tongues

"Researchers at the University of Pennsylvania took brain images of 5 women while they spoke in tongues and found that their frontal lobes, the thinking, willful part of the brain through which people control what they do, were relatively quiet, as were the language centers. The regions involved in maintaining self-consciousness were active. The women were not in a blind trance. It was unclear which region of the brain was driving the behavior."

"The passionate, sometimes rhythmic, language-like patter that pours forth from religious people who "speak in tongues" reflects a state of mental possession, many of them say. Now they have some neuroscience to back them."

Information from Tribune Wire Services, November 7, 2006
Published in "The Tribune", San Luis Obispo County, California.

My thoughts – The first time my daughter and I heard a religious group of people speak in tongues was in South Carolina in the late 1970's. There were about 200 people. It gets your attention very quickly! The sounds are very unusual. We were stunned.

A Fringe Church

Protesting funerals of troops killed in Iraq is done by members of the Westboro Baptist Church (WBC) of Newport News, Virginia over the past few years. They use profane signs, which state that deaths in Iraq are retribution triggered by America's tolerance of homosexuals. They also were planning to picket services for the victims of the Virginia Tech shootings.

The church news release said "God is punishing America for her sodomite sins. The 33 massacred at Virginia Tech died for America's sins against WBC (Westboro Baptist Church). Just as United States soldiers dying in Iraq each day for America's sins against WBC."

Virginia Attorney General Bob McDonnell is warning protestors that they could be arrested if they interrupt the funerals.

Information from an article in "The Tribune" by Tribune wire services, April 20, 2007, published in "The Tribune", San Luis Obispo County, California.

My thoughts – I hope this is a teeny tiny church to match their brain size! We don't need or want people with these views. Drop counterfeit money in their collection baskets with a note, this is phony and so are you! I like fringe but not a fringe church.

Gay Movement Within Conservative Judaism

A panel of rabbis gave permission for:
    A. Same-sex commitment ceremonies
    B. Ordination of gays within Conservative Judaism

This is a wrenching change for a movement that occupies the middle ground between orthodoxy and liberalism in Judaism.

The complicated decision by the Conservative Movement's Committee on Jewish Law and Standards leaves it up to individual seminaries whether to ordain gay rabbis and gives individual rabbis the option of sanctioning same-sex unions.

Article in "Nation Roundup", New York, Published in "The Tribune", San Luis Obispo County, California, December 7, 2006.

49

The $190 Million Catholic Church

Completion date is Fall 2008 for the Cathedral of Christ the Light in downtown Oakland, California. It will be one of the nation's most expensive religious sites. The Roman Catholic Diocese of Oakland lost it's old Cathedral in the 1989 Loma Prieta Earthquake.

The 1,300 seat Cathedral on a 2-½ acre site will have offices, a bishop's residence, a conference center and a garden plaza. The Cathedral is being financed by donations; $100 Million has been pledged as of June 2007.

Oakland saw a 57% increase in homicides last year.

Last January it was announced that a fund raising campaign for a new Catholic high school in Livermore, California would be halted so officials could focus on raising money for the Cathedral's completion.

The Architect is Craig Hartman of San Francisco, California. Many people are unhappy about the building of this Cathedral.

> Information from an article in "The Tribune", San Luis Obispo County, California, by Louise Chu, Associated Press, September 2, 2007.

> My thoughts – I'd rather have 20 or more Catholic high schools and grade schools built and staffed. The need is great.

A will is a dead giveaway.

> On a sign in Grover Beach, California, author unknown.

50

This will make You Proud

The following information is taken from an e-mail received in May 2008.

Why would newspapers carry on a vendetta of one of the most important institutions that we have today in the United States, namely the **Catholic Church?**

Do you know – the **Catholic Church** educates millions of students everyday **saving the American taxpayers billions of dollars**? Graduates go on to graduate studies at a much higher rate than most public schools.

The **Catholic Church has 245 or more colleges and universities** in the United States with an enrollment of tens of thousands of students.

The **Catholic Church has a non-profit hospital system of 550 hospitals**, which account for hospital treatment of thousands of people – **not just Catholics** – in the United States today.

But the press is vindictive and trying to totally denigrate in every way the Catholic Church in this country. They have blamed the disease of pedophilia on the Catholic Church, which is as irresponsible as blaming adultery on the institution of marriage.

Pedophiles and sexual advances are a problem in all denominations but Catholic Priests have been targeted and made the public aware of this inexcusable problem.

This is not just a Catholic problem.

The Catholic Church is bleeding from self-inflicted wounds. The agony that Catholics have felt and suffered is not necessarily the fault of the Church. You have been hurt by a small number of wayward priests that have probably been totally weeded out by now.

Walk with your shoulders high and your head higher. Be a proud member of the most important non-governmental agency in the United States. Be proud to speak up for your faith with pride and reverence and learn what your Church does for all other religions. Be proud that you're a Catholic.

> My thoughts – Finally some good news about the Catholic Church! It's about time!

Pope Benedict XVI

Pakistan's legislature unanimously condemned Pope Benedict XVI. Lebanon's top Shite Cleric demanded an apology. In Turkey, The ruling party likened the pontiff to Hitler and Mussolini and accused him of reviving the mentality of the crusades.

Across the Islamic world yesterday, Benedict's remarks on Islam and Jihad in a speech in Germany unleashed a lot of rage. Will violent protest ensue? The Pope cited an obscure Medieval text that says some of the teachings of Islam's founder are "evil; and inhumane."

Fears of a new outbreak of anti-Western protest because the Pope inflamed Muslim passion.

> Information from an article "Istanbul, Turkey" published in "The Tribune", San Luis Obispo county, California, September 16, 2006.

> My thoughts – Live with it Muslims! Your words about us are disgusting and we don't throw temper tantrums!

The (Anti-Religion) Bigotry of the Elites

In 9 Western states the courts have ruled it Constitutional for public schools to require a 3-week course on the Islamic faith. In this course all junior-high students are mandated to pretend they ARE MUSLIMS and offer prayers to Allah.

This is the same court that infamously ruled that it is unconstitutional for students to mention "under God" in the Pledge of Allegiance, (in the case brought by Atheist activist Michael Newdow).

This information is from Newt Gingrich's e-mail of November 13, 2007 - HumanEvents@HumanEventsOnline.com - Subject "The Anti Religious Bigotry of the Elites.

My thoughts – This is another very good reason to always know what is happening in your child's classroom, from kindergarten through high school.

There are 1.2 Billion Muslims in the world.

Heard on television – July 2008.

But according to IslamicPopulation.com the total Muslim Population is 1.84 billion in the year 2007.

Knick Knack

There are 6 million Muslims in America, 150,000 Muslims live in Minnesota. In Minnesota 3/4th's of the cab drivers are Somali Muslims.

Heard on Television early 2007

The "Plain People"

A visit to Lancaster county or Pennsylvania Dutch County is where you see shiny black horse-drawn buggies, towns named Mount Joy, Intercourse and Bird-In-Hand. The Amish and Mennonites live here, only 60 miles west of Philadelphia, Pennsylvania.

Today the "Plain People" make up over 10% of the population of the area, with numbers almost tripling since 1960. The Amish are stricter than the Mennonites. They do not use electricity or motors; they use their horse-drawn buggies for travel and tilling their farms. The Amish avoid fancy clothing, jewelry, and other adornment. They believe that posing for pictures is an unacceptable act of pride. They are extraordinarily devoted to God and family.

Visitors are fascinated by these people and like the hearty food and deserts from their kitchens. Small shops throughout the area serve local delicacies, hand carved toys, beautifully stitched quilts.

The Amish choose to live simply to give all honors to God; they choose a rural life so they don't expose their children to the distractions of the secular world, therefore their society thrives.

This is their recipe for "Buttons" (Dumplings) that are dropped into "Schnitz and Knepps" (apples and buttons).

Buttons (Dumplings)

2 cups sifted flour
4 tsp. Baking powder
½ tsp. Salt
3 T. unsalted butter
1 egg, beaten
About ½ cup milk

Sift flour, salt and baking powder together.
Cut in butter.
Stir in egg.
Slowly add enough milk to create a moist, fairly stiff dough.
Drop dough by the tablespoon into boiling ham and apple liquid.
Cover and simmer until dumplings are done, about 15 minutes.

Schnitz and Knepp (Apples & Buttons)

3 lbs. Smoked ham, bone-in
4 cups dried apples, tart
1 large onion, finely chopped
3 T. brown sugar
2 medium potatoes, cubed

Place ham in a large pot.
Cover with water and bring to a boil.
Reduce heat and simmer until ham is tender, approximately 2 hours.
While ham is cooking place apples in a bowl and cover with water.
Soak apples at least 2 hours.
Remove ham from bone and cut into medium pieces, return pieces to water.
Add apples and most of apple liquid to ham.
Add onion and brown sugar.
Cover and simmer for 30 minutes.
Add potatoes, simmer for 30 additional minutes.

Information from an article by Mary Dixon Lebeau in the "Harris' Farmer's Almanac for 2008," first published in 1692. Featuring weather forecast, planting tables, predictions, nostalgia, Mysteries of the Universe, Facts and Folklore, issued September 13, 2007.

My thoughts – Why not drop the dumplings into homemade chicken broth if you don't like ham?

I think I would like to live there for a week or two, visit all the stores and buy quilts. Of course I would hire a horse and buggy and driver. Who wants to go?

Michelangelo's Private Room in St. Peter's Basilica

Vatican experts say that a 450-year-old receipt provides proof that Michelangelo kept a private room in St Peter's Basilica while working as the Pope's Chief Architect.

Michelangelo was put in charge of the restoration of St. Peter's Basilica by Pope Paul III at age 71 in 1546 and held the job until his death in 1564 at age 89.

Michelangelo is the Renaissance painter whose frescoes adorn the ceiling of the Sistine Chapel in the Vatican. His greatest contribution to the Basilica was his design for the central dome or cupola, an architectural triumph.

In the Basilica Archives researchers found an entry for a key to a chest, "in the room in St. Peter's where Master Michelangelo retires. Now they must find the room and the chest. The receipt does show that Michelangelo had requested a very expensive key. The price of 10 scudos for the key in the 1550's was more that the monthly salary of many of the artisans working on the Basilica. "The key was surely meant to keep that chest tightly locked," said the manager of the office where the basilica's archives are kept.

2006 was the 500th anniversary of the Catholic Church.

Information excerpted from an article by Daniels Petroff, Associated Press, published in "The Tribune", San Luis Obispo County, California, February 18, 2007.

My thoughts – What a mystery! What is in the chest?

CITIES

Top 10 Top Cities

1. Florence, Italy
2. Buenos Aires, Argentina
3. Bangkok, Thailand
4. Rome, Italy
5. Sydney, Australia
6. New York City, New York, USA
7. Udaipur, India
8. Istanbul, Turkey
9. San Francisco, California, USA
10. Cape Town, South Africa

Information from Travel + Leisure's 2007 readers' poll, "The Top Cities in the World," published in "The Tribune", San Luis Obispo County, California, September 2, 2007.

Top 10 Adventure Cities

1. Chicago, Illinois
2. Nashville, Tennessee
3. Austin, Texas
4. Huntsville, Alabama
5. Gainesville, Florida
6. Overland Park, Kansas
7. Albuquerque, New Mexico
8. Tulsa, Oklahoma
9. Springfield, Missouri
10. Hattiesburg, Mississippi

According to National Geographic Adventure Magazine the above are the nation's top cities for adventure.

Published in "The Tribune", San Luis Obispo County, California, September 16, 2007

The Icebox of the Nation

The temperature in International Falls, Minnesota fell to 40 below zero on February 11, 2008, a few days after the town won a federal trademark making it officially the "Icebox of the Nation". By late morning, the temperature had risen to 18 below zero.

Information from an article by the Associated Press in "The Tribune", San Luis Obispo County, California February 12, 2008.

There are 6.4 square miles in the city. The total population was 6,703 in the 2000 census. Information from Wikipedia, the free encyclopedia.

St. Louis, MO, # 1 of Unsafe U.S. Cities

This Midwestern city of about 330,000 people is listed as the most dangerous city in the United States. It was listed just days after the St. Louis Cardinals won the top honor in Major League Baseball.

Cities are ranked based on more than just their crime rate, according to Morgan Quitno Press. Crimes are weighted based on their danger to people.

Most Dangerous
1. St. Louis, Missouri
2. Detroit, Michigan
3. Flint, Michigan
4. Compton, California
5. Camden, New Jersey

Most Safe
1. Brick, New Jersey
2. Amherst, New York
3. Mission Viejo, California
4. Newton, Massachusetts
5. Troy, Michigan

Santa Barbara, California ranked 115th in a ranking of 371 cities, with # 1 being the safest and 371 being the most dangerous. Santa Maria, California ranked 178th.

Information from an article by Morgan Quitno Press, (Source), October 30, 2006.
Published in "The Tribune", San Luis Obispo County, California.

If our dad is a policeman will we grow up to be police dogs?

60

Fresno's Chinatown Tunnels

Fresno, California--------City officials and Chinatown shopkeepers have long known that basements beneath Fresno's historic Chinatown were interconnected, though entrances were kept secret to prevent break ins.

Last August 3, 2007, a team of archaeologists, hired by the city, started using ground-penetrating radar to document what lies beneath Chinatown before redevelopment changes the area.

The researchers were looking for the connected basements, built from the 1880s through the early 1990s, but also for a larger network of tunnels long rumored to exist under all of Chinatown and beyond.

> Information from an article in "The Tribune", San Luis Obispo county, California, Associated Press, September 14, 2007.

Greenwich, Connecticut

The town has 61,000 residents, is Connecticut's richest town. Through March 31, 2007 presidential contenders have received $1.038 million in gifts. Several of the current contenders want to raise $500 million each to stay competitive so the town's richest residents are being wooed more than ever.

Greenwich has joined New York, Los Angeles, and Silicon Valley as positive stops by the contenders.

> Excerpts from an article published in "The Tribune," San Luis Obispo County, California, May 28, 2007 Tribune Wire Service.

> My thoughts – If you have a Greenwich zip code be prepared to donate some of your money. Wealth equals popularity!

Santa Fe, New Mexico

A sculpture of more than 100 old refrigerators, stacked and arranged in a ring like England's Stonehenge, was removed by the city May 30. It was 80 feet high.

Adam Horowitz created the public art nearly a decade ago. It had become a health and safety hazard.

It was a cult phenomenon, a tourist destination and in print worldwide. It started out as a statement about American consumerism and waste, then it became waste itself.

> My thoughts – Did you know this art existed? Did you see it? I have misplaced the article, written in June, 2007 or before.

Knick – Knack

Bill O'Reilly said on his TV show March 24, 2008. A black gang member, just let out of jail, killed a 17-year-old black high school football player! He also said Los Angeles, California is out of control, it is a sanctuary City and Mayor Antonio Villaraigosa is a weak leader.

Expansion of the Panama Canal

Panama City, Panama---------Cost = $5.25 Billion. This expansion will accommodate a new class of ships that will be able to carry more than twice the number of containers as are now used. Completion is set for 2014. The expansion started September 3, 2007.

> Information from a Tribune wire services article September 4, 2007 in "The Tribune" San Luis Obispo County, California.

> MY thoughts – I wonder who is doing the expansion? Will this mean double the goods that will come into the United States from China?

Is $15 Billion Too High A Cost?

Congress has appropriated $7.1 Billion to repair and upgrade the New Orleans flood-protection system by 2011. But now Federal Officials outlined plans for a significant improvement to the New Orleans flood-protection system by 2011. It would be more than double the $7.1 Billion, spending an additional $7.6 Billion.

The Army Corps of Engineers could build higher, tougher floodwalls and gates to seal off waterways from storm surges. Permanent pumping stations at the mouths of the city's drainage canals would block surging water from Lake Pontchartrain and effectively pump water out of the city during storms as well.

> Information from an article by the New York Times, August 23, 2007 in "The Tribune", San Luis Obispo County, California.

> My thoughts – Is it worth it? I guess that depends if you live there. What's another $15 Billion? We give that much to other countries, why not to New Orleans? Ask Angelina Joli, she and Brad Pitt bought a home in New Orleans in 2007.

> So let's take care of New Orleans so it doesn't happen again!

Leaky Levees

The Army Corps of Engineers said improving New Orleans flood defenses to help it endure future storms like Hurricane Katrina will cost $14.7 Billion, more than twice what Congress has appropriated!

But even that much investment will not keep the city dry. Two feet to four feet of rainwater could still inundate some neighborhoods in a bad storm. If the reinforced levees hold, it would be pumped out again in a matter of hours.

> Information taken from an article in "The Tribune", San Luis Obispo County, California, August 26, 2007 from The New York Times.

63

San Francisco Cable Cars

One year ago the Municipal Railway imposed a 67% fare increase on cable cars. Now a one-way ride costs $5.00 that starts at the Powel Street turn around to Fisherman's Wharf. If you want to return you pay another $5.00.

City officials raised the fare to ease a $57 million deficit. Bus and streetcar fares went up 25 cents, to $1.50. Cable car fares nearly doubled. To operate a cable car the cost is $312.00 per hour, $188.00 for a streetcar and $126.00 for a diesel bus.

The ridership has dropped. The $5.00 one-way cable car fare is turning off riders. Revenue is up 20% over the past year because of the increased fare but it is unclear how much ridership has dropped because Muni doesn't track ridership on individual cable cars.

Information from an article by Rachel Gordon of the San Francisco Chronicle, published in "The Tribune", San Luis Obispo County, California, September 17, 2006.

My thoughts – A cable car ride is real life – more fun than a carnival ride. I remember the happy rides with relatives.

Where are we going?
Why are we running?
Is the end in sight?
I haven't finished my life yet
I still have things to do.
Leave me alone.
Come back later
when I have time
to talk to you.

CGC 7-20-08

CRIMES

Los Angeles is the Nation's Gang Capital

One study counts 40,000 members in 700 gangs! Los Angeles, California, Mayor Antonio Villaraigosa says it is the national epicenter for gang activity. The city is the originator and exporter of dangerous gangs gone national, such as "Bloods", the "Crips", and "Mara Salvatrucha 13 – (MS13)."

FBI spokesman, Kenneth Smith, said, "We have Blood and Crips sets in Indianapolis, Indiana, Chicago, Illinois, Cincinnati, Ohio, Louisville, Kentucky, that middle part of the country where people don't think they have a gang problem." Smith was an Indianapolis policeman for 8 years until 1997.

Chicago Crime Commission President Jim Wagner acknowledged Los Angeles as a breeding ground for gangs that are now in Chicago's western suburbs. "We are seeing in the suburban areas a growth in the presence of MS13," he said.

After more than 20 years trying to eradicate Los Angeles gangs – whose violence influenced American culture from video games to movies – officials are being sharply rebuked for ongoing failures in a new study by a local civil rights group. Gang fighting has turned racial between blacks and Latinos.

Officials insist the city is as safe as it was in 1956 when Los Angeles had the same overall crime rates as 2006's. On February 7, 2007, local officials and the FBI's Los Angeles office will host a long-planned summit with law officials from the United States, Canada and Central America on "Transnational" gangs such as MS13, which has ties to El Salvador.

Information from Michael Martinez of the Chicago Tribune published February 4, 2007, in "The Tribune", San Luis Obispo County, California.

My thoughts – Another good reason to close our borders and build the fence along the Mexican border. 40,000 gang members are equal to and surpass the population of many small towns in America!

Knick Knack-Underground Economy

"There is a 1 Trillion dollar underground economy in the United States."
From Lou Dobbs, Lou Dobbs TV show, February 28, 2008.

From Wikipedia, the free encyclopedia.
The underground economy or black market is a market consisting of all commerce on which applicable taxes and/or regulations of trade are being evaded. The market consists mainly of prohibited commerce, that is, drugs, prostitution, weapons and gambling, and tax-evasive trade of legal goods and services that is, money laundering. They are typically cash transactions.

2,000 Fake Emergency Calls

Vallejo, California – A man calling himself, Nomar, has phoned 911, on a donated cell phone, almost 2,000 times. He says he is a victim of a drug overdose, possible heart attack, a robbery, attempted suicide, etc.

Each of his calls could result in a single misdemeanor. His calls are all fake emergency calls over the past 6 months.

His calls tie up dispatchers; send the police and fire fighters on wild goose chases.

Information from an Associated Press article in "The Tribune", San Luis Obispo County, California, September 4, 2007.

My thoughts – What is a just punishment? Fine him, time in jail for every call, volunteer work for 2000 hours.

Top Spots for Stolen Cars

According to the National Insurance Crime bureau, California contains six of the ten areas in the United States with the highest rates of auto theft:

1. Modesto, CA
2. Las Vegas/Paradise, NV
3. Stockton, CA
4. Phoenix/Mesa/Scottsdale, AZ
5. Visalia/Porterville, CA
6. Seattle/ Tacoma/ Bellevue, WA
7. Sacramento/Arden-Arcade/ Roseville. CA
8. San Diego/ Carlsbad/ San Marcos, CA
9. Fresno, CA
10. Yakima, WA

Information from an article in "Parade", published in "The Tribune", San Luis Obispo County, California, August 6, 2006.

Medical Information Breached

Los Angeles, California – "An indictment accuses Lawanda Jackson, 49, of one count of illegally obtaining individually identifiable health information for commercial advantage." She allegedly received $4,600 from a media outlet for giving the private medical information. She is a former UCLA Medical Center employee. At least 61 patients at UCLA's hospitals medical information was breached, including Farrah Fawcett, Britney Spears and First Lady Maria Shriver.

Information from an article in "The Tribune", San Luis Obispo County, California, April 30, 2008 by the Tribune wire service.

Rob a Bank – Win a $1 Million Lottery

A convicted bank robber won a $1 million lottery prize. He gets to keep it but now has to pay a $65 a month probation supervisory fee because he used to be indigent but now he isn't. He is Timothy Elliott, 55. He lives in Bourne, Massachusetts under the supervision of the Department of Mental Health. He violated his probation by buying a ticket but a judge says he can keep the money, as did the lottery commission as did the probation department.

Information from an Associated Press article in "The Tribune", San Luis Obispo County, California, January 19, 2008.

My thoughts – I concur with the judge, probation department and the lottery commission that he should keep the prize. If the money had been denied he probably would have become a bigger crook. Now he has a chance to pay his monthly fee and help others. So be it.

Beware!

Ontario, California – Police arrested 31 year old Francisco Santiago Ramos at his Pomona home accused of telling a woman staying at an Ontario hotel that he was a security guard to get inside her room, then robbing and raping her. The 25-year-old woman told police he confronted her at the front door of her hotel room early Monday morning on December 24, 2007. He was arrested after being recognized from parking lot surveillance camera footage that was broadcast on television. He's being held on $600,000 bail.

Information from an Associated Press article in "The Tribune", San Luis Obispo County, California, December 29, 2007.

My thoughts – Thank God for cameras! Always stay alert! Beware of strangers! Take a self- defense class. Don't open doors for strangers. If you must travel alone carry a licensed gun after taking classes in self-protection.

Pure Evil

Joliet, Illinois. Police arrested Christopher Vaughn, 32, at the funeral home where his wife and 3 children lay, on charges of gunning down his family in their sport utility vehicle.

He works as a computer forensic adviser and had been shot in the thigh. His wife, 34, was shot once, each of his children 12, 11, 8, two girls and a boy, were shot twice. His handgun was found at the scene.

Information from an article in "The Tribune" San Luis Obispo County, CA, June 24, 2007, Nation Roundup, Tribune Wire Services.

My thoughts – He is Pure Evil that I indicated in the title. What do you think he deserves? The death penalty? Or life in prison? Or maybe a lifetime of hard labor where he can think about his sins. How could a human being kill his 3 children and their mother?

Murders – Black on Black, White on White

Washington – Nearly half of the nation's murder victims in 2005 were black; the number of black men who were slain is on the rise. Mostly, the victims were between 17 and 29, said the Justice Department in a study released August 9, 2007.

In 2005 Black people represented 13% of the population but were the victims of 49% of all murders and 15% of rapes, assaults and other non-fatal violent crimes nationwide.

Most of the black murder victims – 93% - were killed by other black people, the study found. About 85% of white victims were slain by other white people.

In 2005, 16,400 (est.) people were murdered in the United States, down from a peak of 21,400 a decade ago. Also the number of black people slain dropped over the last 10 years from 10,400 in 1995 to almost 8,000in 2005.

Tribune Wire Services, August 10, 2007, "The Tribune", San Luis Obispo County, California.

My thoughts – Too many murders are committed each year! What is the solution? Better education, more moral training?

United Nations Owes $18 Million in Traffic Fines to New York City

The new United Nations secretary-general, Ban Ki-moon, South Korea, supports the recovery of nearly $18 million in traffic fines owed by U.N. diplomats and members of the consular community to New York City.

Most of the debt came prior to a city crackdown four years ago on envoys that routinely were cited for illegal parking on city streets but rarely paid because of diplomatic immunity.

Egypt owes the most, $1.9 million; Kuwait owes $1.3 million, South Korea owes $17,000. In all 177 countries have yet to pay city fines.

Information from "World Roundup," Tribune Wire Services
Published January 18, 2007 in "The Tribune", San Luis Obispo County, California.

My thoughts – They should pay or get out and stay out until their fines are paid.

Knick – Knack

"It currently costs an average of $43,000 a year to house an inmate in California."

Taken from an article by Andy Furillo, The Sacramento Bee, in "The Tribune", San Luis Obispo County, California, November 1, 2008.

476 Homicides in 2006

Los Angeles, California – Los Angeles had 392 homicides in 2007 down from 476 in 2006, that is 84 less. In 1970 there were 394 homicides. Police Chief William Bratton said the department has 9,608 officers – the highest number since 1998.

Information from as article by the Associate Press in "The Tribune", San Luis Obispo county, California, January 4, 2008.

DRUGS

Illegal Drugs

Mexican Gangs make 80% of the methamphetamine consumed in the United States.

Many United States users are switching from cocaine to meth. In the first 21 days of April 2008, $30 million worth of meth was confiscated by United States officials, which was headed for Atlanta, California, Dallas, Kansas City and Washington. In 2007, at 6 border crossings from Mexico into California, 2,000 pounds of Methamphetamine, worth $220 million, was stopped by border agents.

The chemicals used to make methamphetamine are so common that the biggest bust linked to meth manufacturing in 2007 was of an unknown Chinese businessman, Zhenli Ye Gon, who had $207 million in cash stashed in his Mexico City home. To produce $20 worth of methamphetamine the cost is only 20 cents, which equals Big Profits!

Information from an article by Franco Ordonez, McClatchy Newspapers, in "The Tribune", San Luis Obispo County, California, April 30, 2008.

My thoughts – Outrage! Get that Border Fence built and use all other means to stop meth coming into America! The United States has to have control of its borders to keep out illegal aliens and terrorists and drugs. Remember there are idiots that want open borders. DO NOT VOTE FOR THEM!

In case you are very, very young and don't know what "open borders" mean, it means exactly that, "open", ANYONE can come into our Country. Do you keep your doors at your home open and unlocked so anyone can come in?

Knick Knack

Since the year 2000, an average of 500,000 illegal aliens have entered the United States and **settled permanently per year!**

"Immigration Watch", January 2008 by "Americans for Immigration Control, Inc.", P.O. Box 738, Monterey, Virginia 24465

Massive Anti-Drug Package Between U.S. and Mexico

Washington – This plan resembles a U. S. aid plan for Columbia. Mexican President Felipe Calderon is negotiating a massive counter-drug aid package with the Bush Administration worth hundreds of millions of dollars! The talks have been taking place quietly for several months. Bush and Calderon met in Quebec August 20 and 21, 2007.

Mexican officials have been reluctant to go public with the discussions, because of the anti-U.S. sentiments harbored by many Mexicans. The conservative Calderon believes he has little choice but to enlist U.S. help given the cross border nature of drug trafficking and the ruthlessness of Mexico's drug gangs.

In public U.S. officials say little other than to acknowledge the discussions. Drug-related violence-most of it between rival cartels- has cost the lives of 3,000 Mexicans in the past year and forced the intervention of 20,000 federal troops.

Roger Noriega with the American Enterprise Institute think-tank says the Mexicans realize it's going to get worse before it gets better and "they can't do this alone and should not have to do this alone."

U.S. law enforcement agencies are wary of sharing crucial intelligence information with their Mexican counterparts who are viewed as splintered and infiltrated by drug gangs.

The Drug Enforcement Administration believes 90% of cocaine consumed in the United States comes from Mexico. Mexico also supplies the U.S. with large quantities of marijuana, heroin and methamphetamine.

> Article in "The Tribune", San Luis Obispo County, CA, July 28, 2007
> From McClatchy Newspapers.

> My thoughts – Hmmm, quiet talks, don't want publicity, anti American thoughts by many Mexicans. How is it we are so lucky to get to help Mexicans with their drug problems??? We do a substantial amount of good for Mexico-what do we get for it? More Illegal Alien immigration, more of everything that U.S. taxpayers must give to help Mexico!

> We have 20 million Illegals in our country. Mexican workers here in the United States have wired to Mexico City since January 2006 over $22 Billion dollars! U.S. taxpayer's cost of Social for Illegal Aliens since 1996 is over $397 Billion Dollars! And they don't like us! Ridiculous!

73

Did You Hear?

A veteran counterterrorism detective claimed he flunked a drug test because his wife served him marijuana-spiked meatballs!

He has been fired by the New York Police Department. These claims "simply were not creditable." So much for the meatball defense.

Police Commissioner Raymond Kelly rejected an earlier recommendation by an administrative judge that the detective, Anthony Chiofalo, be reinstated. Kelly has final say on firings.

> Article in "The Tribune", San Luis Obispo County, California
> August 24, 2007 by the Associated Press.

> My thoughts – What do you think, did she or didn't she?

Sierra Vista, Arizona

She loves bingo.
She's 62.
She's a grandmother.
Her name is Leticia Vilareal Garcia.
She had 214 pounds of marijuana stashed in her car trunk.
She was going to a bingo game.
She gets 3 years in prison, and a $150,000 fine.
She ran drugs to support her bingo habit.
State police stopped her in February 2005.
She told the judge at her sentencing that she was unaware of the marijuana.
She maintains her innocence.

> Information from an Associated Press article published January 28, 2007,
> in "The Tribune", San Luis Obispo County, California.

> My thoughts – I guess she was bored at home! I'd rather be bored at home than in prison.

A Mexican Drug Lord

San Diego, California------Francisco Javier Arellano Felix, 39, a notorious Mexican drug lord pleaded guilty to running a continuing criminal enterprise and conspiracy to launder money. Arellano Felix helped run a Tijuana, Mexico-based drug cartel that brought into the United States:
1. hundreds of tons of cocaine
2. hundreds of tons of marijuana
3. laundered hundreds of millions of dollars.

After prosecutors said they would not seek the death penalty, he pleaded guilty September 17, 2007 in United States District Court to crimes that carry a mandatory life sentence. Officials in Washington agreed not to pursue the death penalty.

> Information from an article in "The Tribune", San Luis Obispo County, California, 9-18-07, Associated Press.

> My thoughts – Besides the life sentence he should be fined millions of dollars and do hard labor. What sorrow he has wrought to families of those using drugs. He should work in drug rehab facilities cleaning and scrubbing and doing laundry, working for his food.

Cocaine Use Drops

Washington – Cocaine use by U. S. Workers is at its lowest rate in a decade, said the White House Office of National Drug Control Policy on August 9, 2007.

It cited a 16% drop in positive workplace drug tests for cocaine in the first 6 months of this year. Tight supplies and raising prices in many U.S. cities are contributors.

> Tribune Wire Services, "The Tribune," San Luis Obispo County, California, August 10, 2007.

> My thoughts – Good news for America!

75

EMERGENCIES

Earthquakes

Earthquake magnitude is a logarithmic measure of earthquake size. In simple terms, this means that at the same distance from the earthquake, the shaking will be 10 times as large during a magnitude 5 earthquake as during a magnitude 4 earthquake.

Yesterday's Weather and The Quake Report
Published in "The Tribune", San Luis Obispo County, California,
November 17, 2006

Earthquakes up to 15 Times Larger

Released research says the Los Angeles, California area may be in the midst of a prolonged seismic lull.

Going back 12,000 years geologists examined the size and frequency of earthquakes finding patterns of heavy and lighter seismic activity every 1,000 to 1,500 years.

In the journal "Geology" in a paper, scientists from the "Southern California Earthquake Center" argue that when the lull ends, metropolitan Los Angeles will experience temblors up to 15 times larger than the destructive Northridge earthquake of 1994. That could be soon or 500 years from now. "We've been having fewer earthquakes than our long-term average'" said James Dolan a USC geologist and the lead author on the paper.

Article in "The Tribune", San Luis Obispo County, California,
August 26, 2007, Tribune Wire Services.

My thoughts – I'm happy that I live on the Central Coast of California about 5 hours north of Los Angeles. I do not want to be in Los Angeles for the big one!

Hide The Cash

Include in your family's financial plan cash that you hide at home in a safe or a fire-resistant lock box. The amount depends on your family's need for food, fuel and other necessities. You need enough to last two weeks for daily expenses in case of an earthquake, hurricane or terrorist attack.

Cash remains KING when disasters happen and power may be disrupted for days or weeks. ATM's run dry. Without power, electronic commerce is powerless; debit card, credit card and check verification machines are useless!

> Information from an article by Jeff D. Opdyke in "The Tribune", San Luis Obispo County, California, June 25, 2006.

> My thoughts – Bring the cash and also have a supply of bottled water, canned and packaged foods for 2 weeks along with a portable battery operated radio and extra batteries, flashlights, blankets, etc. The variety and amount of foods depends on the size of your family and ages of your children. Don't forget the silverware and bowls. Also have a First Aid Kit and a bag with prescriptions ready to go. Decide ahead of time the fate of your family photographs and albums.

> Have a cat carrier ready and whatever you need for your dog, collar, leash, and bed. Take 2 or 3 gallons of water and dog and cat food.

> Also try to keep your car gas tank on full at all times to be ready for a quick getaway.

A Portable Hospital

Long Beach, California – A 200-bed portable hospital ordered by Governor Arnold Schwarzenegger can be deployed to the scene of a large-scale disaster. There are 2 more. Each hospital provides 23,000 square feet of hospital space and treatments from triage and emergency room services to surgery and extensive care.

> Article published in "The Tribune", San Luis Obispo County, California, August 26, 2007, Tribune Wires Services

> My thoughts – A marvelous idea!

Hurricanes Killed 320 Million Trees

Washington – "The Washington Post"

320 million trees were killed or severely damaged in Mississippi and Louisiana by Hurricanes Katrina and Rita, new satellite imaging has revealed. This is the largest single forestry disaster on record in the United States. It is an unreported ecological catastrophe.

The die-off caused by wind and later by weeks-long pooling of stagnant water was massive. Researchers say it will add significantly to the global greenhouse gas buildup. It will put as much carbon from dying vegetation into the air as the rest of the nation's forest takes out in a year of photosynthesis.

Also it has opened vast and fragile tracts to several aggressive and fast growing exotic species that are squeezing out far more environmentally productive native species.

Information from an article, in "The Washington Post" in "The Tribune", San Luis Obispo County, California, November 16, 2007.

My thoughts – Okay, what say you Al Gore, winner of the Nobel Peace Prize for your movie about Global warming? What's your solution?

$2.00 to $138.00

It cost the Saudis $2.00 to produce a barrel of crude oil.
They charge us $138.00 a barrel!

Bill O'Reilly said we must do the following to help alleviate our energy crisis.
1. Drill in Anwar for oil.
2. Use Flex Fuel cars (gasoline and electric) and increase fuel efficiency in vehicles.
3. Use Nuclear power for energy.

Heard on Bill O'Reilly cable TV show "The Factor" at 5 and 8 PM P.S.T. June 9, 2008.

My thoughts – Where have Congress and the President been for the last 30 years? Well, they're still there!!!

We let the environmentalist like the Sierra Club cheat us out of lower cost gasoline and the use of nuclear power! What are we, United States Citizens doing about it? Run for office, tell the Sierra Club to donate their millions of $$$$$ to fund private schools so children may learn about the Sierra Club and all the harm they do to the United States of America and how they get millions of $$$$$! It is our tax money that they are given every time they win an environmental lawsuit against our government!

FAMOUS

PEOPLE

&

BIG

BEN

Father Flanagans' Boys' Home

Father Edward J. Flanagan, a Roman Catholic priest and Irish immigrant, borrowed $90 from a friend to open a home for wayward boys.

On December 12, 1917, he opened Father Flanagan's Boys' Home. His home became a symbol of help, healing and hope for boys of all races, creeds and colors.

In 2000, residents voted to change the organization's name to Girls and Boys Town. Girls have been a part of the Family since 1979. Boys Town became an incorporated village of the state of Nebraska in 1936. It has 900 acres of land with 70 homes that care for about 550 children.

It has fire and police departments, Catholic and Protestant Chapels, 2 schools, a farm and a U.S. Post Office.

The Village of Boys Town is a National Historic Landmark and remains the National headquarters for all Girls and Boys Town operations.

Besides living in a safe structured family, youth in the Long-Term Residential Program enjoy many other benefits that contribute to their success. They attend state-accredited schools, and many have access to programs like "Reading is Fame", a specialized reading instruction course for students who have fallen behind or are struggling in the classroom.

Youth who have been diagnosed with mental health disorders receive counseling and treatment through the Behavioral Health Services program. Also provided are individual and group counseling for youngsters with alcohol or drug problems.

Positive outcomes – Direct Care Programs and Services – Helped 47,170 children. Parent Training Programs and Professional Workshops – Affected 929,805 children. Girls and Boys Town National Hotline – Served 444,546 callers.

Girls and Boys Town – 1-800-217-3700, www.girlsandboystown.org

Information from Girls and Boys Town sheet of stamps 2007

My thoughts – Can you believe a borrowed $90 started all these great outcomes! Wouldn't it be great if we heard more of these great successful stories! Children and youth need places to play with supervision. They need buildings to learn to dance, appreciate music, play instruments and make crafts. Tell Bill Gates to use some of his Foundation's money and that of Warren Buffet to start places where youth can go to be safe, learn arts and crafts and be successful, to learn how to use their time and not be bored.

Tony Snow 1955 – 2008

Tony Snow died today, July 12, 2008. He was 53 years old. He died of complications of cancer. He had been fighting Colon Cancer for 3 years. He was one of the best people living on earth. Tony Snow was the "Stuff" of which Presidents should be made! He had character, brains, personality, and a flawless family life. He was no fraud, he was the real thing, and the best human being a person can be!

He has a wife and 3 children. I've listened to Fox News for hours today as many people talk about his life. Everybody loved him and spoke endearingly of him. He had all the qualities of a perfect human being.

His mother died of colon cancer when he was 17. He knew he had to be vigilant about himself getting cancer. He was, but it overtook him anyway.

He had many careers in the broadcasting field. He was a radio talk show host, a commentator, Anchor of Fox News Sunday, speechwriter. In 2006 he was the White House Press Secretary, which he gave up after about 18 months because he felt he had to make more money for his family. He had taken a salary cut when he took the job as Press Secretary.

Someone said he was the best Press Secretary there ever has been! I loved to listen to him on his radio talk show.

Why is it – the good die young? This country needs people like Tony Snow! Why was he taken and despots live to old age!

Carolyn Cavolt, July 12, 2008

Knick – Knack

Carl Icohn of Carl Icohn Associates Corporation is the 24th richest man in the United States worth $14 billion. He made $300 million in one deal.

Heard on TV "60 Minutes" March 9, 2008.

83

Britain's Tony Blair, a regular at Mass

London – The ex Prime Minister of Britain is now a Roman Catholic. His wife Cherie, convent educated, and 4 children are Catholics. 6 months after stepping down as Prime Minister he has completed his long-expected conversion from Britain's established church, Anglicanism.

Blair is a Middle East envoy and was received into the Catholic Church during a Mass, December 21, 2007, at a chapel in the residence of the leading Catholic in Britain, Cardinal Cormac Murphy-O'Connor.

Information from an article in "The Tribune", San Luis Obispo County, California, December 23, 2007, by The New York Times.

My thoughts – Good for Tony! I once sent him a note thanking him, but I forget why. I really like Tony Blair; I believe he was a great leader.

Fight or Flight

Fight, fight for the right to blast detractors. Blast the liberals (what is theirs is theirs, what is ours is theirs) who want to smother us with illegal aliens, millions and millions of them! Who do the liberals, such as Hillary, and **MOST DEMOCRATS**, think will take over their jobs and their children's jobs and our country when these illegal aliens become legal through amnesty and climb up the ladder of success? They'll take over the liberals' jobs and their children's jobs and our country. They'll become members of Congress. They'll vote for what **THEY** want!

We owe our ancestors, the people who fought in the wars to keep this country free from other foreign countries a lot of honor and respect. They worked and sacrificed to make this country GREAT and FREE! They did not want us, the people following them, to give this country to the citizens of Mexico, who come to the United States of America as illegal aliens. They as illegal aliens should have no rights here. They should return to Mexico and clean up their own country, Mexico.

Carolyn Gerdink Cavolt May 30, 2008

On His First Visit to California

Mexican President Felipe Calderon made his first visit to California on February 13, 2008 since becoming Mexico's President in 2006.

Calderon told a joint session of the California Legislature that tensions existed between the United States and Mexico over illegal immigration but stressed that both countries have an interest in ensuring their citizens could cross the border legally and safely. "Our nations will never find prosperity by closing their doors," Calderon said. "I know that immigration is a controversial issue today in this great nation. But I strongly believe that Mexican and Mexican-American workers are a large reason for the dynamic economy of California," Mexican President Calderon said.

Information from an Associated Press article in "The Tribune", San Luis Obispo County, California, February 14, 2008.

My thoughts – So we have Mexican and Mexican-American workers to thank for our dynamic economy! That is Bull-Shit! The United States Citizens pay $338.3 Billion a year to take care of illegal aliens, most of them from Mexico, and we must thank Mexican and Mexican-Americans for our dynamic economy in California!

63 California hospitals were forced to close because of taking care of illegal aliens and birthing their babies free of charge! They can go to any Emergency Room of a hospital and get FREE care!

What a preposterous statement from a visiting foreign President to say on our soil!

Pants, pants, pants

When will we see females wear dresses again?

Do Pants rule?

Have women forgotten how they look in dresses?

Do 18 million women want to look like Hillary?

People watching isn't so much fun anymore.

Too many big butt behinds are flaunted which would be better viewed in a dress!

CGC
8-19-08

85

Lydia Hearst Shaw

Her mother is Patricia Campbell Hearst who was kidnapped and terrorized while attending Berkeley University in Berkeley, California in the 1970's. Her family lived in Hillsborough, California, a rich suburb in Northern California, 30 minutes south of San Francisco.

Lydia is the great granddaughter of William Randolph Hearst who built Hearst Castle at San Simeon, California. She is an heiress to the publishing fortune established by her maternal great-grandfather.

Lydia is a successful model. She was born September 19, 1984 in Wilton, Connecticut. Her father is Bernard Shaw, who was her mother's bodyguard before the couple's marriage. He is now head of security for the Hearst Corporation.

Information from Wikipedia, the free encyclopedia, may 2008.

My thoughts – I remember the kidnapping. We lived in Hillsborough in the 1970's. I remember driving by the Hearst home. The street was packed with News vehicles for weeks.

A British Landmark

London – Big Ben has been silenced for repairs only three times before this repair, in 1934, 1956, and 1990. Old age will silence Big Ben's bongs for repair in August 2007 for 4 to 6 weeks of maintenance work.

This is the first time since 1956 that both the sonorous hourly bongs and the chimes that mark each quarter-hour will be silent which is one of London's most distinctive sounds. Sometimes it can be heard for a mile and a half away. It did not stop during WWII bombing raids.

The famed bell sounds the hour at Britain's House of Parliament and will be silent for only the 4th time in 150 years.

House of Common officials said a team of specialist "industrial rope-access technicians" would rappel down the Tower's south clock face. The team will spend a day cleaning and repairing the clock's 4 faces.

A back up electric system will keep the clock running as technicians replace the bearings on mechanisms that operate the hour bell and drive the clock. This is the first replacement since the clock was installed in 1859.

Online Big Ben: www.parliament.uk/about/history/bigben.cfm

Information from an article by Associated Press, August 10, 2007 in "The Tribune", San Luis Obispo County, California.

The clock tower picture is from Wikipedia.

Mitt Romney, Former Governor of Massachusetts

He's buying a home in La Jolla in Northern San Diego, California. One of his five sons, Matt, lives in San Diego. A son, Josh, lives in Salt Lake City, Utah.

His other homes are in Belmont, Massachusetts; Wolfeboro, New Hampshire; and Deer Valley, Utah.

His wife, Ann, likes riding horses on the West Coast. The property will be closing at the end of May 2008.

> Information from an article by the Associated Press in "The Tribune, San Luis Obispo County, California, May 25, 2008.

> My thoughts – Welcome to California Governor! We need more good people to live here.

Knick Knack

Mitt and Ann Romney have a vacation home in Deer Valley, Utah, which is outside Salt Lake City, Utah. They have 5 sons. They are all married. They have 10 grandchildren. They all gather here for a 10-day ski vacation. He is the former Republican Governor of Massachusetts.

> Information from an article in "The Tribune", San Luis Obispo County, California, December 23, 2007, Associated Press.

> My thoughts – It appears they have many good things in life, a lasting marriage, a large family, 10 grandchildren, a vacation home where they all gather for a holiday.

Knick-Knack

Republican Mitt Romney said he would likely donate his salary to charity if elected president, a financial freedom he described as a byproduct of a successful business career."

> Article published in "The Tribune," San Luis Obispo County, California, May 30, 2007.

> My thoughts – I hope he handpicks 4 students to receive this money to use for college education. The money goes in their college trust fund. No overhead expenses need to be paid to a charity.

88

He's 93!

Former President Ford received a cardiac pacemaker at the Mayo Clinic, Rochester Minnesota. He was resting comfortably and his wife and children were with him. He'll stay for several days.

The pacemaker is designed to enhance his heart's performance.

Information from an article published in "The Tribune", San Luis Obispo County, California, Associated Press, August 22, 2006,

Note - President Ford died December 26, 2006 in Rancho Mirage, California

My thoughts –Our friend of 52 years, Jack Snellgrove, has a pacemaker. He was 70 when he received his first pacemaker. Seven years later a new battery unit was installed. He said the battery unit is replaced but not the implanted wires into the heart. He's now about due for the third battery unit. He said it's a "Piece of Cake." He reminds us that he is now 84. He plays bridge, was a Marine, drinks gin martini's daily, and still goes on a few gambling trips. He and his wife, Elaine, live in Kerrville, Texas.

Don't tell anyone he's an ex-Marine because he considers himself a Marine NOW and ALWAYS! He was one of the first men to land on Florida Island, over looking and covering the landing on Tulagi, which was a part of the Guadalcanal Campaign in WWII.

Knick - Knack

The New Gerald R. Ford 41 Cent Postal Stamp

The Postal Service will issue the new 41 cent stamp August 31, 2007.

Information from an article published in "The Tribune", San Luis Obispo County, California, June 12, 2007, Tribune Wire Services.

$30 Million A Year and Counting

Gillette executives declined to say how much these athletes will be paid. They are Tiger Woods, Roger Federes and Thierry Henry who will team in an endorsement deal with Gillette that will put the trio in TV commercials around the world. This combination of star power is in golf, tennis and soccer.

Woods already endorses an array of products. Last year he renewed his deal with Nike that will pay him about $30 million a year!

> Information from "Tribune wire reports", published February 5, 2007 in "The Tribune", San Luis Obispo County, California.

> My thoughts – If you don't like endorsements by celebrities, don't buy the products! The celebrities already make millions, why honor them with more money? Give the public a less expensive product and do away with giving celebrities millions of dollars.

Outrun Beckham?

London – According to the Royal Society scientific academy (www.royalsoc.ac.uk) published September 6, 2007 the Tyrannosaurus rex would have been able to outrun soccer star David Beckham. Expert's earlier thought that the 18-foot-tall T. rex's bulk would have meant it was a slow-moving scavenger. New calculations using a supercomputer suggest the T. rex could run nearly 18 MPH.

> Information from an article by Associated Press in "The Tribune", San Luis Obispo County, California, August 23, 2007.

> My thoughts – T. rex didn't make millions and wasn't on a team. But he was 18 feet tall and could run 18 miles per hour (mph).

Knick - Knack

Lisa Ling, former co-host of ABC's "The View", married Dr. Paul Song, a Chicago-based radiation oncologist, on Memorial Day Weekend. Lisa is a correspondent for National Geographic Channel.

> Published in "The Tribune" San Luis Obispo County, CA
> May 31, 2007, Tribune Wire Services.

> My thought – She was wise to leave "The View" when she did!

90

A Wedding – May 10, 2008

Bride – Jenna Welch Bush, 26, daughter of President George W. Bush and Laura Bush.

Groom – Henry Chase Hager 29, son of the head of the Republican Party in Virginia. He was an aide to Bush's former top political advisor, Karl Rove.

They met during George Bush's 2004 re-election campaign. He graduated from Wake Forest University.

Jenna has a twin sister, Barbara. They are the only children of President and Mrs. Bush.

Jenna will wear a designer gown, an Oscar de la Renta with a small train.

200 friends and relatives will attend the outdoor ceremony with dinner and dancing. A tent is being erected at the family's 1,600-acre ranch in Crawford, Texas.

The bride will have 14 attendants. Her sister, Barbara is the maid of honor.

Barbara helped the groom make decisions about the ring, which is a Hager family heirloom. It was reset in a ring that features sapphires.

Jenna will be the 23rd. child of a President to be married while their father was in office.

> Information from an article in "The Tribune", San Luis Obispo County, California, May 7, 2008.

> My thoughts – May they live happily ever after! Her grandfather, George H. W. Bush was the (41st) President of the United States.

> Heard on TV, May 9, 2008. Today is Henry Hager's 30th birthday. The population of Crawford, Texas is 751.

Sunday Freebie

Avoid basic illness traps by visiting www.whattoexpect.com for your free copy of "What to Expect: Guide to a Healthy Home", by Heidi Murkoff. The biggest mistake is forgetting that a through hand-washing can prevent many illnesses. From salmonella in the kitchen to flu in the sink, your home can be an unhealthy place.

> Information from "Intelligence Report" by Lyric Wallwork Winik, "Parade" January 14, 2007, in "The Tribune, San Luis Obispo County, California.

The Movie Star - Jimmy Stewart's Last Home

He lived in it about 50 years. He also bought an adjacent lot to use as a post-World War II victory garden. He died in 1997. The house was torn down in 2000.

A mansion built on the site of the house and garden has been sold for its $25 million asking price, the buyer is a businessman.

The new 12,000-square-foot house uses most of the 1.3-acre property.
The Mediterranean-style house has
> 7 bedrooms
> 12 bathrooms
> a projection room
> a sauna
> a basement
> an attic
> a library
> an elevator
> a service entrance
> a detached guest house with
>> 2 bedrooms
>> 2 bathrooms
>> a living room
>> and a kitchen.
>> Outside is a pool
>> A spa
>> Terrace and a loggia.

Many stars used to live on this street, Lucille Ball, Jack Benny, Rosemary Clooney, George Gershwin, Ella Fitzgerald, Paul Neuman, Joanne Woodward. In recent years Madonna and Diane Keaton.

By Ruth Ryon, Los Angeles Times-Published in "The Tribune" San Luis Obispo County, California, August 6, 2006.

My thoughts: Jimmy was one of the best examples of an actor. If you haven't seen his movies rent some, they are what movies should be, the finest examples of acting. He volunteered for service during WWII. He was one of the finest examples of a movie "star" and a patriot!

If you don't know what a victory garden is, ask someone in their 60's or 70's!

20 Richest Women in Entertainment

1. Oprah Winfrey, $1.5 billion.
2. J. K. Rowling, $1 billion. "Harry Potter" author who is finishing the 7th and final installment in the boy wizard series.
3. Martha Stewart, $638 million, lifestyle guru.
4. Madonna, $325 million.
5. Celine Dion, $250 million.
6. Mariah Carey, $225 million.
7. Janet Jackson, $150 million
8. Julia Roberts, $140 million.
9. Jennifer Aniston $110 million
9. Jennifer Lopez, $110 million.
11. Mary Kate and Ashley Olsen, twin actresses of the 80's comedy "Full House" created a multimedia empire, combined net worth around $100 million.

They are followed by Britney Spears, Judge Judy Sheindlin of TV's "Judge Judy", Sandra Bullock, Cameron Diaz, Gisele Bundchen, Ellen De Generes, Nicole Kidman, Christina Aguilera, and Rene Zellweger.

Forbes richest women needed a minimum net worth of $45 million amassed over the course of their careers to make the list. It was posted January 18, 2007 on the web site www.forbes.com

Information from Associated Press article, published in "The Tribune", San Luis Obispo County, California, January 20, 2007.

Were You Invited?

Barbra Streisand had a fundraising dinner at her Malibu, California estate April 12, 2007 for the Democratic Congressional Campaign Committee. Barbra welcomed Nancy Pelosi and 120 invited guests who paid up to $50,000 a couple for a dinner party inside a large white tent. $1.3 million was raised.

Article in "The Tribune", San Luis Obispo County, California, April 14, 2007.

A Wonderful, Courageous Woman!

1. Barbara Hillary, at age 75, is one of the oldest people to reach the North Pole.
2. Believed to be the first black woman to reach the North Pole.
3. The North Pole is the northern most point on earth.
4. She lives in Averne, New York, grew up in Harlem.
5. She raised thousands of dollars for the trip and on April 23, 2007 she started the trip on skis with two trained guides. They left Longyearben, Norway where people carry guns to ward off hungry polar bears.
6. The hazards are many in getting to the North Pole. Frostbite, polar bears, and the shifting ice beneath frozen feet.
7. She had a nursing career and was a community activist. At 67, during her retirement she battled lung cancer and survived.
8. At 72 she went dog sledding in Quebec and photographed polar bears in Manitoba.

Information from an article in "The Tribune" San Luis Obispo County, CA by Meghan Barr, Associated Press, May 7, 2007.

My thoughts – This lady has no fear! She is a model for all women.

Actor Glenn Ford

Glenn Ford died August 30, 2006 at his home in Beverly Hills, California. He was 90 years old. His Hollywood career lasted 53 years. The Film Encyclopedia, a reference book, lists 85 films from 1939 to 1991.

He appeared in "The Blackboard Jungle," "Gilda," "The Big Heat." He was a leading man.

Sidney Poitier also starred in "The Blackboard Jungle." He said Ford had magical qualities and was a Movie **Star.**

Obituary-Associated Press, published in "The Tribune". San Luis Obispo County, August 31, 2006.

My thoughts-The old movies were (are) the best! Who can ever forget the movie, "Gilda"?

Chelsea Clinton

Chelsea gets a new job in New York working with Avenue Capital Group, a hedge fund that manages about $12 billion in assets, the agency that represents Clinton confirmed.

New York based Avenue Capital specializes in trading in distressed debt or debt of companies that are nearing or have filed for bankruptcy. Clinton, 26, had been working as a consultant for McKinsey & Co. since 2003, reportedly for a 6-figure salary.

She received a Master's degree from Oxford University after graduating from Stanford University in California in 2001.

Federal records show Avenue Capital founders Mark Lasry and Sonia Gardner have donated thousands of dollars to Democratic lawmakers, including Senator Hillary Rodham Clinton of New York, as well as to Democratic campaign committees.

> Information from an article from the Associated Press, New York, November 6, 2006, published in "The Tribune", San Luis Obispo County, California.

> My thoughts – Is that old adage true? It's not what you know but whom you know! In case you don't remember, Chelsea is the only child of Hillary and Bill Clinton.

Kennebunkport, Maine

President George W. Bush visited his parents' century-old summer home on the Maine coast.

He got a loud reminder of the unpopularity of his Iraq policies. About 700 anti-war demonstrators marched to within half a mile of the Bush compound.

The protesters sang, beat drums, waved signs, played fiddles to call on Bush to bring the troops home.

> Information from an article, Associated Press, in "The Tribune", San Luis Obispo County, California, August 27, 2006.

> My thoughts-We saw this home from the road in the 1990's. I wish many Americans could be so fortunate to inherit a family vacation home on a coast. A very good tradition.

Paris Hilton, an entitled life!

She has been famously portrayed as an airhead, heiress, party girl and sex tape victim. Her first full CD, "Paris" has been released. "I've been singing and playing piano since I'm 6 years old," she reports, as if the world should know this by now. "This is something I'm really good at. I can really sing. (So) whatever people really believe, I don't really think about it." Her first single, "Stars Are Blind," cracked the top 20.

Hilton says she performed in the school orchestra and the choir growing up. She's already bubbling with ideas for CD # 2. She'll even do a tour. Hilton calls music her most personal expression; she has no plans to ease up on her broader empire building. There's a new movie coming called "The Haughty and the Naughty." She's "Curating" a cartoon series about her life. She's also working with "Spider-Man" creator Stan Lee to create her own superhero. So, what superpowers might that character possess? "Basically," Hilton says, "She can do anything."

> Information from an article by Jim Farber, New York Daily News, Published in "The Tribune", San Luis Obispo County, California, August 23, 2006.

> My thoughts – She is proving herself to be capable of almost anything she wants to do. I wish she would build a school, naturally called "The Paris Hilton School" to give struggling children a chance. This would be Paris Hilton's greatest act of the century. It has been estimated that she will inherit $150 million. Her sister will also. Plus Paris will have the money from her many successful enterprises.

This is How it's Done Now!

First, the two revealed they were expecting their first child together.

Later he presented his bride-to-be with an engagement ring.

Brooke Burke, 34, a "Baywatch" beauty will marry her former co-star, French actor/musician David Charvet.

She has two daughters from her marriage to Garth Fisher, a plastic surgeon featured on ABC's "Extreme Makeover."

Charvet, 34, played lifeguard Matt Brody on "Baywatch," and also starred on "Melrose Place."

> "People" – published August 22, 2006 in "The Tribune", San Luis Obispo County, California.

Albert Ellis

New York – Albert Ellis developed rational emotive behavior therapy, which stresses that patients can improve their lives by taking control of self-defeating thoughts, feelings and behaviors. Many consider his work to be part of the foundation of cognitive behavior therapy.

Ellis is the founder of a renowned psychotherapy institute. He died July 24, 2007 at the age of 93. His wife said he died of kidney and heart failure after a long illness. He was a provocative figure in modern psychology.

> Article in "The Tribune", San Luis Obispo County, California, July 25, 2007, Tribune Wire Services.

> My thoughts – He must have practiced what he preached to have lived such a long life.

Oprah Tops Forbes TV List

Oprah (need I add Winfrey) made $206 million between June 2006 and June 2007, the Forbes.com salary survey shows.

> Here's how her money was accumulated:
> 1. her daytime show
> 2. her satellite radio program
> 3. women's service magazine
> 4. the Broadway show, "The Color Purple" which she produced
> 5. she has an interest in Dr. Phil McGraw's and Rachael Ray's syndicated shows
> 6. she's producing 2 reality-TV programs.

Her 2 protégés McGraw and Ray are # 7 and # 13 on the list.

> Information from an article by the New York Daily News in "The Tribune", San Luis Obispo County, California, September 29, 2007.

> My thoughts – Will anything or anybody ever stop Oprah? I say she's unstoppable. Congratulations to her! She's also doing many good deeds with the money! I wish she'd build more schools here in America. We surely need great schools and instructors.

97

Liz Claiborne

New York. Liz Claiborne died June 26, 2007 of a rare cancer that affects the lining of the stomach, which she was told she had in 1977. She was 78.

She was the designer of Career Clothes for professional women entering the workforce beginning in the 1970's. She became the most successful women's apparel designer in America of the time. She had already worked for 20 years in the backrooms of Seventh Avenue sportswear houses

> Information from an article in "The Tribune" San Luis Obispo County, California, Nation Roundup, Tribune wire services, June 28, 2007.

Put a Lid on Malibu Parties!

Would you believe that one Malibu Party lasted 22 hours! The corporate-financed celebrity parties that Malibu residents say clog their streets, create too much noise and invite a swarm of paparazzi to their well-heeled beaches.

Malibu leaders are drawing up an ordinance that would limit corporate beach house parties.

Companies rent mansions in the summer in order to link their products to hot young celebrities who show up and indulge in freebies. Then there are the paparazzi ready to photograph celebs next to the latest flat screen TV's, jewelry and other products.

Renny Shapiro, a Malibu resident, said they've had 26 parties at the house next to them. Half have been parties with hundreds of people. She lives on Malibu Beach next to what is now known as the "Polaroid Beach House." Nearby are the LG Beach House and the Silver Spoon Beach House.

City officials say that the parties have led to noise, illegally parked cars blocking driveways and fire hydrants, and seemingly non-stop action. They want to draft an ordinance that would limit the corporate gatherings but would still allow weddings, barbecues and bar mitzvahs.

> Article in "The Tribune", San Luis Obispo County, California by Associated Press, August 26, 2007.

> My thoughts – More proof that rules are always needed. I wonder how easy it would be to crash one of these parties?!

The Goldman Family vs. O.J. Simpson

Simpson gave them a fake; it was supposed to be a gold submariner Rolex watch, estimated to be worth between $12,000 and $22,000. The luxury watch was a knock-off made in China, worth maybe $125. The Goldman's attorney will return the watch to O.J. Simpson, saying, "it's a people's Rolex, it was made by the finest craftsman in China." A Santa Monica, California judge had ordered Simpson to give it to the Goldman family because a jury found him liable for the killings of Ron Goldman and Niclole Brown in 1994, although he was acquitted of murder charges. He was ordered to pay $33.5 million.

He is currently being charged with armed robbery and kidnapping in a September 13, 2007 incident at a Las Vegas hotel. He and 5 other men are charged with bursting into a hotel room at gunpoint to steal signed footballs etc. from memorabilia dealers.

> Information from "People" in "The Tribune", San Luis Obispo County, California, October 6, 2007.

> My thoughts – I believe he should be in prison for killing Nicole Brown and Ron Goldman. The evidence I saw as I watched the trial on TV seems to point to him. I will always remember I was in San Antonio, Texas in a hotel near "The River Walk" when I heard the "Not Guilty" verdict on TV and was outraged and incredulous!!

Dolly Girl Scout

Dolly Parton is a
1. Country singer
2. Songwriter
3. Movie Star
4. Amusement Park owner
5. Philanthropist
6. Girl Scout

She was named a lifetime member of Girls Scouts of Tanasi Council before 1,000 Girl Scouts at her Dollywood theme park. She accepted a lifetime membership pin and led the audience in the Girl Scout Promise.

> Information from an article published in "The Tribune", "People" San Luis Obispo County, California, June 18, 2007.

> My thoughts – Having no girls of her own, Dolly has been blessed with a thousand good Girl Scouts!

Drunken Astronaut Claims Untrue

NASA said on August 29, 2007 that they found no evidence that any of its astronauts ever flew while inebriated, or even showed up for work impaired, as was recently asserted by an outside investigative panel.

Agency Administrator Michael Griffin said an account of an unnamed astronaut flying drunk on a Russian Soyuz flight was false. A 45 page internal review was released. He said, "I think our guys are doing a heck of a job." Go to sanluisobispo.com/topnews to read NASA's report.

This article from "Los Angeles Times", August 30, 2007, published in "The Tribune", San Luis Obispo County, California.

My thoughts – What a relief to know that the drunken astronaut claims are untrue.

Wrongly Accused

Atlanta – Richard Jewell died August 29, 2007 at age 44. He was the former security guard who was wrongly linked to the 1996 Olympic bombing. He was found dead in his west Georgia home. He had been home sick with kidney problems for 6 months.

Article from the Tribune Wire Services, in "The Tribune", San Luis Obispo County, California, August 30, 2007.

My thoughts – He was relentlessly featured in the news as the Olympic bomber. He was not guilty. Poor Guy! He surely died young.

Model Behavior

Model Kate Moss referred to as "Cocaine Kate" by the British Press, was named model of the year at the British Fashion Awards, November 2, 2006, in London. But as the Daily Mail put it so kindly, Kate, 32, couldn't "be bothered to show up" for the applause.

In "People," Tribune Wire Services, November 4, 2006.
Published in The Tribune, San Luis Obispo County, California.

My thoughts – It seems that those who are given much don't know how to live with it! She needs a Nanny!

100

The Son of Princess Grace Kelly

Prince Albert said he doesn't see marriage in his future. The 48-year-old Monarch said, "I have no plans in the near or distant future." "Anytime I'm seen with a pretty young woman by my side more than once, then everybody flashes the "M" word as you say."

The Prince is the second child of Prince Rainier and American film star Grace Kelly. He was visiting the U.S. this weekend to attend an international leadership conference and a celebration of the 50th anniversary of his late mother's last movie, "High Society."

> Information from an article in "The Tribune", Associated Press, San Luis Obispo County, California, published August 14, 2006.

> From Wikipedia – Grace Kelly was born in Philadelphia, Pennsylvania, November 12, 1929, died September 14, 1982 (Age 52) Monte Carlo, Monaco, in an automobile accident.

> The American Film Institute ranked Grace Kelly # 13 amongst the Greatest Female Stars of All Time. She married Prince Rainier III of Monaco on April 19, 1956 (600 guests). They had 3 children, 2 girls and a boy.

> Some of her films were, "High Noon" with Gary Cooper; "Mogambo" with Clark Gable; "Dial M for Murder"; "Rear Window" with James Stewart; "The Country Girl" with Bing Crosby; "To Catch a Thief" with Cary Grant. Her film career lasted only 5 years and 11 films because she gave it up for Marriage but she is remembered as a premier actress.

Hawaiian Crooner Don Ho

He died April 14, 2007 of heart failure at age 76. A sunset memorial was held at Waikiki on a beach with thousands of fans. City officials said the crowd was one of the largest ever. His signature tune was "Tiny Bubbles".

> Information from article in "People" published in "The Tribune", San Luis Obispo County, CA, May 7, 2007.

> Information from Wikipedia – Don Ho was born Donald Tai Loy Ho, August 13, 1930 in the Honolulu, Hawaii, neighborhood of Kaka'ako. He was a graduate of Kamehameha School. He also graduated from the University of Hawaii. He was in the United States Air Force (1954 – 1959) flying fighter jets. He had 10 children. He was a very famous entertainer.

> My thoughts – I remember listening to him sing "Tiny Bubbles", when we visited Waikiki in the 1970's. His rendition stays with listeners forever.

Baron Rothschild of the French Banking Dynasty

Baron Guy de Rothschild, the patriarch of the French branch of the famous banking dynasty, who rebuilt and expanded its Paris bank after it was seized during World War II. The bank also survived another government takeover in the 1980's. Baron Rothschild died in Paris on June 12, 2007. He was 98.

Lean and charming, the aristocratic Rothschild was an heir to the house of Rothschild, whose several branches were financiers of kings and princes when Europe was a royal family affair.

He was celebrated in Paris, London, New York and elsewhere for the family wine, chateau Lafite Rothschild, also for his thoroughbred racehorses.

Extravagant costume balls and dinners were held at his enormous country home outside of Paris, the Chateau de Ferrieres.

After the fall of France in 1940, the pro – Nazi Vichy regime seized the family bank. The next year, the baron slipped away to New York and then to London where he joined General Charles de Gaulle's Free French forces. 40 years later in 1981, history repeated itself, the newly elected Socialist-Communist coalition of President Francois Mitterrand nationalized the bank that the baron had reclaimed and built up again after World War II.

He had retired as chairman of the bank in 1979. He was so disgusted by what France had done to his family for a second time that he again returned to New York where he helped run a small Rothschild business. Before leaving Paris he published a famous front-page article in Le Monde accusing the Socialists of pandering to French anti-Semitism.

> Information from an article from the New York Times, published in "The Tribune" San Luis Obispo County, California June 14, 2007.

The Search

Minden, Nevada. The search for aviator and adventurer, **Steve Fossett**, 63, included 45 airplanes and helicopters. 25 are under the jurisdiction of the civil air patrol; the remainder are flown by private pilots operating from a ranch owned by hotel mogul Barron Hilton, about 80- miles southeast of Reno, Nevada. It has been nearly a week since his plane disappeared in Nevada's high desert.

> Information from an article in "The Tribune", San Luis Obispo County, California, by Tribune Wires Services, September 9, 2007.

> My thoughts – I pray he is found.

O. J. Simpson

Las Vegas, Nevada---------- Police arrested O. J. Simpson on September 16, 2007, saying he was part of an armed group that burst into a Las Vegas hotel room and snatched memorabilia that documented his own sports career.

10 years ago he was acquitted of the slaying of his ex-wife and a friend. Plainclothes officers took Simpson, 60, away in handcuffs from the Palms casino-hotel. Simpson said there were no guns involved. He said they were retrieving items that were stolen and belonged to him. His golfing buddy was arrested the day before. This buddy was with him with a gun in the hold up.

The expected charges, according to Clark County, Nevada, District Attorney David Roger:

1. Conspiracy to commit robbery, a felony, 1 to 6 years in state prison.
2. Burglary with the use of a deadly weapon, a felony, 2 to 15 years in state prison.
3. Assault with a deadly weapon, 2 counts, felonies, 1 to 6 years in State prison on each count.
4. Coercion with a deadly weapon, a felony, 2 to 12 years in state prison.
5. Robbery with the use of a deadly weapon, 2 counts, a felony, 2 to 15 years in state prison on each count plus an enhancement of up to 15 years.
6. Conspiracy to commit a crime, a gross misdemeanor, up to 1 year in county jail.

Excerpted from an article in "The Tribune", San Luis Obispo County, California, September 17, 2007, Associated Press.

My thoughts – I hope this person finally gets a just punishment. I believe he was guilty of killing Nicole, his ex-wife, and Ron Goldman, who was just doing a good deed when he returned Nicole's mother's glasses, after the dinner at a restaurant, to Nicole's house.

It is with difficulty that I look at Simpson on the TV screen. I'll never understand why a judge gave custody to him of his and Nicole's 2 children. Where is the justice in this country? He is rich so will he get off again? My disgust for this male is unbounded!

Up Yours!

Don't pull a Britney Spears when you go to Wal-Mart to do your shopping. Alejandro Valdez, 24, of Fremont, California was arrested on suspicion of unlawful peeping with an electronic instrument after a 30-year old San Jose, California woman said she noticed him crouching behind her in the produce aisle.

She whirled around and grabbed his phone when she saw her thighs on the screen of the cell phone. She went to the store pharmacy to call police as Valdez trailed behind pleading to get the phone. She was wearing a skirt and he was trying to snap pictures under her skirt.

> Rewritten information from "State Roundup", Associated Press, published January 21, 2007 in "The Tribune", San Luis Obispo County, California.

> My thoughts – Some people in our country are really weird! Can you imagine this happening 15 years ago? If you don't remember about Britney Spears – I believe she forgot to wear underpants and the paparazzi went nuts with their cameras.

A Soccer Player's Worth

David Beckham, the renowned English soccer player who has signed with the "Los Angeles Galaxy" will be paid a base salary of $5.5 million per year. This is a 5-year contract.

The Major League Soccer season ends in November 2007. He will be going to the "Los Angeles Galaxy" after his contract with Real Madrid ends June 30, 2007, when he will take a short holiday before joining the Galaxy.

> Information from an article in "The Tribune" San Luis Obispo County, California, Associated Press article May 31, 2007.

> My thoughts – Parents pray that your child wants to play soccer. It is a lucrative sport and the whole neighborhood can practice together with the parents also. Buy a house with a large backyard or live near a park.

> Another article of September 1, 2007 stated his salary as $6.5 million a year. He is married to a Spice Girl.

Soccer's David Beckham

The 32-year-old English midfielder is out of play for 6 weeks with a sprained right knee to go along with his famously injured left ankle. He sprained his medial collateral ligament in a tackle during the Galaxy's loss to a Mexican team. His injuries threaten to deflate the Hollywood hype that propelled Beckham and his Spice Girl wife to A-list celebrities. His Galaxy coach is Frank Yallop.

For Beckham's time – 310 minutes in 6 of 12 possible games – Beckham earned $20,967 a minute from a yearly salary of $6.5 million.

His minutes in 3 MLS games totaled 198, worth $32, 828 a minute.

Information from an associated Press article September 1, 2007 in "The Tribune", San Luis Obispo County, California.

My thoughts – I didn't realize Soccer players received so many injuries. He must just be having a bad year. Maybe he should have stayed with England's national team. This article stated his salary as $6.5 million a year.

Roseville, California

Summer Sanders' family home in nearby Granite Bay burned. She was in town for the "Summer Sanders Invitational" at the Roseville Aquatics Complex in Suburban Sacramento. Her brother, Trevor Sanders, said the fire destroyed his sisters NCAA trophies from her years at Stanford University, as well as her Goodwill Games medals and her 1992 Babe Zaharias award for amateur women athletes. No one was injured not even the family cat. The cause is under investigation. Sanders, 34, lives in Park City, Utah where her four Olympic medals – two gold, silver and a bronze – are stored.

Information from an article published in "The Tribune", San Luis Obispo County, California, by Tribune Staff Wire Reports, published June 12, 2007.

105

FREEDOM

&

NUCLEAR

POWER

Freedom

1. There are 193 Countries in the world.
2. 90 Countries are free, representing 47% of the world's countries.
3. 60 are partly free.
4. 43 Countries are judged not free.
5. 36% of the people in the world are not living in freedom, about half of them in China.
6. Numbers according to a survey by a private democracy watchdog organization.

Information from an article by the Associated Press (Washington) in "the Tribune", San Luis Obispo County, California, January 16, 2008.

My thoughts – There are 6.6 Billion people in the world.

Do You Know The United States Has 103 Nuclear Power Plants?

There are 103 nuclear power plants in the United States. There are at least 7 applications for more. France's power is 90% nuclear.

The Sierra Club stops the United States from building more nuclear power plants. They file lawsuits to stop the building of nuclear plants.

Heard on the Bill Wattenberg radio program – KGO, 810AM San Francisco, California, 10 PM to 1 AM every Saturday and Sunday night, May 2008. Dr. Bill Wattenberg is one of the country's brilliant men.

United States Largest Nuclear Power Plant

The Palo Verde Nuclear Generating Station is the nation's largest nuclear power plant located in Wintersburg, Arizona. The containment domes where the plant's nuclear material is stored are about half a mile from the entrance.

Information from a Tribune wire services article in "The Tribune", San Luis Obispo County, California, November 3, 2007.

GIFTS

A gift of 15 Surfboards

Jerusalem----Dorian Paskowitz, a Jewish surfing legend from Hawaii, who is an 86-year-old retired doctor with 75 years of surfing experience gave 15 surfboards to a few Palestinians surfers waiting on the other side of the Erez Crossing between Israel and Gaza. He hopes Israelis and Palestinians will catch a peace wave! "When a surfer sees another surfer with a board, he can't help but say something that brings them together", said Paskowitz. He had read a newspaper article about 2 Gazans who couldn't enjoy the waves because they had only one board between them. A surfer from Tel Aviv, said Paskowitz's project was part of a larger effort called "Surfing for Peace" aimed at bringing Middle East surfers closer together.

> Article in "The Tribune" San Luis Obispo County, California
> Associated Press, August 22, 2007.

> My thoughts – I pray the good doctor's idea works. There's always another great idea from someone.

A Cell Call

A call from a grown-up grandson can change a day from sad to sunny! A 30-minute call on his way to work is better than a bowlful of Bing cherries or eating a whole watermelon. Grandchildren, don't ever forget about your power of changing a grandparents' day from so-so to happy.

Carolyn Gerdink Cavolt - May 25, 2008 - Thanks, Derek!

Knick - Knack

Have two families.
One to grow up with.
One to grow old with.
Then old age won't be so lonesome and scary.

CGC 7-20-08

109

$50 in a Card

Christmas came early for bus riders in Spokane, Washington when a woman hopped aboard buses, greeted passengers with "Merry Christmas" and handed each an envelope containing a card and a $50 bill. The woman repeated the kind act on several buses and did it so quickly that descriptions varied among surprised Spokane Transit Authority passengers on several routes, 4 days before Christmas. The Spokesman Review newspaper reported this story.

The bus driver said he couldn't remember ever seeing her and that she kind of kept her head down. One young man in the back of the bus looked like he was going to cry.

> Information from an article from the Tribune Wire Services "Nation Roundup" Published in "The Tribune", San Luis Obispo County, California, December 24, 2006.

The Reward

He found an envelope with a $185,000 check. He is **Reggie Damon**, 47, of Jewett City, Connecticut. He took a bus from his home to the bank to return the check to the niece of the landlord whose name was on the check. He remembered his mother's words: "If you take something, you lose 3 times that amount, and if you do something good, something good comes back to you." Damon receives food stamps and works at McDonalds. His reward from the niece was a $50 bill.

> Information from an article by the Associated Press in "The Tribune", San Luis Obispo County, California, January 2, 2008.

> My thoughts – A very honest man who received a stingy reward from the "loser" who should have been taught about generosity and appreciation. I think $1,000 or more would have been a better reward with the offer to help him find a more profitable job or help to learn a more profitable profession.

> I imagine that lady really felt good!!! Her Christmas came 4 days early also.

New Series of Stamps

Washington. The Post Office is launching a new series of stamps featuring the flags of the United States and territories.

The first 10 of the 60 planned flag stamps will be issued spring 2008 and a second set in the fall. The first stamps to be issued will feature the Stars and Stripes and the flags of Alabama, Alaska, American Samoa, Arizona, Arkansas, California, Colorado, Connecticut and Delaware. Each stamp will feature a scene related to each state, such as Alabama shrimp boat, Arizona cactus, Colorado mountains and a Delaware beach.

> Information from an Associated Press article in "The Tribune", San Luis Obispo County, California, August 11, 2007.

> My thoughts – Sounds like a beautiful idea. Buy a sheet to use as a birthday or Christmas gift.

A Dear Abby Question

A husband and wife received a wedding invitation from her nephew's son. Included was a deposit slip to a bank savings account "in lieu of gifts"!   Everyone on the guest list received a deposit slip, even the grandmother. She asks if this is proper? Frankly they were insulted. Puzzled in Colorado.

Dear Abby's reply – Please waste no more time feeling offended. The family who issued the wedding invitation is obviously grossly ignorant about the basic rules of etiquette! According to "Emily Post's Etiquette" (17th Edition) when issuing wedding invitations, "any mention of gifts or listing of gift registries is unacceptable." I am sure that you dealt with the solicitation you received as you would any other. Just be glad they didn't have your bank account number, or you would have found enclosed with your invitation a notice stating that your account had already been debited $125 to cover the cost of the dinner.

> Information from a "Dear Abby" column, August 17, 2007 in "The Tribune", San Luis Obispo County, California. Jeanne Phillips writes under the name Dear Abby. Write to her at www.dearabby.com or P.O. Box 69440, Los Angeles, California 90069.

> My thoughts – Now that is a straightforward answer! Dear Abby must have given that family a headache, which they deserved! A wedding invitation is an invitation to come and share our joy and have a good time with us on this day.

Sell or Swap Gift Cards

A well-intentioned friend gives you a gift card to a bookstore but you crave new clothes. What do you do?

1. Toss the card
2. Give it to someone else or
3. Go on line and swap the present.

The National Retail Federation estimates gift card sales will total $25 billion this holiday season. Some analysts estimate that as much as $3.5 billion of that will never be spent on goods. You don't have to contribute to that eye-popping loss.

Cardavenue.com lets people auction or trade gift cards. Registration is free, but you need an account with Pay Pal, eBay's online payment system. Sellers and traders pay a fee equal to 3.95% of the cards value, plus an additional 50-cent closing fee. For auctions, you can specify a minimum bid.

Fees are flat at Plastic Jungle.com, a sell or trade site that also uses Pay Pal. You can list a card for 90 days for $3.99, no matter the value. Rather than an auction process, you set sell prices upfront. You can also sell some cards directly to the site. Gift Card Buy Back.com is another service where you can sell cards to the company rather than other individual shoppers. The site will pay 60% to 80% of the cards value, but doesn't accept all retailers. Checks usually arrive within 10 days of sending the card.

If you're looking to BUY gift cards, you may be able to get them on line for 10% to 25% off. Although buying from a third party increases the risk of fraud, most of the sites say they have safeguards to protect consumers.

Information from an article, "Tip of the Week" by J. B., published in "The Tribune," "The Wall Street Journal Sunday", December 24, 2006.

My thoughts – Personally I'm not fond of gift cards unless they're from a store where I shop. Why not just give cash to the person you want to give a gift?

Getting the Boot

The West's best boot makers will ensure that you are well heeled.

I. In Colorado, Telluride's "Bounty Hunter" is the requisite stop for celebrities who want customized, handmade Lagarto Black Jack's. They have an Ostrich and Calfskin boot for $1,015. – 226 West Colorado Avenue – 970-728-0256.

II. Aspen's "Kemo Sabe" – 434 East Cooper Avenue – 970-925-7878 – kemosabe.com. Offers burnished-leather Lucchesses.

III. Axel's, Vail, Colorado – 201 Gore Creek Drive – 970-476-7625 – axelsvail.com. Known for its specialty work. adding precious stones and silver to traditional leather tooling. A crocodile and buffalo boot $3,850.

IV. Santa Fe, New Mexico "Back At The Ranch" sells examples from high-end makers as Rocketbuster, Kemmel and Liberty, and it's own private label. – 209 East Marcy Street, 888-96-Boots – backattheranch.com.

V. Schwarz Custom Boots, Dillon, Montana – 120 South Montana Street – 406-683-6652. Dan and Keni Schwarz are a father-daughter team. There is an 18-month wait for their creations and a compulsory fitting at the shop.

VI. Millsap, Texas, ½ hour outside Fort Worth, by appointment – 2112 Poe Prairie Road – 817-341-9700. The showroom of Stephanie Ferguson, the state's only solo female boot maker. Her "dress western" creations start at $950.00, are made for exotic skins and can feature tops depicting humming birds, parrots and morning glories. A kangaroo boot is $3,080.

Information from an article by Sally Horchow, Town and Country magazine, October 2006.

My thoughts – The boots are dazzling, some inlaid with colors. Choose your boot maker.

Please Respond by Due Date!

Wedding invitations with response cards must be answered. "Response Cards" are included with invitations so that the hosts will know how many people to plan on and the quantity of food and beverages that will be needed.

When an invitation is sent, it is meant **only for the person (or persons) whose names are on the envelope.**

This means NO extra guests, and that includes children or dates. If you feel you cannot abide by that, then send your regrets.

Information from "Dear Abby Advice", published in "The Tribune", San Luis Obispo County, California, October 9, 2006.

My thoughts – A very frustrating situation for the hosts. If guests don't return the response cards and attend anyway I'm sure the hosts would like to say, okay you may stay but stand in the back of the line, you may not eat or sit until all the responders have done so. If you brought children take them home and hire a baby sitter, and then return.

Remember, the hosts must order the food, if it is not eaten the hosts still must pay for it. If the reception is in a hotel or restaurant they pay per person, perhaps $50.00 or more per person. Some caterers charge much more, $200 per person.

Put yourself in the host's position – if you don't let them know you're coming they won't have enough food if you come. If you respond and say you'll be there and don't attend they'll still pay for the food. If only 10 people do this the host will pay $500 or $2,000 extra because of your lack of consideration, bad manners and rudeness.

Personally I think not returning the response card should be the 11th Commandment. If you break the 11th you go to Hell!

The Perfect Gift

When a baby is born you can give the perfect gift. Save the newborn stem cells. They can be preserved. When your baby or family needs them the stem cells from the baby's cord blood are readily available. Stem cells are being used to treat over 75 diseases.

Consider the gift of cord blood banking with Cord Blood Registry, cbr cord blood registry.

For information call 1-888-587-4395, or online at www.cordblood.com/perfectgift

An ad in "Town and Country" magazine, July 2006.

My thoughts – Sounds like a good idea to me.

An $8,800 Bag

The season's most desirable is a gem-encrusted metallic tote, a Marc Jacobs bag, $8,800. The most coveted accessories are often the most opulent and the most copied.

This bag is picture in the January 2007 issue of Harper Bazaar magazine, page 63. Fashion Editor Ana Maria Pimentel, Photographer Charles Masters Phone # for bag 212-343-1490

My thoughts – Wrap it!

Knick Knack

Ex-President Jimmy Carter has been given $20 Million of taxpayers' money for his Carter Center since 2001.

Heard on Fox News, April 17, 2008.

My thoughts – Why??? What a waste of taxpayers' money! I can think of a hundred places where that money **should** have been given! Who authorized this gift to Carter?

GOVERNMENT

Your $$$$$ Thrown Away – Again

The United States government wasted hundreds of thousands of $$$ in Hurricane Katrina's (8-29-05) aftermath.

Missing - more than 100 laptop computers.
A dozen **boats** bought by Homeland Security Department employees after the storm.

More than 10,000 Homeland Security Department employees carry "Purchase Cards" for business-related expenses with a spending limit of $250,000 each! Twenty-two (22) agencies make up the Homeland Security Department.

The Homeland Security Department spent $435 million with the "Purchase Cards" in the 2005 budget year, compared to $296 million in 2004, a difference of $139 million more in 2005.

Some Stupid Buys:
> 2,000 sets of dog booties, costing $68, 442, which equals $34.22 per set, are still in storage, not-used, not-needed!
> 3 portable shower units for $71,170 from a contractor who investigators said overcharged the government!
> A beer brewing kit and ingredients for more than $1,000 for a Coast Guard official to brew alcohol while on duty as a social organizer for the U.S. Coast Guard Academy.

> Information in an article by Lara Jakes Jordan, Associated Press, published in "The Tribune", San Luis Obispo County, California, July 19, 2006.

> My thoughts – Use this information to complain to your Congressmen and Homeland Security Chief, Michael Chertoff. Do you like to pay taxes? We need oversight.

First a United States Sailor, Now a United States Citizen

A United States Navy sailor, Victor Nwabuzor, originally of Nigeria, took the oath of allegiance to the United States during a naturalization ceremony Tuesday, August 22, 2006 in Coronado, California. 88 servicemen from 29 countries were sworn in as United States Citizens during the ceremony.

> Information in an article published in "The Tribune", San Luis Obispo County, California, August 23, 2006.

> My thoughts – Do you agree? Join the armed forces and you can become an America Citizen.

117

If the United States switches to $1.00 coins instead of using paper $1.00 bills taxpayers will save $522 Million per year!

> Source: Government Accountability Office, published in "The Tribune", San Luis Obispo County, California, July 2008.

> My thoughts – What an easy way to make $522 Million every year! Why wouldn't everyone want to do this? Carry $1.00 coins instead of $1.00 paper bills.

A $1.2 Billion Airplane

A B-2 Stealth Bomber crashed at Anderson Air Base on Guam on February 22, 2008 with both pilots ejecting safely in good condition. Each B-2 bomber costs about $1.2 Billion.

> Information from a Tribune wire services article in "The Tribune, San Luis Obispo County, California, February 23, 2008.

> My thoughts - $100 million, $100 million, $100 million, $100 million, $100 million, $100 million, $100 million, $100 million, $100 million, $100 million, $100 million plus $100 million equal $1.2 Billion!

Knick – Knack

Abortion has taken the lives of nearly 50 million unborn children since 1973.

> Information in Cal Thomas' column of April 16, 2008 in "The Tribune", San Luis Obispo County, California.

> My thoughts – Cal Thomas is a respected newspaperman and TV Fox News person. Abortion is abhorrent. I believe when the Supreme Court confirmed Roe vs. Wade in 1973 that was the start of the devaluation of human life, of children's lives, of babies lives. To me it says, if you don't want it, kill it!

A Liberal

A Liberal knows what's best for all of us.
A liberal is either from Hollywood or an East Coast Liberal or anywhere in between.
Barack Obama is the most liberal person in the Senate.
You might love liberals.
Many people do.
Hillary is a liberal, 18 million people love her.
One day she will be the President of the United States, she thinks.
Many entertainers are liberal.
Do you know why?
I don't either.
They have lots of money; lots of people love and adore them.
They like to tell people who are not liberals that they are wrong.
They want to convert people to liberalism which means people should have everything other people do.
Except how can we all have the millions that entertainers have?
Is that where Liberalism stops?
I don't know.
Ask a liberal!

> Carolyn Gerdink Cavolt
> October 7, 2008

Knick – Knacks

The hearing on February13, 2008 in the chambers of Congress on drugs with Roger Clemens lasted 4 ½ hours. It cost the taxpayers $1 million and gave some Congressmen a chance to be noticed. Clemens said he did not use steroids. His trainer said he injected Clemens.

My thoughts – When will **some** members of Congress grow brains? Did you vote for a wise person to be your Congressman? Think carefully before you vote. $1 million dollars to hold such a hearing is stupidity.

119

Southwestern United States Fence to be Built

670 miles of fence is being built along the southwest United States Border to be completed by the end of 2008 in Arizona, California, New Mexico and Texas. "As of March 17,2008, there were 309 miles of fencing in place, leaving 361 miles to be completed by the end of 2008 to meet the Homeland Security Department's goal. Of these, 267 miles are being held up by federal, state and local laws and regulations", federal officials said.

The Bush administration with the authorization of Congress, will bypass more than 30 laws and regulations to finish building 670 miles of fence. "Criminal activity at the border does not stop for endless debate of protracted litigation," said Michael Chertoff, Homeland Security Secretary. "These waivers will enable important security projects to keep moving forward." In some areas assessments and studies could not be completed in time to finish the fence by the end of the 2008.

An attorney with "Defenders of Wildlife", Brian Segee, told the Los Angeles Times, "It's dangerous, it's arrogant, it's going to have pronounced environmental impacts and it won't do a thing to address the problems of undocumented immigrants or address border security problems."

Information from an article By Eileen Sullivan, Associated Press, in "The Tribune", San Luis Obispo County, California, April 2, 2008.

My thoughts – This fence is over 25 years late! If the fence had been built years ago we wouldn't have all the illegal aliens in the United States that we do today. Remember in 1986, 3 million illegal aliens were given amnesty with the provision that the border would be closed! This didn't happen! Now we may have 20 million illegal aliens here or millions more – who really knows! We do know how much they cost us each year, a whopping $338.3 Billion a year.

This border fence is finally being built because of all the American Citizens and immigration groups against illegal immigration who wanted it, stormed Congress and the President with letters, faxes, e-mails, and phone calls to pass legislation to get it built.

Knick – Knack

65 Million people in the United States are Catholic. Heard on TV 2-14-08

Stop and Think

America is disintegrating while the President and many in Congress sit idly by and watch! They're talking about hiring more foreign workers while Americans are unemployed.

Bill Gates, (Chairman of Microsoft), asked Congress for more H1B visas to get foreign workers to come to America and work here. What's wrong with hiring the unemployed American workers, Bill?

> This is America.
> Hire Americans.
> No More H1B visas.
> No more foreign workers.
> Send all illegal aliens back to their country.
> Stop legal immigration for 5 years so America can "Catch up".
> Most everyone wants to come to America!

Carolyn Cavolt May 2008

Good-by to Spanish Culture

Madrid, Spain – State-run Spanish television has quietly yanked live coverage of bullfighting, ending a decades-old tradition of showcasing the national pastime.

They are concerned that the deadly duel between matador and beast is too violent for children. The television Espanola's first broadcast in 1948 was a bullfight in Madrid. None of the channels have shown live bullfights this season. Taped highlights are on a late night program for those who care.

Many are livid because they see this as a slight to a cherished piece of Spanish culture.

Information from an Associated Press article in "The Tribune", San Luis Obispo County, California, August 23, 2007.

My thoughts – I'll say thank God it's off the air! Yet there are still the taped highlights! What does that mean – the last sword that goes into the bull's body to kill him? If this is culture I'd rather not see it or have it!

121

Courts Struggle to Lure Jurors

A lady was making a quick trip to the grocery store when a Sheriff approached her car in the parking lot and slipped something through her open window. It was a jury summons. The sheriff told her be there or you will be in contempt. This was in Sanford, North Carolina. Fewer than half of all Americans summoned, report for duty, because of apathy or busy lifestyles.

In New York state occupational exemptions have been eliminated, so doctors, lawyers, firefighters, police officers and even judges can no longer get out of jury duty. In Washington, D. C. judges have summoned no-shows to court. They must explain why they missed their date or face up to 7 days in jail and a $300 fine.

In other places courts have tried raising daily fees paid to jurors, limiting jury service to one day or one trial, and reimbursing jurors for parking cost. Nationally about 46% of people summoned for jury duty show up.

> Information from an article in "The Tribune", San Luis Obispo County, California, July 28, 2007, by Denise La Voie, Associated Press.

> My thoughts – What is the solution? Everyone has to do it except those with medical reasons. Pay more to jurors. No shows get the "Slammer!" This includes Paris Hilton, Lindsay Lohan and Nicole Richie. Charge a fee based on a persons income! Charge these ladies and Brittany Spears at least $10,000 to $100,000; such fees could be used to increase the pay to jurors. This will help the Prison system and give the poor taxpayer a break.

Defraud the Federal Government

Boston – A concrete supplier for the "Big Dig" agrees to pay $50 million to end civil and criminal investigations into the matter that it supplied inferior concrete used in the massive highway project, in Boston, Massachusetts

Aggregate Industries NE Inc. also agreed to plead guilty to a criminal charge of conspiracy to defraud the federal government.

> Information from an article in "The Tribune", San Luis Obispo County, California, July 28, 2007, by Associated Press.

> My thoughts – Their name is Mud now! Who's going to hire them after this debacle? It's time for the Victory dance by Massachusetts's taxpayers.

The California Supreme Court Rules

The court ruled that cities and counties have the right to ban big-box retailers and decide where stores can be located.

The court upheld a Hanford City ordinance that banned furniture stores in a commercial district northwest of downtown while allowing big-box stores to sell furniture in that district.

If the ordinance had a "legitimate public purpose", protecting a downtown area, then it was legal, even if it limited competition.

Information from an article in "The Tribune", San Luis Obispo County, California, June 9, 2007, Associated Press".

My thoughts – I think we need more classes about running city government in grade schools. Add an hour to the school day! Take the children to visit city government in action.
1. First show movies of how city governments work.
2. Invite City officials to speak at an assembly.
3. Be sure to invite the Mayor and his family.
4. The teacher's assistant or helper should be able to make all arrangements, or a willing dependable parent.

A Veto For The 5th Time!

Sacramento, California – Governor Arnold Schwarzenegger vetoed for the 5th time legislation that would have made it easier for news reporters to arrange interviews with prison inmates. Senator Gloria Romero, Democrat, Los Angeles, wants to get her latest bill about access to inmates that would have made it easier for news reporters to arrange interviews with prison inmates. It would have broadened a reporter's access to inmates and would have allowed the use of video cameras or tape recorders without prior approval from prison authorities.

The Governor said this bill would "glamorize murders" and "traumatize crime victims and their families."

Information from an article in "The Tribune", San Luis Obispo County, California, Tribune Wire Services, July 28, 2007

My thoughts – Give it up Ms. Romero! Go to your room! A veto means NO!

123

We received the following e-mail on August 13, 2008. It is copied word for word as received. Article reviewed at "Information Clearing House".

545 People
By Charley- Reese – **Date of Publication Unknown**
(Charley Reese is a former columnist of the Orlando Sentinel Newspaper.)

Politicians are the only people in the world who create problems and then campaign against them.

Have you ever wondered why, if both the Democrats and the Republicans are against deficits, Why do we have them?

Have you ever wondered why, if all the politicians are against inflation and high taxes, Why do we have inflation and high taxes?

You and I don't propose a federal; budget, The President does.

You and I don't have the Constitutional authority to vote on appropriations. The House of Representatives does.

You and I don't write the tax code, Congress does.

You and I don't set fiscal policy, Congress does.

You and I don't control monetary policy, the Federal Reserve Bank does.

One hundred senators, 435 congressmen, one president, and nine Supreme Court Justices, 545 human beings out of 300 million are directly, legally, morally, and individually responsible for the domestic problems that plague this country.

Members of the Federal Reserve Board were excluded because that problem was created by Congress. In 1913, Congress delegated its Constitutional duty to provide a sound currency to a federally chartered, but private, central bank.

Also excluded are all of the special interests and lobbyist for a sound reason. They have no legal authority. They have no ability to coerce a senator, a congressman, or a president to do one cotton-picking thing. It doesn't matter if they offer a politician $1 million dollars in cash. The politician has the power to accept or reject it. No matter what the lobbyist promises, it is the legislator's responsibility to determine how they vote.

These 545 human beings spend much of their energy convincing you/me that what they did is not their fault. They cooperate in this common con regardless of party. What separates a politician from a normal human being is an excessive amount of gall. No normal human being would have the gall of a Speaker, who stood up and criticized the President for creating deficits. The president can only propose a budget. He cannot force the Congress to accept it.

The Constitution, which is the supreme law of the land, gives sole responsibility to the House of Representatives for originating and approving appropriations and taxes.

Who is the speaker of the House? They (in this case – she) are the leader of the majority party. She and fellow House members, not the president, can approve any budget they want. If the president vetoes it, they can pass it over his veto if they agree to. It seems inconceivable that a nation of 300 million cannot replace 545 people who stand convicted - - by present facts - - of incompetence and irresponsibility. I can't think of a single domestic problem that is not traceable directly to those 545 people.

When they fully grasp the plain truth that 545 people exercise the power of the federal government, than it must follow that what exists is what they want to exist.

If the tax code is unfair, it's because they want it unfair.

If the budget is in the red, it's because they want it in the red.

If they do not pay or receive social security but are on an elite retirement plan not available to the people, it's because they want it that way.

There are no insoluble government problems.

Do not let these 545 people shift the blame:
- to bureaucrats, whom they hire and whose jobs they can abolish;
- to lobbyist, whose gifts and advise they can reject;
- to regulators, to whom they give the power to regulate and from whom they can take this power.

Above all, do not let them con you into the belief that there exists disembodied mystical forces like the 'economy,' 'inflation,' or' politics' that prevent them from doing what they take an oath to do.

Those 545 people, and they alone, are responsible.

- They, and they alone, have the power.
- They, and they alone, should be held accountable by the people who are their bosses, provided the voters have the gumption to manage their own employees.

- We should <u>vote</u> them all out of office and clean up their mess!
- What you do with this article now that you have read it is up to you, thought you appear to have several choices.
1. You can send this to everyone in your address book, and hope they' do something about it.
2. You can agree to 'vote against' everyone that is currently in office, knowing that the process will take several years.
3. You can decide to 'run for office' yourself and agree to do the job properly.
4. Lastly, you can sit back and do nothing, or re-elect the current bunch.

YOU DECIDE, BUT AT LEAST SEND IT TO EVERYTONE IN YOUR ADDRESS BOOK, MAYBE SOMEONE IN THERE WILL DO SOMETHING ABOUT IT.

<u>SUMMER RECESS</u>

The Bush Administration Plans to Screen Nonprofit Employees

Thousands of people who work with charities and nonprofit organizations that receive U.S. Agency for International Development funds will be screened to ensure they're not connected to terrorist groups.

The organizations must give the government information about key personnel, such as phone numbers, birth dates and e-mail addresses. They will not tell the groups why they are unacceptable.

Officials of Inter Action, representing 165 foreign aid groups think the plan would impose undue burdens and want it withdrawn. The Federal Register notice said the program could involve 2,000 people and become effective on August 27, 2007.

> Published August 23, 2007 in "The Tribune", San Luis Obispo County, California, by the Washington Post.

> My thoughts – They should be thoroughly screened! Why not? It is U.S. money, if the U.S. doesn't screen the people who will? No one!!!

The United States Pledged $50 million

On July 14, 2006, the United States pledged $50 million for Palestinian refugees.

The United States donated the money to the United Nations Relief and Works Agency to aid those residents of the Gaza Strip and West Bank residents impacted by the fighting, so said U.S. Assistant Secretary of State David Welch.

> From an article in the "The Tribune", San Luis Obispo County, California, 7/15/06, by the Associated Press.

> My thoughts - Will they get it?? What other countries donated?

Knick – Knack

President-elect Franklin D. Roosevelt escaped an assassination attempt in Miami, Florida by gunman Giuseppe Zangara, but Chicago Mayor Anton J. Cermak was mortally wounded on this day of February 15, 1933. The gunman was executed 4 weeks later.

> From "Flashback" in "The Tribune", San Luis Obispo County, California, February 15, 2008.

127

Elephant Sized Government Waste

The city of Los Angeles, California, has approved new funding to spur the construction of a long-planned facility to house the TWO remaining elephants at the Los Angeles Zoo.

The Board of Public Works approved $2.1 million in spending for the new exhibit, a 3.7-acre property that will probably cost $40 million. So now the city can start demolishing the old elephant pen. The elephants could have been sent to a sanctuary. Instead the City Council decided earlier this year on an elaborate expansion of the zoo's existing elephant habitat.

> Associated Press, article published in "The Tribune", San Luis Obispo County, California, July 23, 2006

> My thoughts – Send the 2 lonely elephants to the sanctuary to be with other animals to enjoy the rest of their lives. Send the City Council into oblivion without pay or retirement. Let them spend their own money on frivolous building. Let them work for a living. Disband the Board of Public Works to find a job and live on their own salary and not on OPM (Other People's Money).

$3 Billion for National Parks

Washington – A first of its kind pledge drive has secured promises of $216 million to help pay for hundreds of projects at National Parks.

Corporations, nonprofits and wealthy individuals, have all lined up to contribute to the program being unveiled August 23, 2007 at Yosemite National Park. The contributions would fund everything from restoring beat down meadows to rehabilitating old buildings. Congress first has to allot an additional $100 million.

The program would raise $3 billion before the National Park Service's centennial in 2016.

> Article by Associated Press, August 23, 2007 in "The Tribune", San Luis Obispo, County, California.

> My thoughts - $3 billion is enormous – be sure to get it in the hands of very honest, reliable people to hand over to the park managers after receiving their itemized list of where the money will be spent and then they prove it.

128

One Million Computers

Washington.

The FBI said more than 1 million computers are used by hackers as remote-controlled robots to crash online systems, accept spam and steal users' personal information. The government has no way to track down all the computers.

The hackers have massed the computers, both in the United States and elsewhere, into centrally controlled collections known as "botnets". But the FBI has found several botnet hackers or zombies. One man was charged in a scheme that froze computer systems at Chicago-area hospitals in 2006 and delayed medical services.

> Published in "The Tribune," San Luis Obispo County, California, June 14, 2007, Article by Associated Press.

> My thoughts – The solution? Hire more FBI personnel?

Dakar, Senegal

A plurality of Africans say they are better off today than they were 5 years ago and are optimistic about their future, according to a poll conducted in 10 sub-Saharan countries by the New York Times and the Pew Global Attitudes Project. This is despite troubles from deadly illnesses such as Aids, and Malaria to deep-seated poverty. Africans, in the main, are satisfied with their national governments, and a majority of the respondents in 7 of the 10 countries said their economic situation was at least somewhat good.

Face-to-face interviews were conducted in April and May of 2007 with 8, 471 adults in Ethiopia, Ghana, Ivory Coast, Kenya, Mali, Nigeria, Senegal, South Africa, Tanzania and Uganda.

> Article in "The Tribune", San Luis Obispo County, California, "World Roundup", July 25, 2007, Tribune Wire Services.

> My Thoughts – This surely surprises me!

Yucca Nuclear Waste Dump

Las Vegas, Nevada ---- The Department of Energy proposes to double the size of a national nuclear waste repository it plans to build deep below an ancient volcanic ridge in the Nevada desert. The price tag now tops $77 Billion. This is 35% more than the Energy Department projected in 2001.

The federal government is mandated by law to dispose of the nation's nuclear waste and the Nevada site was supposed to open by 1998. But the Yucca Mountain project has been slowed by lawsuits, quality control concerns and funding shortfalls. The target date for opening is now 2017 or later. Democratic Majority Leader, Harry Reid (Nevada), does not want the repository. Ongoing production of waste at nuclear power plants needs a repository.

> Information from an article in "The Tribune", San Luis Obispo County, California, by the Associated Press, October 6, 2007.

> My thoughts – Harry Reid should retire!!! He's one of those "Not in my backyard" people. There are 102 nuclear power plants in the United States now. France is practically all nuclear. They used our plans to build their nuclear power plants. We have to have more nuclear power plants to reduce our dependence on foreign oil and to reduce our trade deficit.

> We live about 12 miles from the Diablo Canyon Power Plant in San Luis Obispo. They have been building sites for waste on their property because the Yucca Mountain repository keeps getting delayed.

> As Bill Wattenberg has stated for years, the nuclear waste for a family of four for 20 years will fit in a shoebox. He has worked on nuclear projects. He is a brilliant person. He is on KGO radio in San Francisco, California on Saturday and Sunday nites 10 PM to 1 AM. **Coal plants** produce more carbon discharge than anything I know about. We do not want coal plants! If the damn environmentalists and the Sierra Club would stop bringing lawsuits we'd all be better off!

> I pray that you give no money to the Sierra Club. They do not have our best interests in mind when they continually bring lawsuits and win – stoking their coffers with thousands and more thousands of dollars!

> When the Sierra Club wins a lawsuit against the United States government it is taxpayers' money that is paid to them! Do you want your money given to the Sierra Club? Thousands and thousands of dollars! The Sierra Club is made up of lawyers! I heard someone on the radio call them two-bit lawyers! Why do you think they sue? To get money!

130

Change for Electoral College is Vetoed

California has 55 electoral votes. 270 electoral votes are needed to elect a President.

A bill, which passed the California state Legislature in the summer of 2006 would commit their 55 electors to cast ballots for the winner of the popular vote in the United States regardless of how their individual electorates voted.

Governor Arnold Schwarzenegger vetoed the bill September 30, 2006.

The bill was devised by John R. Koza, a computer scientist, who envisions a system in which a series of states holding the number of electoral votes needed to elect a President – 270 – would commit their electors to casting ballots for the winner of the popular vote, regardless of how their individual electorates voted. He said the goal was to force Presidential candidates to campaign nationwide, rather than concentrating on a small number of battleground states, like Ohio or Florida, that have a lot of electors.

Information from an article in "The New York Times", published in "The Tribune", San Luis Obispo County, California, October 3, 2006.

My thoughts – The Democrats control both Houses in the California Legislature. If this Bill had been in existence in 2000, Al Gore would be the President of the United States, if other states totaling 270 (with California's 55 electoral votes) had passed a similar bill.

San Francisco Bans Handguns

San Francisco, California – the city can't ban weapons because state law allows them. A city ordinance banning handgun possession in San Francisco will stay off the books, after a state appeals court sides with gun owners and upholds a lower court's decision overturning the law. The ordinance was approved by voters in 2005, but has never been enforced because of the NRA's legal challenge.

Information from an Associated Press article in "The Tribune", San Luis Obispo County, California, January 10, 2008.

Tall and Skinny

It's official; the tall skinny palm trees that define Los Angeles will be replaced with native species, as they die of old age and disease.

The City Council agreed to replace the trees with oaks, sycamores and other native species that provide more shade and are native to Los Angeles.

Large numbers of palms are dying of fungal disease and tree surgeons don't know how to stop the bacteria that gets into the soil.

The news will likely disappoint legions of fans that say the Palms have become synonymous with the city's beaches, warm weather and the movies.

> Information from an Associated Press article, November 19, 2006, published in "The Tribune", San Luis Obispo County, California.

> My thoughts – The tree surgeons should seek help worldwide. Save the Palm Trees! Do something City Council! This is history. We need more tall and skinny things in our environment!

Knick - Knack

On August 14, 1935 President Franklin D. Roosevelt signed the Social Security Act into law.

Highlight in History: On August 14, 1945 President Harry Truman announced that Japan had surrendered unconditionally, ending World War II.

On August 14, 1947, Pakistan was established as a modern state, independent of British rule.

> Information from the article, "Flashback", published August 14, 2006 in "The Tribune, San Luis Obispo County, California.

132

$1.4 Billion Aid Package to Mexico

The **Merida initiative** is a proposed $1.4 Billion United States aid package to Mexico from United States Congress to help them in the war against drug traffickers that has spilled over into the United States territory.

The United States Congress has added human rights conditions that the Mexican officials don't like. So the Merida initiative is a casualty of Mexican public opinion.

The proposal would offer as much as $400 Million in military equipment and technical assistance this year to help Mexico in this drug war. 450 Mexican police have been killed in the 18-month period since President Calderon became President and made the war on drug trafficking a cornerstone of his administration. The drug cartels and their paramilitary enforcers are vicious. They use beheadings to scare people.

>Information from an article by Lawrence Iliff and Alfredo Corchado' "The Dallas Morning News", in "The Tribune", San Luis Obispo County, California June 7, 2008.

>My thoughts – The United States badly needs the Border fence to be completed and the National Guard to stay on the Border!

I.D. Devices Under the Skin

The California Senate passed legislation August 30 that would bar employers from requiring workers to have identification devices implanted below their skin. Senator Joe Simitian, D-Palo Alto, California proposed the measure. The bill has been approved by the Assembly and now goes to Governor Schwarzenegger.

A company began marketing radio frequency devices for humans. The devices are as small as a grain of rice. They can be used by employers to identify workers.

"RFID (Radio frequency identification device) is a minor miracle with all sorts of good uses, but we shouldn't condone forced "tagging" of humans. "It's the ultimate invasion of privacy," said Simitain.

>Article in "The Tribune", San Luis Obispo County, California, Associated Press, August 31, 2007.

>My thoughts – In some businesses this might be a good idea. There are so many stolen Social Security numbers and personal identifications that it might become a necessity for government jobs and the private sector. Who knows?

133

A New President

Congratulations to Barack Obama. He will be our 44th President. The first black President in the history of the United States of America. We pray for his success for all of us, Liberals and Conservatives.

Our Country is in great distress, economically and culturally. If all the illegal aliens are given amnesty, I don't believe America can absorb them. It will cause to many insurmountable problems. There have to be other solutions.

CGC

Veterans

Veterans Affairs Secretary Jim Nicholson at Alexandria, VA pledged yesterday to add mental health services at more than 100 VA medical centers to fight resistance to seeking help for depression and other illnesses. The addition will take effect in 2/3rds of the VA's 153 medical centers.

Article in "The Tribune" San Luis Obispo County, California, Tuesday, July 17, 2007.

My thoughts – Great, veterans deserve all the help we can give them.

HEALTH

Living to 100 Years Old

500 women and 200 men who had reached 100 had phone interviews. 2/3 of them had no age related ailments. The remainder 1/3, called survivors, had an age-related disease before 85, including high blood pressure, heart disease or diabetes. But the survivors were living very well. The men functioned better than the women because ¾ could bathe and dress without help; only 1/3 of women could.

Dr. William Hall of the University of Rochester said his theory is "that their doctors are aggressively treating these older folks' health problems, and not taking an ageist approach that assumes they wouldn't benefit."

Information from as Associated Press article in "The Tribune", San Luis Obispo County, California, February 12, 2008.

My thoughts – I'm happy to hear this news. I'd love to have a huge German Chocolate Cake that accommodates 100 candles. Who else will be there? Family members, 75 to 80 year old children, friends who also live to be 100, grandchildren and great grandchildren!

Eliminate Endometrial Cancer

Women who have more than 2 alcoholic drinks a day double their risk of endometrial cancer compared with those who drink less, says a new study.
1. Researchers examined 41,574 multiethnic post-menopausal women.
2. Followed them for 8 years.
3. Used questionnaires about diet and drinking habits.
4. In that time the researchers found 324 cases of endometrial cancer, the type that forms in the tissue that lines the uterus.

The United States has 40,000 new cases of endometrial cancer cases a year and 7,400 deaths. The researchers found that women who had fewer than 2 alcoholic drinks a day had no increased risk of endometrial cancer.

Those who had more than 2 alcoholic drinks a day had slightly more than twice the risk. It made no difference whether the women drank beer, wine or hard liquor.

Information from an article in "The Tribune", San Luis Obispo County, California, Tribune wire services, September 18, 2007.

My thoughts – Sounds like an easy way to eliminate endometrial cancer.

136

How to Pick a New Doctor

The American Academy of Family Physicians recommends talking with friends and family to find a recommended doctor. Once you have a few names, 1. call their offices and ask whether they accept your insurance, 2. what their office hours are, 3. which hospitals they use.

Health plans limit your choice of physicians to those who participate in your plan. If you have a choice of plans and a preferred doctor you may want to choose a health plan that includes your doctor.

Once you've chosen a doctor, schedule an appointment to meet and go through the following checklist.

Look for a doctor who:

    I. Is rated to give quality health care.
    II. Has the training and background that meets your needs.
    III. Takes steps to prevent illness-for example, talks to you about quitting smoking.
    IV. Has privileges at the hospital of your choice.
    V. Is part of your health plan, unless you can afford to pay extra.
    VI. Encourages you to ask questions.
    VII. Listens to you.
    VIII. Explains things clearly.
    IX. Treats you with respect.

Source: Agency for Health Care Research and Quality.
Article published in "The Tribune", San Luis Obispo County,
December 24, 2006.

My thoughts – The very worst thing about moving is giving up your M.D. and dentist. My doctor for about 30 years was Beverly Thomas, M.D. of Burlingame, California. Even when we lived in Dover, Massachusetts for 4 years I would make an appointment with her whenever I was in California. She is the Best! I also had a dentist for about 30 years, Dr. Charles McGary of Mountain View, California, but he has now retired. He did the best teeth cleaning in the world.

Ask every friend and acquaintance you have about doctors. Ask every Doctor and Nurse you know about recommending a doctor. If you are thinking about surgery, ask everyone you know about surgeons. Ask your present doctor to recommend a surgeon (s) or ask the hospital in your area.

137

Weight-loss Surgeries Improve Survival

In the United States 177,600 obesity operations were performed in 2006 according to the American Society for Metabolic and Bariatric Surgery. The most common method of obesity surgeries was gastric bypass or stomach-stapling surgery, which reduces the stomach to a walnut-sized pouch and bypasses part of the small intestine where digestion occurs.

A BMI (body mass index) over 30 is considered obese. The surgery leads to lasting weight loss, it also dramatically improves survival.

Information from an article by Alicia Chang, Associated Press in "The Tribune", San Luis Obispo County, California, August 23, 2007.

My thoughts – Being overweight is one of the most burdensome problems in life. People who are overweight know that they are being judged because of their overweight. They can almost feel the disdain from others. It can be a word, a look, a judgment, and avoidance!

All the slim people in society must thank their lucky stars that they are slim! I believe that if a person has fat cells as a child those fat cells are forever going to try to rule that body.

I also believe that the older a person becomes the more difficult it is to control body weight. Remember as a person ages they also shrink in height! Also if you have an illness and cannot exercise, for every day down it takes a week to catch up! So 6 weeks down and out equals 42 days, which equals 42 weeks to recover lost time. That is equal to 10 ½ months!

So show a little mercy and tolerance to those who have been unable to exercise but intend to do so.

United States Circumcisions

In 2004, 57.4% of all male newborns born in hospitals were circumcised, down 11.3% from 1980.

Department of Health and Human Services; Circumcision Reference Library Published in "The Tribune" San Luis Obispo County, California, June 19. 2007.

The Hottest Chili Eater

Mexico City --- A most unusual 54-year-old Mexico City taxi driver, Manuel Quiroz, can guzzle down dozens of Mexico's hottest chilies, squeeze their juice into his eyes and rub them round his face without as much as blinking.

He has made thousands of dollars with his talent and wants to become the world champion chili eater. First he needs to find an organization that can crown him with that title.

"Chilies don't sting me. They don't affect me. It's just like eating fruit," Quiroz said. When most people eat raw chilies, they turn red hot, break a sweat and rush for water.

> Information from the Associated Press, "World Roundup", published February 4, 2007, in "The Tribune", San Luis Obispo County, California.

> My thoughts – I say he is one in 100 million! I hope he is crowned World Champion Red Hot Chili Eater.

Drug Resistant Tuberculosis

London, England -----"Drug-resistant tuberculosis is spreading even faster than medical experts had feared," the World Health Organization warned in a report issued February 26, 2008." In some countries 20% of the TB patients are infected with the drug-resistant strain!

> Information from an article in "World Roundup" in "The Tribune", San Luis Obispo County, California, February 27, 2008.

Knick Knack

Take off your shoes, of course, roll a tennis ball under your arches, which stimulates acupressure points to relax your whole body.

> Idea from Positive Thinking, July 8, 2007.

Breast Enhancement Implants

If you've had implants for breast enhancement you're 3 times more likely to commit suicide. Deaths related to mental disorders, including alcohol or drug dependence, also were 3 times higher among women who had the cosmetic procedure, researchers said. Other studies showed women felt better about themselves after getting implants. A professor of medicine said he believed that many of the women had psychological problems before the implants and their condition did not improve afterward.

Previous studies have shown that up to 15% of plastic surgery patients have body dysmorphic disorder, a psychological condition marked by severe distress over minor physical imperfections. These people have a higher rate of suicidal thoughts and rarely improve after plastic surgery.

Most popular cosmetic surgeries in the United States are:
1. Breast Augmentation.
2. Liposuction
3. Eyelid surgery

In 2006, 315, 516 breast enlargements were performed, up 13% from 2005. The latest study analyzed data from 3, 527 Swedish women who got implants between 1965 and 1993. Breast cancer patients who received implants as part of breast reconstruction surgery were not included.

Article from the Los Angeles Times, the report in the August issue of the "Annals of Plastic Surgery" in "The Tribune" San Luis Obispo County, California, August 10, 2007

My thoughts – Do you really want a breast enhancement? Do you want to look like Paris Hilton or Pam Anderson?

Knick - Knacks

1. 40 gallons of tree sap are needed to make 1 gallon of maple syrup.

2. There are 300,00 women in the United States who are strippers.

3. This is an expression I heard a South Carolina relative (Philip) use, "Are you pikin' up what I'm puttin' down?" Which means, "do you understand what I am saying?"

The Shelf Life of Baking Powder

To test baking powder for freshness:
    Add a teaspoon of baking powder to a cup of warm water.
    If it bubbles the powder is active.
    No bubbles-time for a new can.
Baking powder's shelf life:
    6 months if stored properly,
    The lid is on tightly after every use,
    Use a dry spoon to scoop,
    Kept away from heat and moisture.
A substitute for baking powder:
    ¼ teaspoon of baking soda.
    ½ teaspoon of cream of tartar.
    This doesn't store well make as needed.

Do not refrigerate baking powder or baking soda; the moisture from the refrigerator may cause the product to react in the can, making it unusable.

Article by "Hints From Heloise," September 25, 2006.
Published in The Tribune, San Luis Obispo, California.

To receive a copy of Heloise's 4-page pamphlet of substitutes, seasonings and salts, send $3 and a self-addresses envelope, stamped (.63-this is 9/27/06 price of postage.) envelope to: Heloise/sss
    P.O. Box 795001
    San Antonio, TX 78279-5001

My thoughts – The advantage of knowing if baking powder is fresh can be the difference between successful and unsuccessful baking. Why waste time baking a cake using non-fresh baking powder?

Taboos for M.D.s

London, England-------British hospitals are banning:

1. neckties
2. long sleeves
3. jewelry
4. traditional white coats
5. fake nails
6. watches

in an effort to stop the spread of deadly hospital-borne infections, according to New Rules published September 17, 2007.

The Department of Health said in a statement, "Ties are rarely laundered but worn daily, they perform no beneficial function in patient care and have been shown to be colonized by pathogens." These new regulations for doctors take effect in 2008. This means an end to doctor's traditional long sleeved white coats.

The department warned that the fake nails, jewelry and watches could harbor germs.

Information from an article in "The Tribune", San Luis Obispo County, California, September 18, 2007, Tribune wire services.

My thoughts – What a wonderful ban! I wonder why the hospitals didn't do this years ago! I wonder whose great idea it is?

I've often wondered why cooks and food handlers are allowed to wear long sleeves, jewelry and watches. I watch cooking stars on TV and see their long sleeves, watches etc. Maybe now they'll take a cue from London hospitals.

Cell Phone Users

Motorists using cell phones increase all other drivers' drive time by 5 to 10%. Cell phone users drive more hesitantly and 2 mph slower so say University of Utah researchers. So a one hour commute = 12 extra minutes behind the wheel each day because of cell phone users.

Information from the "Los Angeles Times" in "The Tribune", San Luis Obispo County, California, January 6, 2008.

My thoughts – My thoughts are conflicted. Park and call or if you get a call don't answer, park and call back.

Lowest Health Insurance

The company eHealthinsurance surveyed 5,000 basic plans in 100 cities.

People in these cities pay the least per month for a family of four (individuals pay far less):

Grand Rapids, Michigan	$ 159.06
Columbus, Ohio	179.68
Akron, Ohio	191.46
Des Moines, Iowa	194.40
Lexington/Louisville, Kentucky	197.75

Who pays the most per month?

Spokane, Washington	962.00
New York City, New York	916.79
Yonkers, New York	916.79
Boston, Massachusetts	865.18
Wichita, Kansas	773.06

"Hot List" – "Parade" published in "The Tribune", San Luis Obispo County, California August 27, 2006

My thoughts-Why does Spokane, WA have the highest cost? If many of us moved to Grand Rapids, MI would the cost remain the same?

Pfizer Inc., The world's Largest Drug Company
OR
How to get Promoted at Pfizer

Jeffery B. Kindler's, age 51, walk up the ladder.

Before joining Pfizer he was:
*Chairman and CEO of "Boston Market Corp."
*President of "Partner Brands" both owned by McDonald's Corp.
*Executive vice president, corporate relations and general counsel of McDonald's from 1997 to 2001.
*Executive vice president, corporate relations and general counsel of McDonald's.
*From 1996 to 1997 served as senior vice president and general counsel of McDonald's.
*Vice Chairman Kindler was named chief executive officer, said Pfizer Inc. on July 28, 2006. He was also elected to the drug maker's board.

Information from an article published in "The Tribune, "Business Wrap", New York, San Luis Obispo County, California, July 29, 2006.

143

Chronic Anxiety Can Increase the Risk of Heart Attack in Men

Washington, DC ----- This trait, chronic anxiety, is now added to the growing list of psychological profiles, anger or hostility, Type A behavior, depression that can be linked to heart disease in men. Doctors "need to be aggressive about not only taking care of the traditional risk factors…but also really getting into their patients heads" said Dr. Nieca Goldberg of the New York University School of Medicine. "Doctors really are focused very much on prescribing medicine for cholesterol and lowering blood pressure and treating diabetes, but we don't look at the psychological aspect of a patient's care," she said. The research was published by the Journal of the American College of Cardiology.

> Information by an Associated Press article in "The Tribune, San Luis Obispo County, California, January 12, 2008

Osteoporosis

Atlanta, GA---------In the study, there were 28% fewer deaths and 35% fewer fractures in the group that got a once-a-year infusion of the bone drug "Reclast" compared to those who got a dummy treatment.

For the first time an osteoporosis drug has reduced deaths and prevented new fractures in elderly patients with broken hips according to new research. Some experts think other drugs could have a similar effect.

Dr. Kenneth Lyles of Duke University Medical Center, the lead author, said that no other osteoporosis drug study published in at least 15 years has shown such a pronounced reduction in deaths.

The New England Journal of Medicine released this study on line September 17, 2007.

Older women have nearly seven times the risk of osteoporosis on average than men of the same age.

> Information from an article in "The Tribune", San Luis Obispo County, California, "Health Roundup", September 18, 2007.

144

Nursing

There are an estimated 126,000 vacant full-time nursing positions at hospitals across the country, that number is forecast to triple by year 2020, when the number will be 378,000 nurses needed.

Men currently make up about 6% of the 2.7 million nurses in the United States. Traditionally, nursing has been considered a female-oriented field. Now, more men are looking to nursing as an attractive career choice.

> Information from Marian Medical Center, in "The Tribune", San Luis Obispo County, California, Nurses Week Special Section, May 4, 2008, National Nurses Week, May 6 – 12. 2008.

> My thoughts – Sounds like a wonderful opportunity for men to get in an occupation that needs thousands of people.

Wonders of the Human Body

Scientists say the higher your I.Q. the more you dream.
You use 200 muscles to take one step.
The average woman is five inches shorter than the average man.
You big toes have two bones each while the rest have three.
The human brain cell can hold 5 times as much information as the Encyclopedia Britannica. (AS You Get Older The Leaves Fall Out)
It takes food seven seconds to get from your mouth to your stomach.
The average human dream lasts 2-3 Seconds.
There are about one trillion bacteria on each of your feet.
Blondes have more hair than dark-haired people.
Your thumb is the same length as your nose.

> Received as an e-mail, October 30, 2007, author unknown.

Listen Up, Women in Your 20s-30s-40s!

The study of more than 90,000 women found the more red meat the women consumed when they were in their 20s, 30s, 40s the greater their risk for getting breast cancer fueled by hormones in the next 12 years.

Those who consumed the most red meat faced nearly twice the risk of those who ate red meat infrequently. The consumption of red meat is already known to increase the risk of colon cancer.

A serving is roughly equivalent to a single hamburger or hot dog. Those who ate more than 1 ½ servings a day having nearly double the risk for the so called hormone-receptor positive breast cancer compared to those who ate 3 or fewer servings a week. This was a Harvard study of women's health.

> Excerpted from an article by Rob Stein, The Washington Post, November 14, 2006, published in "The Tribune", San Luis Obispo County, California.

> My thoughts – Who needs red meat anyway? Who wants breast or colon cancer?

E. Coli Recalls

There have been 8 recalls related to E. Coli bacteria in food so far this year compared to 7 for all of 2006, said the U.S. Department of Agriculture. 7 of those recalls have involved ground beef. The E. Coli strain 0157:H7 is a bacteria that lives in cows' intestines and which the animals tolerate. Contamination occurs during slaughtering, when feces and intestine material may accidentally come into contact with portions of the carcass that are trimmed for retail beef cuts.

This year's recalls have involved more than 6 million pounds of beef. In 1997, 25 million pounds of ground beef were recalled and in 2002, 19 million pounds of beef were recalled.

The USDA says at least 14 people have become ill this year but some environmental groups say the number is as high as 38.

> Information from an article in "The Tribune" San Luis Obispo County, California by Chicago Tribune, June 24, 2007

> My thoughts – Who wants to eat ground beef after reading this? I don't! I really haven't eaten it for probably 20 years or more with a few exceptions.

146

Abortions

Since the Roe v. Wade ruling on January 23, 1973 there have been roughly 50 million abortions in the United States in 35 years. The Supreme Court's Roe v. Wade decision established a nationwide right to abortion.

1. ½ of the nearly 1.2 million United States women who have abortions each year are 25 or older.
2. 17% are teens.
3. 60 % have birthed at least 1 child.
4. High abortion rates are linked to hard times.
5. A disproportionately high number are black or Hispanic.
6. 13% of American women are black yet they account for 35% of the abortions.
7. Race of the women who had abortions in 2004; white 52.6%; black 35.3%; other 12.1%.

Information from an article by David Crary, Associated Press, article published in "The Tribune, San Luis Obispo County, California, January 19, 2008.

My thoughts – I believe the Supreme Court made the wrong decision on January 23, 1973. I surely wouldn't want that decision on my conscience. Babies have a right to life.

I believe the Supreme Court decision gave people the impression that babies are not valuable. Obviously 50 million people do not believe a baby has the right to life! Women have birthed babies and then put them in a dumpster. Where do they get these ideas? Why do women drown their babies? Why do some men kill their children? Why did a man throw his 4 children off a bridge? Why did a mother throw her children in the ocean? Why did a mother drown her 5 children one by one?

Knick – Knack

Heparin is a drug made in China. 81 people died because they took Heparin.

The FDA is ill equipped to check the plant or plants that make it. The Federal Drug Administration spends $11 million a year now for inspections. It needs at least $70 million a year to do its job properly.

Heard on television, April 24, 2008.

My thoughts – Why does the United States Government let drugs that Americans consume be made in other countries? Someone STOP IT!!! Does the Administration or Congress or anyone care about us, American Citizens?

Daddy?

Now available, March 2008, at Rite Aid stores nationwide is the "Identigene DNA" paternity test, $29.99 – plus $119.99 for laboratory processing. Results are at least 99% accurate in 3 to 5 days.

When Rite Aid started selling the test in November 2007 on the West Coast the company sold 10,000 kits to Rite Aid in 3 months. Identigene is based in Salt Lake City, Utah. Companies are even starting to offer "personalized genomics", tests that offer customers what diseases they are likely to get or even who their soul mate may be.

Users must submit samples of DNA in the form of cheek swabs from the mother, child and purported father. "Technicians at the laboratory analyze 16 locations on the chromosomes for each participant and assign a numeric value to each. The Childs DNA should contain half of the mother's and half of the father's." Negative readings are 100% conclusive, while positive readings are 99% accurate said Douglas Fogg, chief operating officer for Identigene.

> Information from an article by Ylan Q. Mui, The Washington Post in "The Tribune", San Luis Obispo County, California, March 30, 2008.

> My thoughts – Sounds like a good test for people with the need to know. Children would likely benefit the most for health reasons. Now the identity of the father is assured if anyone was questioning his status. If he is wealthy he will be persuaded to share that wealth. If he isn't he will still need to share.

Thoughts for Children, Grandchildren and other Caring People

Thoughts for children, grandchildren and other people who care about their parents, grandparents, older relatives and friends.

"Do unto others as you would have them do unto you." One day, you too will get old and older. Your parents clothed, fed, kept you safe and educated you because they loved you and took their responsibilities seriously. Although we do know some parents do not perform their parental duties. God will handle their cases!

Use the telephone, snail-mail, e-mail, and personal visits to stay in touch unless you just do not care!

By Carolyn Gerdink Cavolt - April 15, 2008

Bottled Water

New York – Some of it comes from the same place as the water in your tap. Pepsi Company Inc. is the latest company to offer some clarity about the source of its top-selling bottled water. It comes from the same source as tap water.

Corporate Accountability International has been pressuring bottled water sellers to curb misleading marketing practices. Aquafina is the single biggest bottled water brand; its bottles are now labeled P.W.S. the new labels will spell out "public water source." Aquafina water is taken from public sources, and then purified.

The accountability group is also pressing the Coca-Cola Co., which owns the Dasani water brand, and Nestle Waters North America; seller of Nestle Pure Life purified drinking water, which gets some of its water from municipal sources.

> Published in "The Tribune", San Luis Obispo County, California, article by Associated Press, July 28, 2007.

> My thoughts – At last! As it should be! Consumers definitely need watch dogs! Bottled water is a bit more expensive than tap water. Send a thank you note to "Corporate Accountability International"!!!

Live 14 Years Longer

London, England ------- According to a study that followed about 20,000 people in the United Kingdom:
1. Don't smoke
2. Eat lots of fruits and vegetables
3. Exercise regularly
4. Drink alcohol in moderation

to get an extra 14 years of life. People who used these 4 healthy habits lived an average of 14 years longer than people who didn't, so said Kay-Tee Khaw and colleagues of the University of Cambridge.

> Information from an article in "The Tribune", San Luis Obispo County, California, Tribune wire services, January 12, 2008.

> My thoughts – How many people are willing to do this?

The World's Largest Soup Maker

The Campbell Soup Company has 12 soups for children. The company is lowering the sodium to 480 mg per serving so now they can legally label the soups as healthy foods for the first time.

In 2003 Campbell's sold $100 million of reduced sodium soups. Today, the lower-salt soups are bringing in $650 million a year in retail sales.

Information from an article in "The Tribune", San Luis Obispo County, California, February 19, 2008, by Tribune wire services.

My thoughts – What an incredible amount of increased revenue for lower-salt soups. Campbell's has found the magic number – lower salt equals millions of $$$$$.

Homemade Shoe Deodorizer

Need: 1 empty film canister
       A piece of panty hose
       Activated charcoal

Buy the <u>activated</u> charcoal at pet stores that sell aquarium supplies. It's inexpensive.
Punch several holes in the lid of the empty film canister.
Put 1 tablespoon of activated charcoal into film canister.
Stretch a small piece of pantyhose over the top. (The pantyhose keep the smaller pieces of charcoal from coming out the holes).
Snap on the lid.
Place the canister in shoes at night or when not being used.

Keep the left over charcoal in an airtight self-sealing bag to keep it fresh.
Replace charcoal in the canister when charcoal starts to lose its effectiveness.

Information in an article "Tackling shoe odor", Hints from Heloise, published in "The Tribune", San Luis Obispo County, California, August 31, 2006.

My thoughts – Knowledge to have in case someone asks. It may be a good friend! Send to the troops.

$15 Million in Advertising

Atlanta, GA---------The American Cancer Society has taken its biggest step ever into politics of health care reform, spending $15 million in advertising on behalf of Americans with too little health insurance or none at all. Ads began airing September 17, 2007. The cancer society traditionally focuses its advertising on encouraging Americans to quit smoking or to get screening tests.

This year's campaign will feature television commercials that portray the challenges of uninsured and underinsured cancer patients. They want people to do something about it.

The cancer society is the richest health charity in donations and volunteers.

Article published in "The Tribune", San Luis Obispo County, California, from Tribune wire services, September 18, 2007.

My thoughts - $15 million seems to me to be an excessive amount to spend on advertising. Why can't newspapers donate space? That amount of money would pay for many people's health care! Or bank it, let it grow and use it as needed for health care.

Physical Activity Appears to Slow Aging in Genes

"Physically active people have cells that look younger on a molecular level than those of couch potatoes" according to new research. 2,400 British twins were studied. Exercise appears to slow the shriveling of the protective tips of bundles of genes inside cells, perhaps keeping frailty at bay.

Tim Spector, a professor of genetic epidemiology at Kings College in London, England said this data suggest that exercising may protect the body against aging. He and colleagues examined structures known as telomerses inside cells which cap the ends of chromosomes that carry genes. Explanation – every time a cell divides, the telomeres get shorter. When the telomeres get too short, the cell can no longer divide. As more and more cells reach the end of their telomeres and die – muscles weaken, skin wrinkles, eyesight and hearing fade. "There was a gradient, as the amount of exercise increased, the telomeres length increased," Spector said.

Information from an article in "The Tribune", San Luis Obispo County, California, January 29, 2008, "The Washington Post".

A Pedometer as a Coach

A pedometer is a device that rides with you, counting your steps throughout the day. A 2005 study published in the journal "Medicine & Science in Sports & Exercise" found that wearing a pedometer meant taking an extra 2,000 steps a day-which could mean the difference between gaining weight and maintaining or losing weight. People should aim for 10,000 steps. People with desk jobs seem to log in 2,000 to 3,000 steps daily. Try adding 500 steps to your daily goal.

1. Choose the right pedometer. Look for a pedometer with a "Clamshell" cover over the reset button so you don't accidentally bump it and wipe out the record of the steps you've recorded.
2. Wear it right. It should hang straight up and down.
3. Position it on the waistband and in line with the hipbone, so every time you take a stride it feels the impact of your foot hitting the ground.
4. With a good pedometer, age should not affect the accuracy unless the battery is wearing out. Accuracy stems from the mechanism inside. If you're paying $15 or $20, it should be fairly accurate.
5. Make sure your pedometer has a string or strap, especially if you wear it all day.
6. It pays to pay. Expect to pay around $20 for a good pedometer. You'll pay more for devices that talk, play music, count calories and keep records. Pedometers under $20 "tend not to be very accurate and they don't have a big life span for accuracy, after a year it starts over-counting or under-counting steps," said Wendy Bumgardner, an avid walker and certified marathon walking coach who writes the walking guide for "About.com".

Information from an article by Jan Uebelherr, Milwaukee Journal Sentinel, in "The Tribune", San Luis Obispo County, California, August 28, 2006.

My thoughts – Give $20 pedometers as gifts.

Knick-Knack   Toys for Tots

The marines who run "Toys for Tots' out of a base in Virginia are now starting "Toys for Tots Literacy Program." They will collect books and deliver them to the country's most disadvantaged children to help break the cycle of poverty and youth illiteracy.

Information from an article in "The Tribune", San Luis Obispo County, California, March 3, 2008 by Tribune wire services.

My thoughts – Hooray for the United States Marines! How great are they!

Medical Facts

By Dr. Isadore Rosenfeld

I. Male-pattern baldness can be inherited from either the mother or father's side of the family – or both. It may or may not skip one or more generations.

II. Taking aspirin after a night of revelry actually may increase the risk of a hangover, because it enhances alcohol's effects and increases its absorption in the stomach.

Aspirin also irritates the stomach lining and may cause gastrointestinal bleeding. The same is true for other anti-inflammatory Painkillers if taken in large doses or with three or more drinks a day.

Tylenol (acetaminophen) isn't a good alternative. When combined with alcohol, it can cause liver damage. Your best bet is to drink several glasses of water before going to bed and when you wake up. The only sure cure for the morning-after aches is time.

> Article by Dr. Isadore Rosenfeld in "Parade", published in The Tribune, San Luis Obispo County, California, December 24, 2006. e-mail factsorfiction@parade.com - Personal replies not possible but may be in future issues.

> My thoughts – Not much you can do about baldness, but you can eliminate the hangover by not indulging to excess.

Another Ending

What does it matter when you come to the end of your life.
It doesn't.
Remember all the famous people who have died.
What difference does it make now – 10 to 15 years later.
Everyone dies.
Some die younger than others.
If you have had a long life you're lucky.
What are you leaving.
How many people really like you.

By Carolyn Gerdink Cavolt, May 18, 2008.

"Flesh -eating" MRSA bacteria

San Francisco, California --------

Researchers reported that "MRSA" bacteria is spreading among gay men in San Francisco and Boston. It is a new, highly drug-resistant strain of the "flesh eating" "MRSA" bacteria. It spreads most easily through anal intercourse but also through casual skin-to-skin contact and touching contaminated surfaces.

The infection could become a wider threat unless microbiology laboratories were able to identify the strain and doctors prescribed the correct antibiotic therapy.

The study was based on a review of medical records from outpatient clinics in San Francisco and Boston and 9 medical centers in San Francisco.

> Information from an article in "The Tribune", San Luis Obispo County, California, by the Associated Press, January 15, 2008.

> My thoughts – What else is there to say?

Pregnant ?

This week the American College of Obstetricians and Gynecologist begin recommending that every pregnant woman, regardless of age, be offered a test for the common birth defect of Down syndrome.

The main reason: Test far less invasive than the long used amniocentesis are now widely available, some that can tell in the first trimester the risk of a fetus having Down Syndrome or other chromosomal defects.

It's a change that promises to decrease unnecessary amnions while also detecting Down syndrome in mothers-to-be who probably would have gone unchecked.

> Taken from the article "Nation Roundup," Washington, Tribune Wire Service, Published in The Tribune, San Luis Obispo County, California, December 31, 2006.

HIGHWAY

ACCIDENTS

&

SHARK

ATTACKS

Driving Drunk

You risk everything!!!

Andrew Kenny, the author of this article was almost hit by a drunken driver on his way to work.

He says drunken drivers are everywhere. They are young, old, male, female, rich and poor etc. They can kill anybody, you, your kids, your parents and your friends.

When you drive drunk, you risk your own life, your future, leaving a legacy, and the negative stigma of having been convicted of drunken driving. You don't have a right to drive drunk and endanger the lives of yourself and everybody else.

More Americans have been killed by drunken drivers than have died in all the wars we have ever fought.

> Article in "The Tribune", San Luis Obispo County, California, August 28, 2007, "Viewpoint," by Andrew Kenny who works with the San Luis Obispo County DUI (Driving Under Influence) Task Force.

> My thoughts – It is unbelievable to realize that more Americans have been killed by drunken drivers than have died in all the wars we have ever fought!!!

Traffic Crashes Cost Billions a Year

Traffic crashes cost United States motorists $164.2 billion a year, about $1,051 per person!

Annual costs from congestion cost $67 billion, about $430 per person. The study found that traffic crashes are more damaging on society and in small cities such as Little Rock, Arkansas, Columbia, South Carolina than the congestion that riles commuters in metropolitan areas.

To calculate crash costs researchers listed property damage, lost earnings, medical costs, emergency services, legal costs and travel delays. Maryland based Cambridge Systematics Inc. conducted the research for the Auto Association.

> Information from an article from the Tribune wire services in "The Tribune" San Luis Obispo County, California, March 6, 2008.

Pigeon Dung

St. Paul, Minnesota – The pigeon problem is one of many problems that added to the bridge's problems. The Interstate 35 W bridge over the Mississippi River that collapsed August 1. 2007 and killed 13 people, injured about 100, is still under investigation. The corrosive guano deposited over the bridge's framework helped the steel beams rust faster. 20 years ago inspectors began documenting the buildup of pigeon dung.

Pigeon droppings contain ammonia and acids. If the dung isn't washed away it dries out and turns into a concentrated salt. When water gets in and combines with the salt and ammonia, it creates small electrochemical reactions that rust the steel underneath.

The Colorado Department of Transportation spent so much time cleaning pigeon manure off bridges that it is starting on a 2-year research project looking for ways to keep pigeons away from its spans.

>Information from an article in "The Tribune", San Luis Obispo County, California, by Martiga Lohn, Associated Press, August 23, 2007.

>My thoughts – This is all news to me! It seems to me there should be a tropical island home just for pigeons. Why did God make pigeons???

Knick Knack

Acapulco, Mexico – A San Francisco man, 24, died (April 28, 2008) after a grey shark bit his right thigh. He bled to death. He was surfing off Mexico's Southern Pacific Coast.

>Information from Tribune wire services, "The Tribune", San Luis Obispo County, California, April 30, 2008.

Keep going.
Don't stop.
Don't fall asleep'
Stay awake
to hear the noise
and laughter of youth.

Shark Attack Kills Swimmer

Solano Beach, San Diego County, Southern California.

Dave Martin, 66, retired veterinarian, dedicated triathlete, swam every Friday with friends. A great white shark estimated at 12 to 17 feet long, attacked and bit both thighs, which led to massive bleeding. He was declared dead minutes after he was pulled from the water on Friday, 4-25-08.

This was the first shark death in San Diego County since 1994. Martin was swimming with members of the Triathlon Club of San Diego.

> Information from an article by the Los Angeles Times in "The Tribune", San Luis Obispo County, California, April 26, 2008.

> My thoughts – We can say a prayer for Dave Martin and thank him for helping animals during his career as a veterinarian.

Los Angeles, California

30 big-rigs and 1 car were caught up in a fiery October 12, 2007 pile up in the Interstate 5 truck bypass tunnel in the Newhall Pass after a fiery chain-reaction collision that killed 3 people. The tunnel is reopening a month later because contractors were inspired by a $2.9 million incentive and it is ready a week ahead of schedule.

California Department of Transportation engineers gave the OK to reopen.

> Information from an Associated Press article in "The Tribune", San Luis Obispo County, California, November 16, 2007.

> My thoughts – Something to think about when driving thru a tunnel. Get in and out! Who gave the $2.9 million incentive?

158

Highway Accidents

43,443 people were killed in accidents on the road in 2005 as a result of an increase involving motorcycles and pedestrians. This is the highest number since 1990.

California, Florida and Missouri had the biggest increases.

> Information from an article published in "The Tribune", San Luis Obispo County, California, August 23, 2006

> My thoughts – Something to think about!

Mexican 18-Wheelers

"The Bush administration is allowing Mexican trucks to continue to travel deep into the United States despite what critics say is a Congressional Mandate to ban the trucks from United States highways. Congress voted in 2007 to halt funding for a pilot program that allows Mexican 18-wheelers to begin traveling freely into the United States as part of the 1994 North American Free Trade Agreement. The Department of Transportation contends, however that the Congressional action permits the current program to continue while banning any new program."

> Information from an article in "The Tribune", San Luis Obispo County, California, Tribune wire services, January 4, 2008.

> My thoughts – I think NAFTA was a mistake signed by then President Bill Clinton. I don't want Mexican 18-wheelers traveling our United States roads. Do you want to travel next to them? Let's think about America first! If we don't who will?

> I want the United States of America to continue to be just that, not the United States of Mexico!

HOMES

250 Square Feet

Los Angeles, California – 250 square feet is about the size of a large double-car garage. Planners want to increase density downtown so proposed sweeping zoning changes to allow construction of apartments and condominiums this small are being made. They would apply to an area about 5 miles around downtown, which are being considered by the City Council.

Critics feel the zoning changes will lead to overcrowding and slum conditions.

> Information from a Tribune wire services article in "The Tribune", San Luis Obispo County, California, July 25, 2007.

> My thoughts – There must be conditions on ownership and renting contracts such as would owner live in it, must work downtown, and if an apartment is rented only 1 or 2 related tenants may live there. Is there space to take a bicycle on the elevator?

Foreclosures

Detroit, Michigan had the highest foreclosure rate of homes in the nation in 2007 at 4.9%.

Stockton, California is second at 4.8% of its homes in some stage of foreclosure.

Las Vegas, Nevada was third with 4.2% rate.

> Information from an article by the Associated Press in "The Tribune", San Luis Obispo County, California, February 14, 2008.

Mel Gibson's Homes

The actor-director-producer has sold, summer 2007, his Malibu home on 155 feet of beachfront for nearly $30 million. He bought the 7,000 square-foot, Mediterranean style estate in the fall of 2005 for $24 million. It was remodeled shortly before Gibson bought it. It was built in 1981. It has:

                6 bedrooms
                10 bathrooms
                1 gym
                1 library
                1 office
                1 elevator
                a lagoon pool
                a cabana
                a bar
                a wine cellar

In July, before this sale, his Tudor-style mansion on 76 acres in Greenwich, Connecticut sold, reportedly, for $39.5 million.

                28 rooms
                13 bedrooms
                16,000 square feet

In May Gibson bought a 400 plus acre agricultural and cattle ranch in Costa Rica for $25.8 million.

Gibson was born in New York but was raised in Australia, where he also has owned grazing and farmland.

He has owned 3 houses in Malibu, including one he bought in 2000 for $3.5 million. It has 4 bedrooms in 2,300 square feet and sits on 50 feet of sandy beach. Gibson, 51, and his wife, Robyn, have 7 children.

Information from an article in "The Tribune", "Hot Property", San Luis Obispo County, California, July 29, 2007.

My thoughts – Congratulations to Mel and Robyn on their 7 children and beautiful homes. My question – How many garages per house?

162

House Swaps

How to protect yourself when swapping houses for your next vacation. Here's what you need to know.

Do your homework:

1. Have several contacts with the person you're exchanging with. E-mail is a starter but also set up phone conversations. It's okay to request additional photos and video. Be clear about your expectations and communicate any rules you have ahead of time.

2. Get references. Since half the people who participate in vacation exchanges have done it before, get the contact information of others who have stayed in their home and ask them questions about their experience.

3. Protect your valuables. Store them with a friend or lock them in a safe or bedroom that your swap mates can't access.

4. Pop in visits. Consider having a friend check up on your home and its visitors once while you are away.

5. Check your home insurance policy. According to Bankrate.com most homeowners' liability coverage allows for short-term home swapping. But if you swap for more than a month, some insurance companies might issue a seasonal surcharge under the logic that the home is being used for business.

6. An exchange based on mutual trust. Karl Costabel, president of Home Link USA, says that problems with home exchanges are rare, especially because "Your protection is that you are in their house." But he admits it's not for everyone: "The whole is based on trust. If you wouldn't feel comfortable turning your keys over to a stranger, this isn't for you."

Information from an article published in "The Tribune", San Luis Obispo County, California, "Your money," Market Watch, November 2, 2006.

My thoughts – I haven't tried house swapping so I can't give first hand information. We've had lots of delightful company though.

Moving to Mexico

Half a million U.S. expatriates and long-term visitors make their homes in Mexico, with another half-million Canadians. Lacking is an English language print journal. Mexico's oldest English publication folded 4 years ago and hasn't been replaced. It was the 53-year-old "News ".

A couple, Aran and Margot Lee Shetterly, started "Inside Mexico" a free, English-language monthly newspaper they launched in November 2006. The 20,ooo papers are distributed at coffee sops, hotels and other tourist friendly venues. They also plan to open a radio station and have started distributing a weekly newspaper, "The Tip", which goes to 10,000 readers.

Their website, www.insidemexico.com attracts thousands of hits.

Most Americans are aware of the growing "Latinization" of the United States, but some Americans are doing the reverse.

Information from an article by Reed Johnson, Los Angeles Times, published in "The Tribune", San Luis Obispo County, California, February 18, 2007.

My thoughts – There are possibly 20 million Illegal Aliens living in the United States with more coming in each day and night. Also Mexican Illegal Aliens are giving birth here daily with no cost to them, and the child becomes a U.S. Citizen!

I don't ever believe there will be more Americans going to Mexico to equal the Mexicans coming to the United States. So don't worry Mexico!

164

ILLEGAL

ALIENS

Illegal Alien Population May Be As High As 38 Million

A new report finds the Homeland Security Department "grossly underestimates" the number of illegal aliens living in the United States. Homeland Security's Office of Immigration Studies released a report August 31, 2007, that estimates the number of illegal aliens residing in the United States is between 8 and 12 million.

"Californians for Population Stabilization" or "CAPS report that the illegal population is between 20 and 38 million.

Four experts contributed to the study by CAPS, James Walsh, a former associate general council of the Immigration and Naturalization Service, said he is appalled that the Bush administration lawyers on the Senate Judiciary Committee, every Democratic Presidential candidate, with the exception of Joe Biden, have no problem with sanctuary cities for illegal aliens. (Hillary Clinton, Barack Obama, Dennis Kucinich, Bill Richardson, and Chris Dodd). "The sanctuary cities and the people that support them are violating the laws of the United States of America! They're violating 8USC section 1324 and 1325, which is a felony –(it's) a felony to aid, support, transport, shield, harbor illegal aliens," Walsh said.

Walsh calculated there are 38 million illegal aliens in the United States by using the conservative estimate of 3 illegal aliens entering the United States for each one apprehended. According to Walsh, "In the United States, immigration is in a state of anarchy – not chaos, but anarchy." (The absence of government)

Information from this article comes from: Illegal Immigration ALIPAC
http://www.alipac.us
October 5, 2007
Jim Brown
OneNewsNow.com

Look Out America!

A Mexican's nationality will be lost if he stays for 5 years in the USA. This is why they want to give Mexicans 5 years to remain in the United States under a "worker's permit". Mexicans will no longer be able to return to Mexico as a Mexican "National". Article 37, Constitution of Mexico

PatriciaSaye@earthlink.net May 4, 2006

My thoughts – Whose country is this? The United States has laws also and Illegal Aliens do not belong here. They are not our responsibility!

166

Benefits for Illegal Aliens 12-4-07

1. $11 Billion to $22 Billion spent on welfare to illegal aliens each year.
http://tinyurl.com/zob77

2. $2.2 Billion dollars a year is spent on food assistance programs such as food stamps, WIC, and free school lunches for illegal aliens.
http://www.cis.org/articles/2004.fiscalexec.html

3. $2.5 Billion dollars a year is spent on Medicaid for illegal aliens.
http://www.cis.org/articl;es/2004/fiscalexec.html

4. $12 billion dollars a year is spent on primary and secondary school education for children here illegally and they cannot speak a word of English.
http://transcripts.cnn.com/TRANSCRIPTS/0604/01/ltd.01.html

5. $17 Billion dollars a year is spent for education for the American-born children of illegal aliens, known as "Anchor Babies".
http://transcripts.cnn.com/TRANSCRIPTS/0604/01/ltd.01.html

6. $3 Million dollars a DAY is spent to incarcerate illegal aliens.
http://transcripts.cnn.com/TRANSCRIPTS/0604/01/ltd.01.html

7. 30% of all Federal Prison inmates are illegal aliens.
http://transcripts.cnn.com/TRANSCRIPTS/0604/01/ltd.01.html

8. $90 Billion dollars a year is spent on illegal aliens for Welfare and Social Services by American taxpayers.
http://transcripts.cnn.com/TRANSCRIPTS/0604/01/ltd.01.htlm

9. $200 Billion dollars a year in suppressed American wages are caused by the illegal aliens.
http://transcripts.cnn.com/TRANSCRIPTS/0604/01/ltd.01.html

10. The illegal aliens in the United States have a crime rate that's two-and-a-half times that of white non-illegal aliens. In Particular, their children are going to make huge additional crime problems in the United States.
http://transcripts/.cnn,com/TRANSCRIPTS/0604/01.html

11. During the year of 2005 there were 4 to 10 Million illegal aliens that crossed our Southern Border, also, as many as 19,500 illegal aliens from Terrorist Countries.

Millions of pounds of drugs, cocaine, meth, heroin and marijuana, crossed into the United States from the Southern Border. Homeland Security Report.
http://tinyurl.com/t9sht

12. The National Policy Institute, 'estimates that the total cost of mass deportation would be between $206 and $230 billion or an average cost of between $41 and $46 billion annually over a five year period.
http://www.nationalpolicyinstitute.org/pdf/deportation.pdf

13. In 2006 illegal aliens sent home $45 BILLION in remittance back to their countries of origin.
http://www.eense.com/general175/niht.html

14. "The Dark Side of Illegal Immigration: Nearly One Million Sex Crimes Committed by Illegal Immigrants in the United States."
http://www.drdsk.com/articleshtm

Total cost is a whooping … $338.3 BILLION A YEAR!!!

Snopes is provided for doubters:
http:///www.snopes.com/politics/immigration/bankofamerica.asp

Knick – Knack

Rush Limbaugh said on his radio program, October 9, 2008, that 5 million illegal aliens got mortgages for homes!

Illegal Voters

Tens of thousands of illegal aliens voted in the 2000 elections said the Heritage Foundation. 3% of the United States population are illegal aliens that vote!

The United States Census does not distinguish illegal aliens from citizens. They are counted together. Some states may gain seats in the House of Representatives because of higher totals of illegal aliens living in those states, such as Arizona, Texas, and Florida.

Heard on the Lou Dobbs television show, July 20, 2008.

168

Immigration From Mexico

Center for Immigration Studies

Information from the reports of the Center's, Director of Research, Steven A. Camarota, July 12, 2001.

In 1970, the Mexican immigrant population in the United States was less than 800,000, compared to 8 million in 2000. Prices for consumers has only been reduced by .08 to 2% in the 1990's. The impact is so small because unskilled labor accounts for only a small bit of total economic output.

Author Steven Camarota said, "Mexican immigration is overwhelmingly unskilled, which reduces wages for workers who are already the lowest paid. This cheap labor comes with a high cost; continued unskilled immigration significantly increases the size of the poor and uninsured populations, and the number of the people using welfare."

Mexican immigrants who have lived in the United States for more than 20 years, who are legal residents, still have DOUBLE the welfare use rate of natives. (The natives being people born in the United States).

Mexican immigration acts as a subsidy to businesses employing unskilled workers, holding down labor costs while taxpayers pick up the cost of services to the poor and low-income Mexicans.

The United States needs to reduce unskilled legal immigration, stop illegal immigration and enforce the ban on hiring illegal aliens. The guest worker program will not work either. "Legalizing illegal aliens, through a guest worker program, an amnesty, OR some combination of the two, would not change the fundamental problems associated with high levels of unskilled immigration."

Knick Knack

Since the year 2000, an average of 500,000 illegal aliens have entered the United States and **settled permanently per year!**

"Immigration Watch", January 2008 by "Americans for Immigration Control, Inc.", P.O. Box 738, Monterey, Virginia 24465.

169

CAPS=Californians for Population Stabilization

Illegal Immigration Facts

1. There are an estimated 20 to 30 million illegal aliens residing in our country.

2. California is home to at least 3 million of those illegal aliens.

3. All of the 9/11 hijackers were in the United States legally, having entered on temporary visas.

4. Between1993 and 2003, 60 California hospitals were forced to close from the financial burden of providing free health care for uninsured illegal aliens.

5. Illegal immigrants that enroll in the University of California system are charged in-state tuition.

6. Each year the border patrol makes more than a million apprehensions of persons unlawfully crossing United States borders to work and to receive public assistance, often with the aid of fraudulent documents. Such entry is a misdemeanor, and if repeated becomes punishable as a felony.

Information from www.capsweb.org - Facts May 2008.

Knick – Knack

The President of Mexico, Felipe Calderon, says he has relatives and friends living in the United States who are illegal aliens! He was in New Orleans, Louisiana with President George W. Bush and Prime Minister of Canada, Stephen Harper. He opened a Mexican Consulate in New Orleans. There are now 48 Mexican Consulates in the United States.

Calderon said he would name his relatives after the United States passes new immigration laws!

Heard on Lou Dobbs Tonight TV, April 26, 2008.

My thoughts – Why are there 48 Mexican Consulates in the United States? Do Americans need them? Why doesn't the Mexican President offer jobs in Mexico to his relatives and friends living illegally in the United States? How funny does he think he is?

170

6-Hour Walk as an Illegal Alien

Spend a night as an illegal alien. The 20 or so people are tourists; they each paid about $15.00, to be on this nearly 6-hour nocturnal walk. This mock journey takes place in a nature park in central state of Hidalgo, Mexico about 700 miles from the border.

The Mexican government helped finance the creation of the Eco Alberto nature park, which is communally owned. The organizers, members of a Hnahnu indigenous community estimated as many as 90% of their 2,500 person community have made the journey to the United States, most ending up in Las Vegas, Nevada.

The organizers are trying to build empathy for immigrants. The group scaled walls, hid in tunnels, jumped into the backs of pickups and followed a path through a cornfield. A Mexican who has crossed the border more than 5 times says the tourist's experience "is not even 10% of the real trip." Some people think it could improve the often-conflicted attitudes of Mexicans toward their compatriots who migrate.

> Article by Jeremy Schwartz, Cox News Service, PARKONLINE-PARQUE ECO ALOBERTO: http//parqueecoalberto.com_mix – Information from an article in "The Tribune", San Luis Obispo County, California, August 23, 2006.

Another Jailhouse

Santa Barbara, California – A second jailhouse is needed in Santa Barbara County because of Illegal immigrant inmates, a county grand jury report said. The cost has been estimated at $153 million!

"Inadequate enforcement of federal immigration laws has resulted in a jail population of which illegal immigrants represents an annual average of 10 to 20 % of the total," the grand jury report said.

> Information from an Associated Press article in "The Tribune", San Luis Obispo County, California, March 30, 2007.

> My thoughts – Another occasion that United States Citizens' tax money must be spent on illegal immigrants. $153 Million should be spent on U. S. citizens children for pre-school and through higher education. When will the needs of illegal immigrants ever stop? They won't, until America's laws are enforced and the illegal aliens return to their homes.

President Bush Wants More Immigrants

He wants Congress to give him legislation that will welcome more foreigners into the U.S. He thinks immigration reform can only be achieved if the get-tough border security to keep people from sneaking (entering illegally) in is combined with opportunities for more immigrants to enter the country legally! He wants to keep America what she has always been -
   An open door to the future
   A blessed and promised land,
   One nation under God.

Bush wants to provide more temporary worker permits for foreigners willing to take low wage jobs and allow illegals working in the U.S., for some time, to become citizens.

Conservatives think the borders should be strengthened to keep Illegal Aliens out! Of the 6,000 National Guard troops he pledged only half are on duty along the border.

   Information from Associated Press article, August 6, 2006 - in "The Tribune", San Luis Obispo County, California.

   My thoughts – President Bush is so wrong on immigration it is hideous! We are being smothered (Invaded) by Illegal Aliens. We should halt legal immigration for 5 years. Our natural resources could become extinct and so could our generation of Americans! Bush is determined and very wrong!

Knick – Knack

175 people were arrested for deportation. Federal authorities swept through Southern California this week, including a Mexican man wanted for murder and a **convicted child molester** who had already been deported once! Most were Mexican Nationals but some were from India, Kenya and the Philippines.

   From an article in "The Tribune", San Luis Obispo County, California, June 23, 2007.

   My thoughts – What imbecile says we do not need a fence on our borders???

172

Secure Our Borders Battle Plan-9/11 Families for a Secure America

With your help, 9/11 Families for a Secure America will fight to:
   A. Reject all calls for additional amnesties for Illegal Aliens.
   B. Demand immediate action where no legislation is required.
      1. Assign troops to patrol the Mexican and Canadian borders, as well as seaports to halt illegal immigration and entry of terrorists.
      2. Enforce existing federal law baring employment of Illegal Aliens.
      3. End immediately all reverse discrimination, quota-filling, and so-called "affirmative action" programs to immigrants. Applying such programs to immigrants puts Americans at a disadvantage to immigrants and gives further incentives to Illegal Aliens to enter the United States.
   C. Cease all incentives for Illegal Aliens to cross our borders, including:
      1. Stop automatic citizenship for children born within the border of the United States to illegal immigrants.
      2. Stop welfare benefits in any form to non-citizens.
      3. Cut off Social Security benefits to Illegal Aliens.
      4. Simplify the currently unenforceable visa system.
      5. Prohibit educating illegal immigrants at United States taxpayer expense.
      6. Denaturalizing citizens who obtain their citizenship through fraud or deception or commit terrorist acts in concert with foreign terrorist entities or governments.
      7. Expand the number of Border Patrol Agents.
      8. Institute enhanced "Whistleblower" safeguards for all federal employees who uncover willful non-enforcement of immigration law.
      9. All state and local law enforcement agencies may deputize their officers to enforce immigration law.
      10. Enact legislation prohibiting banks and financial institutions from establishing accounts for people illegally in the United States.
   D. Re-establish assimilation as the goal for legal immigrants:
      1. Stop non-citizens from voting in federal, state or local elections. Such measures should include requirement of presentation of photo ID at time of voting, ending voter registration by mail and severe criminal penalties to those who violate or aid others to violate voting laws.
      2. Require all ballots to be in English only. Since immigrants must display a proficiency in English to become citizens, there is no need for ballots to be in any other language.
      3. Enforce existing requirements for proficiency in English and knowledge of United States history as prerequisites for achieving citizenship. Require schools that receive federal aid to teach English to students who are not proficient in the language. Establish a legal limit on duration of programs for such children.

173

E. Restore a system for issuing visitors' visas that protects the safety of the United States and its citizens.

    1. Strip the State Department of all visa granting power and transfer this authority to the Department of Homeland Security.

    2. Prohibit any employee of the Federal government from accepting payment from a foreign government or business or any entity controlled directly or indirectly by a foreign government or accepting a gift or thing of value from a foreign government or entity for 20 years after leaving government service.

    3. Enforce consular treaties barring consuls and all other diplomats and employees from participating in political affairs in the United States, this includes lobbying of state and local officials or aiding or abetting illegal immigration.

    4. Prohibit contributions of any kind by non-citizens to candidates for federal, state or local office and to political parties, either directly or through third parties.

    5. Prohibit federal aid to public colleges and universities that grant in-state tuition rates to Illegal Aliens or those enrolled or funded by foreign governments.

All this information is from the pamphlet "Secure Our Borders Battle Plan", "9/11 Families for a Secure America."

9/11 Families for a Secure America
Post Office Box 96196
Washington, DC 20090-6196

My thoughts – These are all very important actions that every American Citizen must fight to achieve! Otherwise, we will lose our country, which is happening now. The United States taxpayer paid $70 billion a year in 1997 for illegal immigration so what do you think it is today??? I hope you will send a donation to the 9/11 families.

Knick – Knack

The Washington Post newspaper has sympathy for Illegals who are here in the United States illegally. The Washington Post is the newspaper associated with the "Philip L. Graham Fund" which has provided funds to "Casa de Maryland", an illegal Alien support group.

Information from Special Report, Andy Selepak, June 5, 2007, "Accuracy in Media" for "Fairness, Balance and Accuracy in News Reporting."

Police Chief William Bratton of Los Angeles, California

He faulted his department for using poor communication and planning at a May Day immigration rally. Officers fired rubber bullets and swung batons to disperse a crowd.

The police did what they did after being pelted with rocks and bottles. Bratton said the clash embarrassed the department.

> Information from an article in "The Tribune," San Luis Obispo County, California, May 30, 2007.

> My thoughts – I wasn't there but I am embarrassed by Chief Bratton's remarks! Why is he so intent on blaming his officers? The police said they had rocks and bottles (Filled with what?) thrown at them. Doesn't he believe them???

> I also heard that the police didn't give the command to disperse in Spanish!!! Isn't this America?!! English is our language isn't it???!!! So if the police want a crowd to disperse how many languages should they use?? Two, ten, 15?!! I guess they'll have to carry a very loud recording of 15 languages screaming "Disperse" or maybe just in Spanish!

> Isn't it enough the taxpayers have to pay for all this crowd control everywhere? What happens if 20 million, plus their families, are given amnesty to become citizens of the United States? Will they march whenever they want their way?

> There are legal ways to come to this country!!

Immigration Smuggling Ring Accusation

Laredo, Texas. Three National Guardsmen assigned to the Texas – Mexico border were accused of running an immigration smuggling ring. Twenty-four immigrants were found inside a van that one of them was driving, said a U.S. attorney. The three were arrested and arraigned on a Federal charge of conspiring to transport illegal immigrants. They are Pfc. Jose Rodrigo Torres, 26, Sgt. Julio Cesar Pacheco, 25, both of Laredo and Sgt. Clarence Hodge Jr., 36, of Fort Worth, Texas.

> Information from an article published in "The Tribune" San Luis Obispo County, California, June 12, 2007, Tribune Wire Services.

> My thoughts – What were they thinking?

175

FAIR (Federation for American Immigration Reform) Report

More than 13 million Illegal Aliens reside in the United States! This represents an 88% increase since 2000. This is in a new report (October 30, 2007) by FAIR. In 2000 there were a little more than 7 million Illegal Aliens according to the INS.

Dan Stein, president of "FAIR" said "almost from the day the Bush administration took office, they made it clear that their AIM was to **reward** illegal immigration with amnesty and assorted other benefits. As a result we have had record increases in illegal immigration, mounting burdens on taxpayers and unprecedented public concern about this issue."

This Illegal Alien population of 13,175,000 people is now larger than the entire population of Illinois, the nation's 5th most populous state! 24 states now have Illegal Alien populations that exceed 100,000!

About 60% of all illegal immigrants – nearly 8.4 million people are settled in 6 states, California, Texas, New York, Florida, Illinois and New Jersey. Recent reports by "FAIR" indicate that the **combined cost of K – 12 education, health care and incarceration of criminals to those 6 states exceeds $27 billion annually**.

Dan Stein says, "The American public strongly supports an enforcement-first approach that discourages new people from coming illegally and encourages millions who are here to return home. Lack of enforcement and proposed amnesties has only exacerbated the problem!"

This information is from "FAIR", October 30, 2007 –
www.fairus.org/site/PageServer

My thoughts – The people who want Illegal Alien immigration thought that they would overwhelm the people of the United States by letting thousands and millions of Illegal Aliens to come here. They may have won, we don't know yet. We do know we have to elect a President who is against Illegal Alien Immigration! Many of the liberal Democrats want Illegal Aliens in our country.

Knick Knack

New Haven, Connecticut is the first city to issue illegal aliens identification (I.D.) cards. The illegal aliens can use them to get some city services but they cannot use them to vote.

Heard on Lou Dobbs TV show May 1, 2008.

Search for Illegal Immigrants Extends to Interior

Pearl, Mississippi-----------Detective Nick McLendon on stake out duty along eastbound Interstate 20 stopped a cherry Chevy Suburban without a light over its rear Texas license plate and 800 miles from the Mexican border. Inside were 14 illegal immigrants, 2 suspected smugglers and a notebook listing the passengers and their destination in Spanish-

1. Arterio Ramires to Nuy Yersey,
2. David Luna to Nueba York,
3. Marcelina and Jasmin to Carolina del Norte,
4. Jose Aguilar to Alabama,
5. Josefina Ortega to Chicago,
6. Gustavo Ribera to Florida.

More than week into "Operation Uniforce" they have arrested 300 immigrants and suspected smugglers. This is a trial 2-week crackdown; about 40 Border Patrol and custom agents have been temporarily assigned to the crackdown. After two weeks they return to their regular jobs and evaluate what they have learned. They may return but hope the immigrant smugglers will give up by forcing them to take longer, slower and more costly detours.

Most of the illegals are Mexicans headed for the East Coast where they get jobs in agriculture, construction and manufacturing.

One Mexican paid a smuggler $400 to get him home to avoid a murder charge in Chicago.

The agents uncovered vital information about smuggling rings and a popular Texas stash house where illegals are stashed after crossing the border.

Information from an article by Alicia A Caldwell, Associated Press, in "the Tribune", San Luis Obispo County, California, January 25, 2008.

My thoughts – I hope when we finally get the Border Fence in place that it will lessen the number of illegals that have to be chased and picked up all over the United States. Obviously until the Border Fence is operational and more Border Guards are hired the illegals are still coming over every year – who knows the number 500,000 to a million a year. They'll keep coming as long as they can get work and think they can get amnesty. In America they get all the freebies, education, healthcare, have a baby who will become a citizen, hospital care and everything is free. But a U.S. Citizen has to pay to have a baby.

Extremely unfair! American taxpayers pay all the costs for illegals.

177

Farmworker Ride-Sharing

An expanding ride-share program for unlicensed and uninsured farmworkers is being criticized by opponents who say the system benefits illegal aliens.

Ventura and Santa Barbara Counties were granted $3 million in state funds to purchase vans and cover operating expenses for 3 years. But critics said the state should not subsidize a program that appears to benefit workers who can't get insurance and licenses because they are in the county illegally! A spokesman for the Federation of American Immigration Reform, Ira Mehlman said, "The reason we have the large-scale illegal immigration is that we keep coming up with ways to accommodate people who are breaking the law rather than enforcing it!"

Officials said the program would make roads safer by getting uninsured and unlicensed drivers off the street, local growers said it would help ensure a stable and reliable work force.

Keith Millhouse, a Ventura County Transportation Commissioner said, "From a transportation policy standpoint, this is a good program." Ventura County's Transportation Commission is set to vote next week on whether to contract with a private company to operate its program. Santa Barbara County already has contracted with a nonprofit group to run its program.

> Information from an Associated Press article in "The Tribune", San Luis Obispo County, California, January 6, 2008.

> My thoughts – This is another travesty upon American taxpayers! It would seem to me that we must hire Americans to do the farm work, pay more and also use machines. By the time we pay for illegals to be farmworkers, we pay their health care, education and all myriad costs of illegals we are really losing money and our country! They stay in the country, have babies, all costs are paid by us and their babies become citizens. (Check the costs of illegals in other articles in this book) Eventually they will outnumber United States Citizens.

> Do you speak Spanish?

Knick – Knack

If you want illegal immigration news be sure to watch the Lou Dobbs Cable TV show, on CNN, 5 days a week, California time 4 PM.

It has more information about Illegal Immigration than any other TV show.

1 Million Sex Crimes by Illegals

This information is from a WorldNetDaily article posted May 31, 2006. To view the entire article online please visit
http://www.worldnetdaily.com/news/article.asp?ARTICLE_ID=50441

Based on a one-year in-depth study, a researcher estimates there are about 240,000 Illegal Immigrant sex offenders in the United States who have had an average of four victims each.

The highest number of sex offenders, according to the study, came from Mexico. El Salvador was the original home to the next highest number.

Previous Stories:

5 illegals face deportation after killing a principal
"Illegal runs red light," kills popular principal
Illegal-alien offenders flout United States justice system
Illegal "Hits American jackpot" with $44,000 job, crime spree
Murder suspect – an illegal with driver's license
Illegal, 17, runs down hero cop
3 illegals beat pregnant woman
Illegal alien accused of triple homicide
Illegal alien wanted for hunter murder
"Cop-killing" illegal snagged in Mexico
Alleged cop killer an illegal immigrant

Words of Advice

Let all those who want 12 to 20 million illegal aliens given amnesty and all the free benefits of the United States of America while living in the USA go to Mexico, take all the illegals with them, live there and help the Mexican people get aid in Mexico.

I have no problem with that, all the liberals and entertainment people who are in favor of amnesty and benefits for illegals can go also, build a house, make movies in Mexico, hire Mexicans to be their publicity agents, security guards, household help, nannies, and gardeners. And live happily ever after!

Carolyn Cavolt, July 11, 2008.

Smuggler Kidnappings in the United States

Phoenix, Arizona -----A woman is grabbed in a parking lot by 4 men who force her into a pickup truck. They demand $900,000 ransom. The police soon discover that the woman's family are Marijuana smugglers and her family arranges the woman's release. This is a common crime in Latin America that has moved across the border into the United States.

In the Phoenix area these abductions are happening at the rate of almost one a day!!! Police believe they have also led to killings where bound bodies have been found in the desert with bullets. The victims are criminals, drug dealers or human smugglers or a close family member.

"Immigrant smuggling is a lucrative line of work: A ring that moves a load of 30 illegal immigrants through Arizona can gross $45,000 to $75,000." The kidnappers are also fellow immigrant traffickers who do it to punish their rivals or do it for the money.

There were more than 340 such kidnappings in Phoenix in 2007. The San Diego area also has such kidnappings but hostage – taking is most prevalent in Phoenix, the nation's biggest base of operations for immigrant smugglers. In Mexico, kidnappings are common where victims include criminals as well as legitimate businessmen.

Information from an article by Jacques Billeaud of the Associated Press in "The Tribune", San Luis Obispo County, California, January 12, 2008.

My thoughts – I believe this should not be happening in the United States. If the United States President and Congress would get the promised border fence built it would eliminate many kidnappings while also eliminating illegal aliens coming into our country.

It is ridiculous that the President and many in Congress don't believe it is important to stop illegal immigration. **It costs us $338.3 Billions every year**, it changes our culture, it changes our schools, and it robs us of our tax money.

Would you want to live in the city where these kidnappings are taking place? Wouldn't it frighten you? What if these kidnappers picked the wrong person!

Do we need more crime in America?

Let me Make This Perfectly Clear!

This IS MY COUNTRY!

And, because I make this statement
DOES NOT mean I'm against immigration
YOU ARE WELCOME HERE IN MY COUNTRY.
Welcome to come through like everyone else has.
Get a sponsor
Get a place to lay your head!
Get a job!
Live by OUR Rules!
Pay YOUR taxes!
And
Learn The Language Like All Other
Immigrants Have In The Past!!!
AND PLEASE DON'T DEMAND THAT WE HAND OVER OUR
LIFETIME SAVINGS OF SOCIAL SECURITY FUNDS TO YOU
TO MAKE UP FOR "YOUR" LOSSES.
If you don't want to forward this for fear of offending someone,
Then YOU'RE PART OF THE PROBLEM!
When will AMERICANS STOP giving away THEIR RIGHTS???
We've gone so far the other way … Bent over backwards not to
Offend anyone. But it seems no one cares about the
AMERICAN that's being offended!

Information from an e-mail "Not yours it's mine", received February 2008.
Author Unknown.

Violence Along our Southern Border

Another Border Patrol Agent, Luis Aguilar was killed after being hit by a Hummer driven by suspected drug smugglers in California as he placed spike strips in front of the escaping vehicle.

Aguilar was a 32 year-old father of 2. From 2006 to 2007 violence increased along the border 31%, attacks on agents went up 44%. It will increase as fencing, technology and staff are increased to apprehend illegal immigrants, said Homeland Security Secretary Michael Chertoff.

Information from a Tribune wire services article in "The Tribune", San Luis Obispo County, California, January 23, 2008.

My thoughts – What are the rules of engagement? Why didn't the Border Patrol Agent shoot at the suspected drug smugglers? If they're in California illegally why can't the Border Patrol Agents shoot at them? They certainly killed an agent with their vehicle, didn't they?

The ACLU, AFL-CIO Suit

Los Angeles, California ---- The American Civil Liberties Union (ACLU) has filed a suit to force the Bush Administration to halt the plan to crack down on employers who hire illegal alien immigrants because the increased scrutiny of Social Security numbers will threaten the jobs of legal and American workers.

The AFL-CIO (the nation's largest federation of labor unions) who sued the U.S. government (August 29, 2007) over this plan to start September 14, said the plan would violate workers' rights and impose burdensome obligations on employers.

> Information from an article by the Associated Press in "The Tribune", San Luis Obispo County, California, August 30, 2007.

> My thoughts – The ACLU is a threat to American Citizens, I believe. I wish they would disband. We don't want or need them. The AFL-CIO suit says the "new rules will violate workers' rights and impose burdensome obligations on employers" is totally wrong in my opinion. Employers who hire illegal alien immigrants are putting burdensome obligations on ALL United States taxpayers! They hire them at lower wages than U.S. workers and then we the taxpayers, have to pay the balance, their health care, social services, education, and incarcerations if they commit a crime.

182

President Bush and his Immigration Bill

The immigration bill is his top domestic priority. The bill was sidelined 2 weeks ago. "The measure would tighten borders and workplace enforcement, create a new guest worker program and provide pathways to legal status for most of the estimated 12 million illegal alien immigrants in the country."

Information from an article in "The Tribune", San Luis Obispo County, California, June 24, 2007, Tribune Wire Services.

My thoughts – Here we go again! He'll never give up even though 80% of Citizens of the United States don't want 12 million more illegal aliens to get amnesty! His brother, Jeb, married a Mexican National (I heard on the radio). We can't afford them and probably 8 million plus in family members or maybe 20 million illegal aliens plus their families. Who knows? Nobody really knows! Why should the USA be the dumping ground for Mexico?

Shouldn't Mexico take care of their own? They have rich people in Mexico! Can't they do anything? What does the President of Mexico do to alleviate the situation? We know the last President, Vincente Fox, wanted them to come to America! Did he say "Good Riddance"? They had comic books that directed them how to get into the United States, the best places to cross the borders etc.

Immigrant Rights Activists

Los Angeles, California – Demonstrators protest the deportation of illegal alien immigrant, Elvira Arellano, who stayed inside a Chicago Church for a year to avoid being deported and separated from her U.S. born son. She was deported once before.

Arellano, age 32, was sent back to her native country, Mexico, a week ago after traveling to Los Angeles to attend a rally for the overhaul of U.S. immigration laws.

Organizers said more than 2,000 demonstrated, but authorities said it was about 600 who demonstrated in the streets.

Information from an article in "The Tribune", San Luis Obispo County, California, Tribune Wire Services, August 26, 2007.

My thoughts – A sanctuary church is wrong and so is a sanctuary city! Illegal Aliens should be deported. A nation without borders is not a nation.

183

Danger to Border Patrol Agents

The United States Border Patrol Agents are increasingly under attack from people on the Mexican side of the border. Sometimes the Border Patrol has retaliated by firing tear gas.

A metal wire was found strung between 2 border fences in San Diego – "An apparent effort to inflict serious injury to Border Patrol Agents." "An agent found the wire on the ground, strung about 150 feet between San Diego's 2 border fences leading through a hole into Mexico. The wire would be about 4 feet high if someone pulled it from the Mexican side – high enough to strike an agent on an all terrain vehicle in the neck."

Information from an "Associated Press" article in "The Tribune", San Luis Obispo County, California, February 14, 2008.

My thoughts – This is not a game for fun obviously! This is on the United States/Mexican Border! We need the double wall and quickly before an agent gets hurt or killed!

A Houdini

A 22-year-old male from Mexico has been arrested 15 times in the United States as an illegal alien. He uses a different name each time he returns to the United States after being deported. The last time he had 13 illegal aliens in his trunk.

Heard on Fox TV News, February 19, 2008.

My thoughts – I wonder how many other illegal aliens have their own business. Good ole' United States of America! A ready-made business opportunity for any illegal alien that wants to be an entrepreneur. Keep coming back into America and bring more illegals with you to make big money.

700,000 immigrants became United States citizens in 2006, 100,000 more than in 2005.

So said Lou Dobbs, January 24, 2007 during his TV show on CNN.

Knick – Knack

The total cost for illegal aliens in the United States is $338.3 BILLION a year that American taxpayers must pay.

My thoughts – And still people complain about the treatment of illegal aliens!

Illegal Alien Fights

Lancaster, Southern California – Rioting illegal aliens at a county-run detention center had to be subdued with tear gas, authorities said. There were hundreds involved. The fight started between the illegals from rival gangs, said a spokeswoman for United States Immigration and Customs Enforcement. The illegals were waiting to be deported.

Information from an Associated Press article in "The Tribune", San Luis Obispo County, California April 24, 2008.

My thoughts – Many Liberal Democrats in Congress want to give illegal aliens amnesty so they can live in America and fight in our neighborhoods!

Fines to Increase For Hiring Illegal Workers

Increased employer fines take effect March 27, 2008.

1. Minimum penalty is $375 from $275.
2. Maximum penalty would rise from $1,000 to $3,200.
3. $5,000 to $16,000 for repeated violations.
4. Fines are per person.
5. Workers using invalid Social Security numbers may be arrested for identity theft.
6. One Missouri poultry plant director now faces a 10-year prison sentence.
7. The owner of an Indiana construction company was sentenced to 18 months in jail and forced to forfeit $1.4 million.
8. There is increasing violence along the Southwest border by "alien smugglers, drug smugglers, gun smugglers" said Chertoff and Attorney General Mukasey. They want Congress to provide more funds to combat it.

Information from an article by Nicole Gaouette, Los Angeles Times, in "The Tribune", San Luis Obispo County, California, February 23, 2008.

My thoughts – It is past time! What has Congress been waiting for all these years while millions more illegals come into the United States and taxpayers have to pay for them?!

185

<u>Dear Bill,</u>

Hi Bill, as the administrator of your Foundation and also Warren Buffet's Foundation would you please consider giving $1,000 or more, what ever is feasible and practical, to every illegal alien and his family in the United States to return home to Mexico, sign a contract not to return, to be finger printed, given passage back to Mexico, their home, where the family can start a business, find a home and help to make their country very successful.

Mr. Gates, this would be your great legacy! You could save America for Americans so we can have our country back. You would also be saving the country of Mexico, help them start over with all their natural assets, great weather, beaches, the ocean, their oil. To each his own! Mexicans have their country and Americans have theirs! They have their own language, Spanish, and we have our own language again – English!

I realize we would have to pull some troops out of some of the 155 countries they're in now to guarantee safe passage for the Mexicans. These troops have dedicated a certain part of their lives to their country. I believe they would willingly volunteer to help save America again.

You must be a great man to have Warren Buffett choose you to administer his Foundation also. Your legacy and Warren Buffett's would be forever in history books as saving 2 countries. As Americans we want our own country, our own language! Our ancestors fought and died for this land. We want to keep it for our children, grandchildren and great grandchildren! If you think this is an impossible feat my alternative plan would be to have the United States government do it under the leadership of General Patreus.

Although I do believe it would be more difficult for the government to be involved!

We spend $338.3 Billion every year to feed, clothe and take care of the illegals in our country. If we used that money to help them and Mexico start again the benefits would be enormous for them and us. We could be friends again. We feel like we are being pushed out of our neighborhoods and our country!

Carolyn Gerdink Cavolt
November 6, 2008

<u>Organizations</u>

The National Council of La Raza (NCLR) is the
<u>Largest</u> – <u>National</u> – <u>Hispanic</u> - <u>civil rights advocacy organization</u> in the United States of America. Janet Murguia is the President and CEO as of April 2005.

LEGAL

And

ILLEGAL

IMMIGRATION

Theodore Roosevelt's Ideas on Immigrants and Being an American in 1907

"In the first place, we should insist that if the immigrant who comes here in good faith becomes an American and assimilates himself to us, he shall be treated on an exact equality with everyone else, for it is an outrage to discriminate against any such man because of creed, or birthplace, or origin.

But this is predicated upon the person's becoming in every facet an American, and nothing but an American! There can be no divided allegiance here. Any man who says he is an American, but something else also, isn't an American at all! We have room for but ONE flag, the American flag…. We have room for but one language here, and that is the ENGLISH language… and we have room for but one sole loyalty and that is a loyalty to the American people"

Words by Theodore Roosevelt 1907. He was the 26th President from1901 to 1909.

My thoughts – President Theodore Roosevelt, Republican, certainly had the right message. The present Congress and President need to abide by his words and listen to the majority of the United States Citizens who are being overwhelmed by Millions of immigrants who come to America. Also the Millions of illegal aliens who come here and want to be given everything we have to give. Actually we don't owe them anything. They sneak into our country and take, take, take!

I know we like to help others but when is it our turn? Is there ever a point when we can stop giving and take care of our own country and it's citizens? Or must we keep giving until America has nothing more to give?

Theodore Roosevelt
26th President of the United States
Wikipedia the free encyclopedia   188

The Average Annual Legal Immigration Level

By Numbers USA during:

The Colonial Era 1607 – 1775	3,500
The Nation Building Era 1776 – 1819	6,500
The era of Continental Expansion 1820 – 1879	162,000
The Great Wave 1880 – 1924	584,000
The rise of the Middle Class 1925 – 1964	178,000
The Civil Rights Era 1965 – 1989	507,000

The Average **Annual** Legal Immigration Level Since The Immigration Act of 1990: 1,000,000 – that is 1 million!

Information form Numbers USA, 310 Sixth Street, SE, Washington, DC, 20003, obtained, September 27, 2007. www.numbersusa.com

My thoughts – When will America say **Enough is Enough?** We also have an estimated 20 million Illegal Aliens here in the United States. Do we have boundaries? We have many Americans that need help. Don't they count? Do we need more and more immigrants in America that we must help?

Double

The Latino population will double from 15% today to 30% by 2050.

Hispanics are the United States largest and fastest growing minority group. They have a large proportion of people in their child-bearing years and have slightly more children according to the Pew Hispanic Center.

Information from a Washington Post article in "The Tribune", San Luis Obispo County, California, May 1, 2008.

My thoughts – Also, if they are illegal aliens they get free pregnancy care and free hospital care and the child when born in the United States is now a citizen. I would say they get a lot of benefits! I do not think it is right or fair.

If you are an American Citizen you must pay all your own birthing costs! **Why do Congress and the President value illegal aliens more than they do American Citizens?**

189

Immigrant Children May Become Major Voters

49% of California's children between ages of 12 and 17 have at least one immigrant parent. Of these 1.2 million children, 84% are United States citizens because of birth or being naturalized. As these children turn 18, they could fuel a rise in immigrant voters by 2012.

About 6.5 million immigrants in California are already United States citizens or could be. By 2012 these adults and citizen children who have become adults, could total 7.7 million "potential future voters" or 29% of the electorate if they register.

> Information from an article by "McClatchy Newspapers", in "The Tribune", San Luis Obispo County, California, April 30, 2008.

> My thoughts – It looks like immigrants may decide who is elected to all offices in California. So if they elect other immigrants to run the state, will long time residents of California who are United States citizens still have a say? Everyone must make an effort to be an informed voter and vote at each election. Absentee Ballots are the easiest way to vote, we've decided.

Knick – Knack

650,000 immigrants to the United States became American Citizens in 2007, Reported by Fox TV News March 31, 2008.

United States May See More Foreigners Than Ever

Immigration will be the main reason the population of the United States will be 438 million in 2050! Today the population is 303 million. Thus immigration is 82% of the increase in the nation's population.

> This bit of information taken from an article from "The New York Times", in "The Tribune", San Luis Obispo County, California, February 12. 2008.

> My thoughts – Move over citizens to share your space, your water, land, roads, schools, hospitals and doctors, jobs, recreational facilities, food and prisons! When will we stop immigration?

700,000 immigrants became United States citizens in 2006, 100,000 more than in 2005. So said Lou Dobbs, January 24, 2007 during his TV show on CNN.

Homeland Security Shortcuts

The Department of Homeland Security is ready to grant permanent residency to <u>tens of thousands</u> of applicants before the FBI completes a required background check. This is a major policy shift. 150,000 green card and naturalization applicants have been delayed by the FBI name check. 30,000 have been held up more than 3 years.

Homeland Security wants to reduce the immigration backlog. Immigrants are eligible whose fingerprints have cleared the FBI database of criminal convictions and arrests, but their names have not yet cleared the FBI's criminal or intelligence files after 6 months of waiting.

If an immigrant is granted permanent status, or gets a green card, eventually he'll be expected to clear the FBI's name check if not, he'll have his legal status revoked and be deported (I doubt that).

This new policy was outlined in an internal memo obtained by McClatchy newspapers. Check the Homeland Security Department's web site.

Because United States citizenship is more difficult to revoke than a green card those seeking United States citizenship will continue to be required to clear the name checks before being naturalized.

> Information from an article by McClatchy Newspapers in "The Tribune" San Luis Obispo County, California, February 11, 2008.

> My thoughts – Who made this stupid decision? Why must the United States always be concerned about how immigrants feel? What about us United States Citizens? Our welfare should be first. Think about our safety. Think about how the thousands, millions of immigrants affect our lives!

> Let them pay their own way. Charge them for services to become a permanent resident! After all, it is a privilege. United States citizens spend billions every month on immigrants, legal and illegal. Why are we responsible for every Tom, Dick & Henrietta that comes to this country???

> We may be getting tired of sharing everything we have in this country with outsiders. We don't even have a say. We must share our freedoms, our water, clean air, our highways, our schools, our space for homes, parks, our right to vote, and our money!!!

When can WE say, stop it, slow down. We're getting pushed out. Is it out with the old – in with the new? We should have a say where our money goes – to the new immigrant or take care of the citizens who have been here for generations.

We need a 5-year moratorium on legal immigration and a complete stop to illegal immigration and NO AMNESTY! We also need to stop the use of the 14th Amendment for "Anchor babies"!

If Congress and the President again consider amnesty for 1 to 30 million illegal aliens how will the Department of Homeland Security give them all a background
Check? They would be overwhelmed! They could not cope.

U. S. Immigration Agencies

U. S. immigration agencies say anti-terrorism is their primary mission, but they tried to deport only 12 people on terrorism-related charges from 2004 through 2006, according to a private research study released May 27, 2007. Co-Author David Burnham said, "The right number is unknowable".

The government tried to remove 814,073 people from the country during those three years and 12 is only a tiny fraction. The study's authors acknowledge the figure of 12 understates the anti-terrorism effort by the Homeland Security Department's immigration agencies. Because no one knows how many terrorists are in the United States or tried to get in, there is no way to say if 12 is too low, too high or about right.

"The budget and powers of this agency are influenced by all their talk and rhetoric about terrorism and criminals and if that isn't what they are doing, it should be considered by Congress and the public" said David Burnham, co-author.

Information from an article in "The Tribune," San Luis Obispo County, California, May 28, 2007, Tribune Wire Service.

Knick Knack

Before 1965, the United States admitted an average of 200,000 immigrants and refugees per year. After 1990, the average annual total rose to nearly 1 million.

Information from, January 2008 issue, "Immigration Watch", by "Americans for Immigration Control, Inc.", P.O. Box 738, Monterey, Virginia 24465.

Knick Knack

Since 1970, the leading source Countries of immigrants have been:

1. Mexico
2. China/Taiwan
3. Philippines
4. India
5. Vietnam
6. El Salvador
7. Korea
8. Dominican Republic
9. Cuba
10. Columbia

Information from "Immigration Watch", January 2008 by American for Immigration Control, Inc., P.O. Box 738, Monterey, Virginia, 24465.

My thoughts – Where are the European Countries? Where is Norway, Sweden, and the Netherlands? Where is Australia? Who has made the decisions since 1970? Why do they want to change the face of America?

Knick Knack

The Diversity Visa (DV) immigration category has been labeled a National Security risk by the Government Accountability Office (GAO).

The DV admits 50,000 immigrants to the United States each year simply on the basis of winning a lottery. The GAO charges that the government is not adequately screening those who come. Eligibility for the DV lottery are citizens of all 5 countries that the State Department lists as **terrorism sponsors**: Iran, Syria, Sudan, North Korea, and Cuba.

Since 1995, almost 10,000 immigrants from terror-sponsoring countries have come to the United States.

Information from "Immigration Watch", January 2008, by Americans for Immigration Control, Inc., P.O. Bob 738, Monterey, Virginia, 24465.

My thoughts – Who's in charge of the DV immigration Category? Obviously, no one with brains! Probably one of the terrorists who got in the United States!! How stupid are we? Really stupid!

193

100 Million More
Projecting the Impact of Immigration
On the United States Population, 2007 to 2060

This study uses Census Bureau data to project how different levels of immigration impact population size. The findings show that the current level of net immigration (1.25 million a year) will add 105 million to the nation's population by 2060.

Among the findings:

*Currently, 1.6 million legal and illegal immigrants settle in the country each year. 350,000 immigrants leave each year, resulting in net immigration of 1.25 million. This will add 105 million to the United States population by the year 2060.

*If immigration continues at current levels, the nation's population will increase from 301 million today to 468 million in 2060 – a 167 million increase. Immigrants plus their descendants will account for 105 million of the increase.

*The total projected growth of 167 million is equal to the combined populations of Great Britain, France and Spain. The 105 million from immigration by itself is equal to 13 additional New York Cities!

*If the annual level of net immigration were reduced to 300,000, future immigration would add 25 million people to the population by 2060, 80 million fewer than the current level of immigration would add.

*Net immigration has been increasing for 50 years. If immigration continues to increase, it will add more than the projected 105 million by 2060 that will be added if immigration levels stay the same.

*The nation's ongoing debate over immigration generally has not focused on the effects it has on the United States population size. Yet, increasing the nation's total population is one of immigration's clearest and most direct effects!

Supporters of low immigration point to the congestion, sprawl, traffic, pollution, loss of open spaces, and green house gas emissions that could be impacted by population growth. Supporters of high immigration argue that population growth may create more opportunities for businesses, workers, and consumers.

Whatever one thinks of population growth, the projected 167 million growth in the nation's population in the next 53 years is very large! **It is larger than the entire United States population in 1950.** It is more than the combined populations of: California – Texas – New York –Florida – Georgia Illinois – Pennsylvania – Ohio – Michigan – New Jersey.   194

Even the impact of immigration by itself is enormous.

*The 105 million immigration will add to the population by 2060 **is more than all of the population growth that occurred in the United States in the first 130 years of the nation's history after independence.**

Information from an article by Steven A Camarota, Center for Immigration Studies, August 2007. http://www.cis.org/articles/2007/back707.html

My thoughts – WHY? Why do we need all this added population? **We don't!!!**

I AM

FAIR

APPROVED

WE VERIFY WORK STATUS

ONLY AUTHORIZED

U. S. WORKERS HERE

FAIR means **"Federation for AMERICAN IMMIGRATION REFORM."**

Businesses displaying the FAIR APPROVED SEAL are businesses that care about their community. They obey the laws of our nation and honor U. S. workers by not displacing them with cheap, foreign Illegal laborers.

Published in the February 2007 issue of "Immigration Report" by FAIR (Federation for American Immigration Reform). FAIR Immigration Report is published 10 times a year, a non-profit membership organization.
> 1666 Connecticut Avenue, NW, Suite 400.
> Washington, DC 20009
> 202-328-7004
> 202-387-3447 (fax)
> www.fairus.org

Knick-Knack

President Calderon of Mexico has announced, Mexico will not participate in the next Summer Olympics!

He said, "Anyone who can run, jump, or swim has already left the country!"

Written as received in an e-mail on April 23, 2007 – The author of this joke is unknown.

IRAQ

A United States $740 Million Embassy in Iraq

There is a new $740 million United States Embassy complex in Baghdad, consisting of 26 buildings. There will be 1,000 United States government employees working there. This embassy is in the fortified "Green Zone" in a 104-acre complex. There are many problems with the complex. The buildings will not be accepted from the contractor until all the problems are corrected.

The contractor is "First Kuwaiti General Trading and Contracting Company."

Information from an article by Warren P. Strobel, McClatchy Newspaper in "The Tribune", San Luis Obispo County, California, March 1, 2008.

My thoughts – Why do we need a $740 million United States Embassy Complex in Baghdad, Iraq to employ 1,000 United States government workers? Seems excessive to me! I would rather use that money to repair our roads and bridges in the United States.

What will the upkeep cost us for the 26 buildings plus the payroll for 1,000 United States workers and the upkeep on 104 acres? Will some of these workers be security guards? Does this amount of money include a security fence?

Where are the smart people we thought we hired to run our country?

$1.1 Billion Contracts

Baghdad Iraq --- Iraq wants to award $1.1 Billion in contracts to Iranian and Chinese companies, the Iraqi electricity minister said on October 16, 2007. This $1.1 Billion is to build a pair of enormous power plants. American Military officials fear that Iranian commercial investments can mask military activities at this time of tension with Iran.

Information from an article in "The Tribune", October 18, 2007, Tribune wire services, San Luis Obispo County, California.

My thoughts – Why Iran or China? **Why not use an American company?**

Iraqi Leaders

From The New York Times – Next Spring (2008) when the United States "surge" of extra troop strength in Iraq will have to wind down, a grim new national intelligence estimate finds that Iraqi political leaders "remain unable to govern effectively" and are unlikely to heal deep sectarian rifts.

This is gloomy news but the report foresees even worse outcomes under Democrat plans for a speedier withdrawal of U.S. forces.

> Article in "The Tribune", San Luis Obispo County, California,
> "Week in Review" from The New York Times, August 26, 2007.

> My thoughts – Is there a solution?

LOCAL

NEWS

OF THE

CENTRAL

COAST

Penelope

I would like to tell you a story about a little 6 pound bundle of joy that loves to walk in the sand along the ocean in an area known as the Dunes. The Dunes belong to the California State Parks, which began in 1864. It is the only beach in California where vehicles are allowed to drive.

We, who live nearby are so lucky to live near such a wonderful spot, the ocean on one side and the Dunes on the other. The Dunes are hundreds of hills of sand.

This little 6 pound bundle of joy grew into a 140 pound pot-bellied pig. Penelope has lived in Grover Beach, California for 14 years. Her owner and caretaker, Mark Berry, said Penelope likes to sleep until approximately 2 PM, then she needs exercise and gets upset if she doesn't get her walk along the beach which she and Mark have been doing for 11 years. They walk later in the afternoon because Penelope does not like the hot sun! Penelope does not jog. Mark drives his pickup truck to the Dunes.

Mark is allergic to dogs and cats so that is why he went to a pet shop in the area and bought Penelope who was a small little piglet of 6 pounds. She has a life span of 15 to 18 years.

Penelope is a house pig. She lives inside the house, has her own bed, sleeps with her head on a pillow and with a comforter wrapped around her neck. She snores like a human being!

Mark says a pot-bellied pig is one of the cleanest animals to own. Every two months she gets bathed in their bathtub.

She used to perform at local elementary schools and a retirement home. Penelope played the piano with her nose and did other tricks. She had to give up entertaining because of arthritis. About 5 years ago Mark noticed that she was deaf.

She drinks glucosamine chondroitin, berry flavor, about a bottle a week that Mark gets at Costco for her arthritis. She loves it!

She lies near Mark while he is watching television. She is a light eater, eating only ½ cup of pellets twice a day.

Mark's wife works at a Thomas Kincaid Art Gallery in Solvang, California. Solvang, a small town settled by the Danish, is 45 minutes south of Grover Beach, off highway 101. It is a wonderful place to visit, shop and eat. There are many specialty shops and restaurants. You'll see windmills, horse drawn carriages and Danish bakeries.

Carolyn Cavolt conducted this interview on the Dunes with Mark Berry and Penelope on June 14, 2008.

02/08/2008

Mark and Penelope

06/14/2008

201

Woods Humane Society, San Luis Obispo

1. Started in May 1955.
2. Founded by volunteers to care for homeless animals on the Central Coast, led by Francis Newhall Woods.
3. 8 to 10 full time employees.
4. 200 – plus volunteers.
5. Annual operating budget, $600,000
6. 80% of budget is donated.
7. 22.4% of budget is for overhead.
8. San Luis Obispo County is served.
9. Each year 1,200 homeless animals on the Central coast are given humane care and shelter.
10. There is a 89% placement rate.
11. Low cost canine obedience classes.
12. Humane education at elementary schools.
13. Summer critter camp for 8 to 12 year olds.
14. Pet visitation to local retirement facilities.
15. Low-cost microchip I.D.
16. Dog and cat adoption.

Woods humane Society needs:

1. Financial support
2. Volunteers to help at the shelter with socialization, obedience training, grooming and off-site adventures.
3. If you want a dog or cat, look here.

> Phone 543-9316
> Federal ID95-2058587
> Address 875 Oklahoma Avenue, San Luis Obispo, CA 93401
> Operations Director – Leigh Ann Harms
> e-mail – info@woodshumane.org
> Web-site – www.woodshumane.org

Information from "Spotlight on Service", 781-7902 or e-mail newsroom@thetribunenews.com, April 20, 2007 in "The Tribune", San Luis Obispo county, California.

The Dana Adobe Burros

Polly and Darlene live at the Dana Adobe in Nipomo, California. They need a little help so if you can, send a tax-deductible donation to D.A.N.A. the Burro Fund, P.O. Box 729, Nipomo, CA, 93444 for their feed and veterinary care.

Plan to visit them on Sundays from noon to 4 PM. They love baby carrots and apples. Group tours are available and by appointment. They also like to be brushed.

Information from "The Tribune", San Luis Obispo County, California, in an article by Nick Wilson and Dawn White, "South County Beat" June 25, 2008.

My thoughts – I spoke with Ethel Landers, Administrative Director of the Dana Adobe, 805-929-5679. She said Polly is 24 and Darlene is 27 years old. They love carrots and apples because they're sweet. Sydney Hubbard donated a grooming kit and will train volunteers how to groom a burro. Call the number to volunteer in any way. The Adobe needs members, volunteers and docents. Your help is truly appreciated. You'll be loved by two burros because they love attention and being brushed. Take your out of town visitors.

To visit the Dana Adobe exit the 101 freeway at Tefft in Nipomo, California, 30 miles south of San Luis Obispo, California, go East one block to Oakglen and turn South one mile. There is a sign at the entrance, 671 South Oakglen Avenue.

Nipomo is a derivative from the Chumash word "Nipomah" meaning "the foot of the hills". Nipomo was founded in 1882 from land grants to William Goodwin Dana. To learn about upcoming events and added times to see the burros and tours – www.danaadobe.org - there are special events on 6 Saturdays this summer (2008).

RANCHO NIPOMO
(CAPTAIN WILLIAM G. DANA RANCHO)

RANCHO NIPOMO, ALMOST 38,000 ACRES IN SIZE, WAS GRANTED TO BOSTON SEA CAPTAIN, WILLIAM GOODWIN DANA, IN 1837. THE RANCHO FOR MANY YEARS WAS THE FIRST STOPPING PLACE ON EL CAMINO REAL SOUTH OF MISSION SAN LUIS OBISPO. FROM 1839 UNTIL DANA'S DEATH IN 1858, THE RANCHO WAS KNOWN THROUGHOUT THE STATE AS A HOSPITABLE STOPPING PLACE FOR TRAVELERS, INCLUDING CAPTAIN JOHN C. FREMONT, EDWIN BRYANT, AND GENERAL HENRY W. HALLECK. IN 1847 THE "DANA RANCH" BECAME ONE OF FOUR DESIGNATED EXCHANGE POINTS ON CALIFORNIA'S FIRST U.S. MAIL ROUTE.

CALIFORNIA REGISTERED HISTORICAL LANDMARK NO. 1033

PLAQUE PLACED BY THE STATE DEPARTMENT OF PARKS AND RECREATION IN COOPERATION WITH THE DANA ADOBE NIPOMO AMIGOS, JUNE 9, 2001.

This photo is by Dana Adobe.

Polly and Darlene are waiting for visitors. They need help.

Don't Call My Town SLO; it's S.L.O.

Myra Tompkins, the author of this article, gets upset if someone calls San Luis Obispo, SLO. She says the letters S-L-O (pronounced es-el-oh) are initials, not an acronym.

"Calling it SLO (w) is ignorant, insulting and demeaning. An acronym is a word formed from the first letters of a compound term. NASA is an acronym for National Aeronautics and Space Administration."

"How about U.S.A.? Usa? Please." "San Luis Obispo is a place name, not an acronym. It's a place made wonderful by climate and hard-working people, including 5 generations of my family. Call it San Luis Obispo, San Luis, or S.L.O. SLO (w) is lazy slang invented by people from somewhere else."

Information from the article "Viewpoint" May 11, 2008 by Myra Tompkins in "The Tribune", San Luis Obispo County, California.

My thoughts – I'm happy to know this, thank you Myra! It is good to stick up for your hometown!

HE Killed His Grandmother ?

San Luis Obispo, California ------- A Cayucos man, Mathew James Levine, age 35, turned himself into sheriff's investigators saying he was responsible for the death of his 84-year-old grandmother, Dorothy Vivian Autrey. He lived with her. Her body has not been found! He reported her missing on February 21, 2008.

Information from an article by Leslie Parrilla in "The Tribune", San Luis Obispo County, California, March 29, 2008.

My thoughts – Sad story about a grandmother! Who is safe these days? Why do some people think they have the right to snuff out the life of another? She lived to 84 years and should have had a peaceful death whenever it was her time. Cayucos is Northwest of San Luis Obispo.

Diablo Canyon Nuclear Power Plant

Location – San Luis Obispo County, California (On the Central Coast), north of Avila Beach, along the Pacific Ocean. The entry to the power plant is on the road to Port San Luis Pier past Avila Beach.

Owner – Pacific Gas & Electric Co. (PG&E). PG&E is the county's largest private employer. Diablo has 1,400 permanent, full time employees, plus about 200 contractors and subcontractors year round.

Almost every nine months, one of the two reactor units shuts down for refueling and maintenance, lasting a month or 2, employing around 1,000 or more temporary workers. At this time Diablo is also replacing 4 steam generators. Workers begin arriving in late January and all will have left by early April. About 2,400 contractors have been working at the plant since the middle of January, half coming from outside the Central Coast.

$2,000 to $3,000 is the amount each out of town worker spends locally each month. Wages are from $24 to $42 hour but average overtime is 20 to 32 hours a week at $36 to $84 per hour. Out of state workers also can qualify for per diem travel stipends.

Workers – engineers, welders, electricians, pipe fitters and carpenters, recruiting is done through local unions.

Many workers use RV resorts, hotels and motels. One couple from Texas flies in their plane to San Luis Obispo paying $500 per month hanger fees and $600 a month for a rental car. PG&E arranges discounted rates with motels.

Information from an article by Raven J. Railey, rrailey@thetribunenews.com in "The Tribune", San Luis Obispo County, California, March 16, 2008.

My thoughts – I believe there are 103 Nuclear Power Plants in the United States. We need at least that many more. France is powered 80% by nuclear power plants! Why are we so slow to get them, because many of the environmentalists don't want them, which is totally wrong. We need nuclear power plants.

A 9-Week Youth Leadership Program for Primarily Hispanic Youths

This new Youth Leadership Program serving primarily Hispanic teens in Nipomo, California is a nine-week course led by community leaders who will teach leadership skills, civic activism and college preparedness.

Classes start in February 2008. The program has been organized by the nonprofit organizations "Vision Unida" AND THE Economic Opportunity Commission's "Lifebound Leadership" program.

The program has been supported by the Robert H. Janssen Foundation with a $12,700 grant. Organizers expect up to 20 students this year. They'll have many local Latino leaders speaking to them. Instructors are psychiatrist Silvia Ortiz, Cal Poly professor Bob Flores, and Cuesta Latina Leadership Network Janet Florez. County Superior Court Judge Teresa Estrade-Mullany will speak at the orientation.

The course includes classes in team building, leadership skills, conflict resolution and achieving academic goals. Leaders with "Vision Unida", an 11-year-old adult leadership program intended primarily for adult-Hispanic participants, designed the teen curriculum based on its own course offerings. Linda Villanueva Quesenberry of "Vision Unida" said, "We've had the idea for the teen leadership program for four years. We're hoping to get another program off the ground soon in North County, but we didn't have the funding this year."

Maribel Flores, 15, wants to start a new club at Nipomo High School to celebrate Hispanic heritage. She wants to be more involved in the community. She has joined the new "Youth Leadership Program". "I want there to be a Latino Club at school that celebrates things like Cinco do Mayo." The skills that Flores will learn in the new program could help her to lead such a club, she says.

Jose Gomez, 15, plans to participate. He wants to join leadership programs to help him improve his college application. He hopes to become an architect and believes he'll benefit from the guidance of local leaders.

A free "I Pod Nano" will be given to every Nipomo teen who attends every session of the course. Gift cards from Target, Wal-Mart, and Best Buy will be given to those teens that attend most of the classes. The 9 meetings are from 4 to 5:30 PM at an elementary school every other Wednesday from February 6 to May 28. Orientation is January 30 at 6 PM or call 929-6054.

Information from an article in "The Tribune", San Luis Obispo County, California, January 29, 2008, by Nick Wilson, nwilson@thetribunenews.com

My thoughts – This is a great idea for teenagers. Although I do wish it were for all teenagers, not primarily Hispanic. This is exactly what all American teenagers need. I do hope and pray that some of our older institutions, teacher organizations, parent groups get together and realize the need for all United States teenagers, not only Hispanic, to have these advantages. Would the Bill Gates, Warren Buffet Foundation contribute to help the United States teenagers get help and advice to be able to start clubs, become interested in Politics?

Some of them will become the future leaders of the United States. Looking at our politicians and Congress today we surely need very smart moral men and women and students who have a full knowledge of American History, our culture, our laws, geography and high morals.

Can't we find teachers, parents, business leaders, college students, who are willing to donate time for the sake of continuing and safeguarding the American Way of life.

We need more courses in schools about how our country began and how to safeguard our way of life. We may have to teach these classes after school in Leadership programs. We can have rewards also. Why are we waiting?

$55,318 is California's Median Income

The Census Bureau data showed California median income rose to $55.318 in 2006 up $1,866 from 2005. Fewer Californians are living below the federal poverty line:

12.2% in 2006
13.2% in 2005

The deepening housing slump is hurting California's job market. Industries tied to the housing market – a major driver of California's job growth over the last few years – have lost jobs the last year and the decline is not over.

Information from an Associated Press Article, September 2, 2007 in "The Tribune", San Luis Obispo County, California.

208

Hearst Castle Guides

San Simeon, California

Want a job on weekends, holidays and during the summer?

The pay is good – a guest trainee earns about $10.41 and $12.22 an hour and can work nearly full time during the summer.

After training, guides earn $ 16.33 to $19.86 an hour. They can work up to 1,500 hours per year.

> Article by P. Kim Bui, "San Simeon-Hearst Castle needs a few Good Guides." Published October 9, 2006, in "The Tribune", San Luis Obispo County, California.

> My thoughts – What a dream job, strolling through the castle and teaching about all the treasures that Mr. Hearst collected, beautiful environment in which to work and enjoy. If you live in Cambria, CA, the Castle would be 15 minutes North. From San Luis Obispo, CA, it would be about 45 minutes. Or if you don't live in the area, move here so you can get an unusual job! Where else in the country???

www.centralcoastgrown.org

That's a website to find fresh local foods for you to buy. It is a product of the San Luis Obispo County Central Coast Ag Network established in 2003. Find out what's in season. Listed are the fruits, vegetables, flowers, wine, meats, dairy, spices and nuts that they produce.

The purpose is to buy locally grown foods, which is better for us and healthier for our planet. Steven Knudsen, a Central Coast Grown board member said "If each person in the county diverted just one dollar a day to locally produced goods, it would mean more than $96 million in additional dollars spent here on the Central Coast each year."

> Information from an article by Leah Etling in "The Tribune", San Luis Obispo County, California, February 29, 2008.

> My thoughts – A wonderful idea.

209

Jordan Hasay, A Top County Runner

Jordan Hasay, the 15-year-old Mission Prep student of San Luis Obispo is running September 9, 2007 in the Morro Bay Invitational at Morro Bay High School. Morro Bay coach Cary Nerelli is hosting the invitational for the 25th year and is happy to have Hasay at his event. It has been a low-pressure season opener for 7 state champions over the years.

"I think anytime the local population can see an athlete the caliber of Jordan run, it just adds a special meaning to that event. Our kids are very excited about running the same event with her," said coach Nerelli.

Jordan Hasay's recent big event in July was a second-place run in the 1,500-meter race at the IAAF World Youth Track and Field Championships in Ostrava, Czech Republic. She has limited local appearances. "That's one of the reasons why I'm running this week end as I have a lot of people say they like to come watch me run. It's neat that they all come out and support," said Hasay.

The course is approximately 2.7-miles because the beach portion of the run depends on the tide.

She is a standout on the running circuit. Her local appearances are limited because she has "more important meets that she needs to be peaking for," Hasay said.

From an article in "The Tribune", San Luis Obispo County, California, by Joshua D. Scroggin, jscroggin@thetribunenews.com - September 8, 2007.

My thoughts – She is a champion. I wish her good luck and good health.

Jordan Hasay of Mission Prep, San Luis Obispo, California

Fresno, California ---- Jordan Hasay won the girls championship race in 17 minutes, 23 seconds on October 6, 2007 at the Clovis Cross Country Invitational at Woodward Park. She owns a PR of 17:02 on the 3.1-mile course. This is her 3rd straight Clovis Invitational title. It was her first victory in the championship race, which had 132 runners. The Mission Prep, San Luis Obispo, California junior has become a mini-celebrity. She's been running 7 miles per day in workouts.

From an article in "The Tribune", San Luis Obispo County, California, by Lisa Houk, "Special to The Tribune", October 7, 2007.

My thoughts – Jordon is a champion who happens to have beautiful, swinging blonde hair falling past her hips.

Jordon Hasay – 3rd National Title

Mission Prep distance runner Jordon Hasay picked up her third National award – USA Track and Field Athlete of the Week.

The USATF announced October 21, 2008 that Hasay will be honored as the organization's Youth Athlete of the Year.

Track & Field News magazine named Hasay its 2008 Girls High School Athlete of the Year.

> Information from "The Tribune", San Luis Obispo County, California, October 29, 2008.

Pismo Beach, California City Council Salaries

The monthly salary of City Council members in December 2008 will be $ 514.80, unanimously approved by the Council, an increase of $ 118.00. Their last salary increase was in December 2002.

The Mayor's salary will be $714.80, an additional $200.00 stipend. Mary Ann Reiss is the present Mayor.

Mayors in San Luis Obispo and Paso Robles receive a similar salary, a Pismo Beach staff report stated.

> Information from an article in "The Tribune", San Luis Obispo County, California, June 24, 2007 by Ann Marie Conejo.

> My thoughts - Who wouldn't want to be addressed as "Honorable Mayor", "Your Honor", or just "Mayor", or Councilwoman? Young people prepare yourselves to be a mayor or council members in your city! Prepare yourselves for a political career.

San Miguel, California

Are you a volunteer? Can you donate money & materials? Morningstar Youth Ranch is a nonprofit organization that pairs at-risk children with rescued horses, to promote trust and caring.

Bryce Richardson has earned his Eagle Scout rank by raising money for materials, gathered helpers and built a new horse arena for Morningstar Youth Ranch. His parents are Janet and Daniel Richardson.

The organization needs volunteers and donation of materials and money.

Arcy and Carl Linn have opened their ranch between Paso Robles and San Miguel for the program.

One project is to crossfence 9 acres. To be a fence sponsor, send donations to Morningstar Youth Ranch, 862 Exline Road, Paso Robles, California 93446.

The ranch welcomes visitors to view the program.

For more information visit – http://morningstaryouthranch.org or call 805-226-2859.

Contact Lynne Schmitz at 805-286-8855 or e-mail Lynne_Schmitz@yahoo.com with "San Miguel News" on the subject line. Lynne Schmitz is a long time resident of San Miguel. She is the writer of this column; "San Miguel Scene."

Information from an article in "The Tribune, San Luis Obispo County, California, August 23, 2007, "San Miguel Scene."

My thoughts – Move over Angelina Jolie! Bryce Richardson is certainly a giver! Angelina doesn't think Americans give enough! San Miguel, California is about 45 Minutes North of San Luis Obispo, California.

Another Taboo!

Make a pledge to never again say, **YOU GUYS!!!**

These two words are used by television news people, ad nauseum, and by everyday ordinary people.

You guys means anyone and everyone. Men, women, boys, girls, old people, young people! Since when are girls called guys?

Why has the English language evaporated?

212

CGC 10-06-08

The Tribune
Newspaper of the Central California Coast
Letter to The Editor Published February 28, 2008

Get Rid of Sierra Club

I would like to vote for the dissolution of the Sierra Club. The Sierra Club is a see-and-sue club. See people having fun and sue them. They seem to sue, win the judgment and the taxpayers have to pay. It doesn't sound fair to me.

Why doesn't it sue sex clubs or pornographic booksellers or sex offenders? Do some good while it is sue happy. God knows we don't need the aforementioned.

Let's take a vote. Who wants the Sierra Club to take away the fun of families, horses, walkers and dogs who use the Dunes for fun? Will it sue to close highways because people use vehicles, spew exhaust fumes, have accidents and get killed on the highways?

God made this ocean, sand and the Dunes for people to enjoy. Back off, Sierra Club.

Carolyn Cavolt
Grover Beach

You Know

Please Pledge to never again say these 2 words! **YOU KNOW.**

As heard on TV, in any conversation, by many persons who want to drive the listener crazy! It is a habit to break!

Examples:
Barack Obama, you know, is now, you know, the President Elect, you know, of the United, you know, States! Congratulations!

Or

John McCain, you know, lost the race, you know, to become, you know, the President of the United States!

Sarah Palin, you know, was the bright, new spot in the, you know, campaign. I hope, you know, that we see much more, you know, of her.

Institute Beauty Culture, Inc.

The Institute of Beauty Culture, a school in the Pismo Coast Plaza on 5 Cities Drive is in Pismo Beach. Students supervised by Linda, a friendly teacher do all the work. I've been going here since it opened about 5 years ago. The prices are very reasonable, $8.00 for a shampoo and set. The students are very friendly and competent. They do color, cuts, manicures and pedicures.

CGC

Pismo Clams

Pismo Clams around town are painted for the holidays & Monarch Butterfly Season.

Playing in the Mud

Volunteers made more than 2000 adobe bricks for Mission San Miguel, California. In the 1950's, the author's dad, Jesse Crettol, built a wonderful machine to make adobe. It started the process by digging a trench and finished with rows of bricks in hand-made forms drying in the trench. With the help of his dad, Jess, the author's brother, Ralph Bebout, and many Franciscan brothers and students for the priesthood, thousands of bricks were made to build the retreat center and the wall around the South end of the Mission. They still have the basic machine, but a lot of the pieces have been lost over the years. The author's brother remembers it was quite a job to keep everything running smoothly.

Article written by Lynne Schmitz, a longtime resident of San Miguel, California.
e-mail Lynne Schmitz at LynneSchmitz@yahoo.com
("San Miguel News" in the subject line), or call her at 805-467-3565.
Published in The Tribune, San Luis Obispo, California, September 7, 2006.

My Thoughts – I assume Lynne can tell you how to make the adobe bricks to build your own little Mission church in your own backyard! We drove to the Mission over a year ago and it needs many bricks. They need donations also. It was damaged in the earthquake a few years ago. It is located about one hour North of San Luis Obispo, California. It was an active parish church but not since the earthquake. It is sad to see it in disrepair.

Knick – Knack

If you're in the Pismo Beach area be sure you save time to go to
Ron's Nursery in
Grover Beach
1207 South 13th Street
805-489-4747.

In my opinion it is one of the most beautifully supplied Nurseries in the area, also go at Christmas time, the decorations are gorgeous.

I used to love to go to the Burlingame Garden Center in Burlingame, California and Ah Sam's in San Mateo, California when I lived in that area. Stunning decorations.

Carolyn Gerdink Cavolt

MEMORIES

The Memory of a Grandson

Our grandson died in a car accident on his way to Homecoming festivities at his school. He was a Senior who was well liked by his classmates. He befriended the less popular his father has said. He was thoughtful and kind. The school, Monte Vista Christian, is a private school in Watsonville, California with primary grades through high school.

His brother, Derek, had graduated a year earlier. He and two friends were on their way to the game and happened to arrive on the scene while the police were investigating the accident. The police wouldn't let him get near the car because it had hit a tree and burned. Several people had tried to break open the door but failed. Derek had the responsibility of telling his parents about the accident.

Part of the road to the school is a narrow two-lane road over a mountain. Somehow his car wheel went off the road, he overcorrected, crossed over the other lane, hit a tree and the car caught fire.

Friends and classmates began visiting his parents at their home. They stayed and talked, brought cards and notes with heartfelt remembrances. Everyone was unbelievably kind bringing food, drinks and flowers.

The memorial service was held at the family church with about 700 mourners, many of them classmates. Derek, remarkably, was able to stand in front of the mourners to speak about his brother. He is now a courageous police officer in a large city in California. He is tall, slim and can outrun and overtake any criminal.

Many ladies and friends of the family prepared food and brought it to the church hall to serve all of the mourners after the service.

His parents started a school Scholarship Fund, in lieu of flowers, which has grown to over $50,000. His legacy is the education of boys and girls in the Christian tradition of the United States to become leaders of this country.

There are two memorial benches at the school with Tyson's name. After his death, October 14, 2000, the day before his 17th birthday, many students started wearing red on Thursdays. Red was his favorite color.

40th Anniversary of RFK's Assassination

Senator Robert F. Kennedy declared victory as he talked to campaign workers at the Ambassador Hotel in Los Angeles, California on June 5, 1968. He was running for the office of the United States President and had just won a victory in the state's Democratic presidential primary. He was shot by Sirhan Sirhan June 5, 1968 at the Ambassador Hotel as he was leaving. He died the next day.

> Information from an article by Brian Witte, Associated Press in "The Tribune", San Luis Obispo County, California June 6, 2008.

> My thoughts – It is now 40 years later. The Kennedy name will never die. It is forever a part of America. Sirhan Sirhan is still in prison and will be until he dies.

> I thought Robert Kennedy was the best Attorney General that we have ever had. He was bold and brave. He had 11 children. I remember the Ambassador Hotel because the "Coconut Grove" nightclub was in the Ambassador Hotel. We were there twice. It was the "hot" spot and many movie stars patronized it. Many famous musicians and singers performed there.

> I also remember the Ambassador Hotel because as we were getting on the elevator one of my favorite earrings fell off and dropped between the elevator and the floor and fell to the basement.. I informed the desk and left my name and address, lo and behold, sometime later I received my earring! It was a little bent but I still have it. The hotel has been torn down, but I have memories!

Knick - Knack

On August 14, 1935 President Franklin D. Roosevelt signed the Social Security Act into law.

Highlight in History: On August 14, 1945 President Harry Truman announced that Japan had surrendered unconditionally, ending World War II.

On August 14, 1947, Pakistan was established as a modern state, independent of British rule.

> Information from the article, "Flashback", published August 14, 2006 in "The Tribune, San Luis Obispo County, California.

A Memory

One of the best trips of my life was taken in August 1997 with my 13-year-old grandson, Tyson. We had a 5–week coast-to-coast trip in a High-Rise Ford Van. He was the navigator. I was the driver.

A great disappointment was not getting into the White House in Washington, DC. We had our tour tickets to walk through the White House but we were 10 minutes late and were not allowed to get in line by the Park Service employees. Can you imagine our disappointment? We also had our 9-year-old grandson whom we had picked up in Virginia Beach, VA. I think they could have bent the rules.

We had traveled all the way across the country from California and the Park Service wouldn't let us in!!! I wish I had thrown a fit and gotten arrested! But with my Catholic school upbringing of 10 years, I did not. But I think I would have set a better example by being strong. I really regret it now that I didn't fight for our rights! Here it is 11 years later and I'm upset.

Tyson has been in Heaven since October 14, 2000 because he was in a fatal car accident, the day before his 17th birthday.

Carolyn Cavolt, July 13, 2008.

This is Tyson about age 6. He loved Karate. He took lessons for about 5 years and was about to earn his Brown Belt, Black is next. Red was his favorite color.

220

The Greatest Loss

There is no greater loss than that of a child.
There is no greater pain.
What could possibly hurt more?
It has been eight years now, the pain is still acute.
She was crying when I called.
She had a reminder of him.
And the tears still flow.
When will it end? Never!
Not until we all meet in Heaven.
As the mother of the mother who lost the child.
There is very little I can do to soften the tragedy.
We feel the loss also but we still have all four of ours.
She has only one son left.

    CGC

NAFTA

SUPERHIGHWAY

Foreigners Are Buying U.S. Roads

Roads and bridges built by U.S. taxpayers' dollars are being sold to foreign-owned companies.

In June an Australian-Spanish partnership paid $3.8 billion to lease the **INDIANA TOLL ROAD.**

An Australian company bought a 99-year lease on **VIRGINIA'S POCAHONTAS PARKWAY.**

Texas officials decided to let a Spanish-American partnership build and run a toll road from Austin to Sequin for 50 years.

Chicago has sold a 99-year lease on the 8-mile CHICAGO SKYWAY for $1.83 billion. Macquarie Infrastructure Group of Sydney, Australia, and Cintra Concesiones de Infraestructuras de Transporte of Madrid, Spain are the buyers and are the same group that leased the Indiana Toll Road. Chicago used the money to pay off debt and fund road projects. Skyway tolls rose 50 cents to $2.50; by 2017 the toll will reach $5.00.

The transportation director for the conservative think tank "Reason Foundation" said private investors can raise more money than politicians to build new roads because these kinds of owners are willing to raise tolls.

Plans to sell or lease highways to companies outside the United States, have not met resistance.

John Foote, senior fellow at Harvard's Kennedy School of Government, said the government can take over a highway in an emergency. He objects to selling roads to raise cash. He thinks the Indiana Toll Road lease is a better deal because the proceeds will pay for projects such as road and bridge improvements.

A subsidiary of an Australian Company owns a **bridge in Alabama**. Also the company gets tolls from the tunnel on the U.S. side between **Detroit and Windsor, Canada**.

> Information from an article published in "The Tribune", Associated Press, San Luis Obispo County, California, July 16, 2006.

> My comments – Who Knew??? This is another bomb – **the selling of America!** Tell your Congressman you object! Congress is asleep.

The NAFTA Superhighway

1. **It will cost $ 183 billion in new taxes and tolls**.

2. It will destroy tens of thousands of homes, ranches, farms, business and whole communities in the United States

3. It will signal the end of the US sovereignty and the beginning of a "North American Union" with Mexico and Canada.

THE NAFTA SUPERHIGHWAY

4. The NAFTA Superhighway (North American Free Trade Agreement, NAFTA) will be a huge four-football fields wide highway that will run through the heart of the nation from the Mexican border at Laredo, Texas to the Canadian border north of Duluth, Minnesota.

5. We are being drowned in a sea of Illegal Aliens and at risk daily from Islam Fascist terrorists. The Bush administration is quietly advancing the construction of this massive Superhighway that will almost obliterate our borders with Canada and Mexico.

6. The short-term goal is to make it easier for cheap foreign goods from Asia to be transported from ports in Canada and Mexico into the United States.

224

7. The long-term goal is to form a "North American Union" with Canada and Mexico that will create a single continent-wide entity without borders, tariffs and customs. The developers and government officials promoting this scheme, from the President on down, all deny this. Construction will soon begin in Texas.

8. When Congress and President Bill Clinton pushed through NAFTA in 1994, we were told this would lead to better prices and more fair trade for American businesses. (I, Carolyn Cavolt, remember Ross Perot said, "Don't do it!" He was right. I voted for him. He received 20% of the vote.)

9. We were **not** told that NAFTA would:
   A. Encourage millions of Illegal Aliens to sneak into America for low-paying but abundant jobs.
   B. Lead to the destruction of America's manufacturing base and millions of good paying jobs along with it.
   C. Help drive down the value of the American dollar.

10. The real long-term goal of NAFTA is the dissolution of our borders with Canada and Mexico.
   A. The 1994 NAFTA agreement called for a Massive Corridor that would allow international goods to flow into America through a "Sentri" system of "Fast" lanes that would only do an electronic "security" check on vehicles.
   B. The vehicles would be officially checked at a "Customs Center" located in Kansas City, Missouri, about 1,00 miles from either border! This massive "Border" check center will also soon be under construction.
   C. Eventually, the Nafta Superhighway will be expanded to a system of 80 large, small and moderate size "Corridors" crisscrossing the United States, Mexico and Canada, which will all but eliminate any form of a border between the three nations. If the Nafta Superhighway is allowed to proceed, the end of the United States of America as we know it will be inevitable.

Ever wonder why the President and so many Members of Congress, the media and industry seem unconcerned about the millions of Illegal Aliens flowing into our nation each year?

In their vision of the future, these Illegal Aliens won't be illegal any more because there will be no borders, no more United States of America! In its place would be a "North American Community" with a single "North American Currency" and a single "North American Government". That's the long-term future of our nation if this 4,000 mile wonder isn't stopped!

11. The immediate damage of this globalist creation will also be catastrophic.

A. Millions of homes, ranches, farms, businesses and whole communities will be bulldozed under "eminent domain" as thousands of miles of new highways are paved.

B. Taxes and tolls will go up all across the nation to help pay for the construction of the Superhighway.

C. Americans will be forced to also pay for the Mexican portion of the Superhighway because the corrupt Mexican government claims it cannot afford to pay on its own.

D. There will be literally no security on what was once our borders to prevent the entrance of radical Islamic terrorists and other enemies who wish America and its people harm.

12. Do we really want Canada and Mexico dictating to us on these vital issues?

A. Canada is one of the most-enthusiastic globalist nations in the Western world, signing onto just about every socialist (a system of ownership by society rather than individuals) environmental treaty.

Canada has:

1. Banned the death penalty.
2. Imposed draconian restrictions on gun rights.
3. Legalized homosexual marriages.
4. Refused to cooperate with the United States in both Iraq and the development of a Strategic Defense Initiative (SDI)
5. Most recently, encouraged members of our Armed Forces to desert and seek safe haven in Canada.

13. Mexico, one of the most-corrupt nations on earth, is constantly lecturing America on human rights while actively encouraging their own citizens to sneak into our nation, break our laws and live off our welfare systems.

Why would we want either Canada or Mexico to have any say in our policies?

Should we have to pay for the dissolution of our borders and our nation??? No! No! No!

14. This North American Community would hurt our savings, our retirement, our economy, our security, our independence and us.

A. Canadians and Mexicans would get richer- - at our expense.

B. They have ruined their economies with high taxes, oppressive regulations and massive welfare state programs.

15. All this information is by the Selous Foundation and if we become one with these two socialist nations, Canada and Mexico, it is at our own peril!

A. Through the publications of the Selous Foundation they have been informing the public for years about the need for a strong U.S. military and a pro-freedom, anti-communism, anti-terrorism foreign policy.

B. The Selous Foundation was the first to expose Bill Clinton's drive to place U.S. soldiers under United Nations command and in United Nations uniforms. Millions of Americans know the truth about that betrayal.

C. Now, the Selous Foundation is moving quickly to expose the Nafta Superhighway and to pressure President George W. Bush and his administration into CANCELING this Globalist Nightmare while there is still time.

D. Please send a tax-deductible donation of any amount to the Selous Foundation. The entire nation needs to know about the Nafta Superhighway and the Selous Foundation wants to get that information to the people.

16. The Nafta Superhighway got its final boost when President George W. Bush and the leaders of Mexico and Canada agreed to the creation of the "Security and Prosperity Partnership of North America (SPP). **This organization is designed to speed the absorption of the United States, Mexico and Canada into ONE "North American Community".**

The Selous Foundation is fighting this globalist bureaucracy as well.

Send all donations to:
Selous Foundation
325 Pennsylvania Avenue, S.E.
P.O. Box 97207
Washington, DC 20090-7207

Their phone number is **202-547-6963** – They have a 501 (c) (3) classification from the Internal Revenue Service.

All of the above foregoing information is from a letter from the Executive Director, Morgan Norval, Selous Foundation, December 2006.

The NAFTA Super Highway

The NAFTA Super Highway will run through Texas and use millions of acres. ¾ of the traffic from Mexico comes through Texas. No voter approval is needed to build this project. It is planned. 10,000 people have shown up at these meetings in protest!!! It will cost $183 billion over 50 years.

Who wants it? International Global Companies?

Representative Ron Paul and many others are against it.

News from Lou Dobbs Tonight-TV show, February 19, 2008.

My thoughts – **Who owns America?** I pray this highway is never built! Why do United States Citizens need trucks from Mexico running through America? We don't! Americans should stop this

NAMES

1,200 Joneses

Cardiff, Wales --- "More than 1,200 people with the surname of Jones broke the world record for the biggest get-together of people with the same last name," Guinness World Record officials reported.

The previous record holder, a meeting of 583 people named Norberg in Sweden in 2004.

Jones is the most common surname in Wales and is Britain's second-most common name after Smith. Joneses also came from four other countries, New Zealand, Australia, the United States and Canada.

Information from an article of the Associated Press – published in "The Tribune", San Luis Obispo County, California, November 5, 2006

My thoughts – Who can keep up with the Joneses? What are the first names of all the Joneses?

Unusual Name

Akron, Ohio -------- He changed his name from Daniel Michael Miller II to "The" Daniel Miller Experience.

His first name is	"The" Dan
His middle name is	Miller
His last name is	Experience

Last year about 300 people petitioned the Summit County Probate Court to change a name.

"The" Dan, 24, is a musician and rapper. Said Experience: "I like to do little things in my life that amuse me. This amuses me.

Information from an article by the "Associated Press", January 8, 2008, in "The Tribune", San Luis Obispo County, California.

My thoughts – Well, what will he name his children? Magnificent Experience, Accidental Experience, Permanent Experience, Whatan Experience!!

Baby Names

Washington, Associated Press.

<u>Most popular names for babies.</u>

Emily was the most popular name for girls in 2007, No. 1 for the 12th straight year.

Jacob was No. 1 for the 9th year in a row for boys.

Elizabeth is new to the top 10 list, returning after a 2-year absence. Samantha previously was No. 10, dropped to No. 12. This list is by the Social Security Administration.

Girls	**Boys**
1. Emily	1. Jacob
2. Isabella	2. Michael
3. Emma	3. Ethan
4. Ava	4. Joshua
5. Madison	5. Daniel
6. Sophia	6. Christopher
7. Olivia	7. Anthony
8. Abigail	8. William
9. Hannah	9. Matthew
10. Elizabeth	10. Andrew

Go on line to see the Social Security Administration lists of top baby names for each year since 1880 at www.socialsecurity.gov

Information from an article in "The Tribune", San Luis Obispo County, California, May 11, 2008.

My thoughts – Give your baby a name that is easy to pronounce and spell and won't be subjected to laughter. Think of it as an 80-year name.

NEED

A

LAUGH

Don't Mess with Old Ladies

<u>An older lady gets pulled over for speeding</u>

Older woman: Is there a problem officer?
Officer: Ma'am, you were speeding.
Older Woman: Oh, I see.
Officer: Can I see your license please?
Older woman: I'd give it to you but I don't have one.
Officer: Don't have one?
Older Woman: Lost it 4 years ago for drunk driving.
Officer: I see…can I get your vehicle registration papers please?
Older woman: I can't do that.
Officer: Why not?
Older woman: I stole this car.
Officer: Stole it?
Older woman: Yes, and I killed and hacked up the owner.
Officer: You what?
Older woman: His body parts are in the trunk if you want to see.

The officer looks at the woman and slowly backs away to his car and calls for back up. Within minutes 5 police cars circle the car. A senior officer slowly approaches the car, clasping his half drawn gun.

Officer 2: Ma'am could you step out of your vehicle please! The woman steps out of her vehicle.
Older woman: Is there a problem sir?
Officer 2: One of my officers told me that you stole this car and murdered the owner.
Older woman: Murdered the owner?
Officer 2: Yes, could you please open the trunk of your car, please?
Older woman opens the trunk, revealing nothing but an empty trunk.
Officer 2: Is this your car ma'am?
Older woman: Yes, here are the registration papers.
The officer is quite stunned.
Officer 2: One of my officers claims that you do not have a driver's license.
Older woman digs into her handbag and pulls out a clutch purse and hands it to the officer.
The officer examines the license. He looks quite puzzled.
Officer 2: Thank you ma'am, one of my officers told me you didn't have a license, that you stole the car, and that you murdered and hacked up the owner.
Older woman: Bet the liar told you I was speeding, too.

Received in an e-mail in January 2008. Author unknown.

Catholic Gasoline

Sister Mary, a nun, who worked for a home health agency, was out making her rounds visiting homebound patients when she ran out of gas. Luckily a gas station was only a block away.

She walked to the station to borrow a gas can and buy some gas. The attendant said the only gas can he had, had already been loaned, but she could wait until it was returned.

Sister Mary was on her way to see a patient so she decided not to wait and walked back to her car. She looked for something in her car that she could fill with gas and spotted the bedpan she was taking to the patient.

Always resourceful, she carried the bedpan to the station, filled it with gasoline and carried the full bedpan back to her car. As she was pouring the gas into her tank, two men watched from across the street. One of them turned to the other and said, "If it starts, I'm turning Catholic!"

The writer of this e-mail is unknown. I'd love to meet her, though.

Love Those Nuns

Sitting behind a couple of Nuns at a Detroit Red Wings Hockey Game (Whose Habits partially blocked their view) three men decided too Badger the Nuns in an effort to get them to move.

In a very loud voice, the first guy said, "I think I'm going to move to Utah, there are only 100 Nuns living there."

The second guy spoke up and said, "I want to go to Montana, there are only 50 Nuns living there."

The third guy said, "I want to go to Idaho, there are only 25 Nuns living there."

One of the Nuns turned around, looked at the men, and in a very sweet, calm voice said, "Why don't you go to Hell, there aren't any Nuns there."

Received in an e-mail, author unknown.

Two Ways to Look at Everything

My wife and I were sitting at a table at my high school reunion, and I kept staring at a drunken woman swigging her drink as she sat alone at a nearby table.

My wife asked, "Do you know her?" "Yes," I sighed. "She's my old girlfriend. I understand she started drinking right after we split up those many years ago, and I hear she hasn't been sober since"

"My God!" says my wife. "Who would think a person could go on celebrating that long?"

So you see, there really are two ways to look at everything …..

      Author unknown. Received as an e-mail in February, 2008.

A $300,000 Watch

Do you want a watch for $300,000 that only tells whether it is day or night? The Swiss watchmaker Romain Jerome has made the "Day & Night" watch.

A CEO said studies show that two-thirds of the rich people "don't use their watch to tell what time it is" anyway. Anyone can buy a watch that tells time, he told a reporter but only a "truly discerning customer" can buy a watch that doesn't.

      Information from "NEWSOFTHEWIERD" compiled by Chuck Sheperd in "The Tribune", May 22, 2008, San Luis Obispo County, California.

      My thoughts – Do you agree CEO's are paid too much! How would you like to have this man as the CEO of **YOUR** company?

Knick - Knack

If you are going through hell, keep going.
 -Winston Churchill

Government's view of the economy could be summed up in a few short phrases:
If it moves tax it. If it keeps moving, regulate it. And if it stops moving subsidize it.
 -Ronald Reagan (1986)

I cannot live without books.
Thomas Jefferson

All tyranny needs to gain a foothold is for people of good conscience to remain Silent!
Thomas Jefferson

The problem is not that people are taxed too little; the problem is government spends too much!
Ronald Reagan

All the waste in a year from a nuclear power plant can be stored under a desk!
Ronald Reagan

Advertisements contain the only truths to be relied on in a newspaper.
Thomas Jefferson

Concentrated power has always been the enemy of liberty.
Ronald Reagan

Approximately 80% of our air pollution stems from hydrocarbons released by vegetation; so let's not go overboard in setting and enforcing emission standards from man-made sources.
Ronald Reagan

A pessimist sees the difficulty in every opportunity; an optimist sees the opportunity in every difficulty.
Winston Churchill

Experience hath shown, that even under the best forms of government those entrusted with power have, in time, and by slow operations, perverted into tyranny.
Thomas Jefferson

NO

HEALTH

INSURANCE

New Jersey and Illegal Aliens

New Jersey is saddled with, at least, $2.1 Billion a year to provide education and health care to illegal aliens living in New Jersey, and to incarcerate criminal illegal aliens.

The costs of education, health care and incarceration of criminal aliens amount to about $800 per year to each native – born headed household in New Jersey.

FAIR estimates that 372,000 illegal aliens live in New Jersey, which is about 100,000 more people than the population of Newark. The largest cost is the $1.8 Billion a year that the state must spend providing K-12 education to the children of illegal aliens – including those kids who were born in the United States to illegal aliens.

Un-reimbursed health care for illegal aliens takes an additional $200 Million. Incarceration of criminal illegal aliens adds another $50 Million, (not including the cost of the crimes they commit). If all the other services that the state and local governments provide to illegal aliens were factored in, the total costs would likely be significantly higher than $2.1 Billion a year.

The costs of illegal alien immigration to New Jerseyites can be found on FAIR's website, www.fairus.org

> Information from FAIR, February 2007 issue. FAIR means "Federation for American Immigration Reform."
>
> My thoughts – the people in New Jersey spend all this money on illegal aliens when it should be spent on citizens of New Jersey. The United States Government has not been enforcing the laws of our country! Does the United States belong to America or Mexico?
>
> **The President and Congress are responsible for not enforcing the laws of our country!**

Knick-Knack

34% of immigrants lack health insurance, compared to 13% of natives. Immigrants and their United States born children account for 71% of the increase in the uninsured since 1989. In 2007 there were 10.8 million school-age children from immigrant families in the United States.

> Information from "Center for Immigration Studies", (CIS), November 2007.

238

OUTSOURCING

Outsourcing

Companies are paying others to make the foods we eat, or the ingredients in them, and selling it under multiple brand names.

Caroline Smith DeWaal, Director of food safety for the Center for Science in the Public Interest, a consumer group, said, "If people cannot trace a product back to a supplier, the supplier has no incentives to keep their processes as clean and effective, in terms of food safety, as possible."

The food industry and regulators say it is coincidence the rash of recent major food safety recalls and the consolidation of food production. Dr. David Acheson, who leads the Food and Drug Administration's food safety effort, said he knew of no evidence that outsourcing production is inherently less safe than traditional arrangements.

Store brand products account for much of the growth in food outsourcing. Super markets, drug stores and mass merchandisers get $65 billion in store brand sales annually.

"**Traceability** is critical to ensuring processors use the highest standards of care," DeWaal said. "When their identities are hidden behind multiple labels and poor traceability information, they can use whatever practices they want because they're probably not going to get caught."

> From an article by Andrew Bridges, Associated Press, in "The Tribune", San Luis Obispo County, California, September 3, 2007.

> My thoughts – I think outsourcing is wrong for our country. The recalls we now see are confirming this. We did much better when our products were made in the United States. I want **"Made in America"** products!!!

Avon is Outsourcing

New York ----Avon Products Inc. is cutting 2,400 jobs, part of its multiyear restructuring plan, which will cost more than expected but save the beauty products maker $430 million annually. This plan was revealed in November 2005 which involved steep job cuts, elimination of management layers, the realignment of manufacturing centers, outsourcing to countries with cheaper labor costs.

> Information from an "Associated Press" article, January 9, 2008 in "The Tribune", San Luis Obispo County, California.

> My thoughts – There goes another outsorcerer! I want to use "MADE in AMERICA" products.

240

POLICE

&

FIRE

DEPARTMENT

Defective Pistols

Sacramento, California ---- Some of the pistols of the California Highway Patrol (CHP) jammed during training so new ammunition magazines will be distributed to hundreds of CHP officers. Also their handguns will be upgraded.

Smith & Wesson will replace the defective magazines and provide a stronger spring for the weapons at no cost to taxpayers, so said Fran Clader, CHP spokeswoman, on August 29, 2007.

The CHP bought more than 9,700 of the .40-calibur semiautomatic pistols last year under a $6.6 million contract. 15 of the 664 handguns distributed last month (July 2007) to officers in the CHP's Inland Division in Southern California jammed during an August 7, 2007 training session. 3 others had similar problems.

> Information from an Associated Press article in "The Tribune", San Luis Obispo County, California, on August 30, 2007.

> My thoughts – Smith & Wesson certainly made the right move to replace the defective magazines and provide a stronger spring for the weapons. The CHP protect us and certainly need the best equipment. They are the heroes. They face tragedy daily.

San Diego, California

California's state fire agency said on November 17, 2007 that sparking power lines ignited the largest of the wildfires that burned in Southern California last month. The Witch fire killed 2 people, burned nearly 200,000 acres and destroyed more than 1,000 homes. Along the way, it merged with the smaller Guejito fire, which was also caused by power line sparks, so said the California Department of Forestry and Fire Protection.

> Information from an Associated Press article in "The Tribune", San Luis Obispo County, California, November 17, 2007.

> My thoughts – There must be a way to stop power lines from sparking. What a waste! This would be an excellent project for some of the wacky environmentalists to do something good for our country instead of continuously filing lawsuits that cost U.S. taxpayers millions!

242

Earn Over $71,000 a Year!

"Earn over $71,000 a year. Apply today and discover why more men and women are proud to wear our uniform than any other law enforcement agency in the Nation."

Information from an ad in "The Desert Sun", Southern California Desert Cities, January 17, 2007-California Department of Corrections and Rehabilitation. www.cdcr.ca.gov/jobs - 1-866-232-jobs

My thoughts – Sound intriguing?

Wildfires in 2007

A. In 2007 Wildfires scorched an area the size of Yellowstone National Park – 14,000 square miles burned!
B. 52 plus buildings were destroyed which ranks second, in 2003 5700 buildings were destroyed, since the current counting method began in 1999.
C. One of the nation's worst fire seasons.
D. A record amount of retardant dropped by aircraft.
E. The federal government spent more than $1.8 billion fighting wildfires.
F. 2007 was the second costliest season on record.

These figures reported by the Boise, Idaho based National Interagency Fire Center.

Information from an Associated Press article in "The Tribune", San Luis Obispo County, California, January 6, 2008.

My thoughts – **What a waste** of forests, buildings, money and manpower! Our forests should definitely be cleaned of underbrush so these fires don't get out of control. **How much responsibility do the environmentalists take?**

243

POLITICAL

NEWS

Oprah's Party for Obama!

Santa Barbara, California – Oprah's home is in Montecito, California, close to Santa Barbara. The $2,300 tickets, per person, to the event September 8, 2007, were sold as soon as they were offered to Democratic and entertainment industry activists. Obama's campaign is now wealthier by $3 million.

The mostly black crowd included Basketball superstar, Bill Russell, Academy Award-winning actor, Sidney Poitier, Comedian Chris Rock, Motown's Stevie Wonder, singing his hits from the 1970's and 1980's. Cindy Crawford and husband Randy Gerber, Kenneth "Baby face" Edmonds, Hill Harper, Tom Joyner, Tyler Perry, Ellen Popeo, Cecily Tyson, Forest Whitaker, and Winfrey's beau, Stedman Graham.

"Winfrey's staff had sent out memos to ticket buyers urging them to wear "garden" attire and warning women not to wear heels that would sink into the meadow. Most of the women dressed for a chic cocktail party and wore heels, which many kicked off to dance on the grass."

"Guests spread their complimentary green and white "Obama'08" blankets on the lawn to drink, chat and listen to the music. Some had their pictures taken with Oprah, Obama and his wife." Oprah wore an olive blouse and long, white skirt. She mingled with the crowd.

> Information from an article by Tina Daunt of the Los Angeles Times, in "The Tribune", San Luis Obispo County, California, September 9, 2007.

> My thoughts – Oprah's home in Montecito reportedly cost $55 million for which she wrote a check, reportedly. It is on 2 acres (or I have also read it is on 42 acres) is 14,000 square feet, 6 bedrooms, 14 bathrooms. I wonder how often she vacations here.

Knick – Knack

George Soros, billionaire financier, is one of the most dangerous men in the world thinks Bill O'Reilly, heard on "The Factor", May 7, 2007.

Knick – Knack

There are **35,000 lobbyists in Washington, D.C.** said Mike Huckabee on his TV show, October 12, 2008 on Fox News Channel.

Lou Dobbs Tonight on CNN TV

United States imports $14.5 Billion in fruits and nuts. Our food imports are up 70% since 2002. **Our United States food inspectors check just 1% of food imports!!!**

70,000 more Chinese products recalled today, October 12, 2007.

The United States has **postponed the labeling** of products of Country of origin **for 1 year**!

Information from Lou Dobbs CNN TV show on October 12, 2007

My thoughts – Why is our government letting all of this happen??? **We need to know the country of origin of every product we use.** Soon we won't be able to buy anything made in the USA!!! We need to produce our own food products.

Check everything you buy before you buy it. **If it doesn't say made in the USA it probably isn't.** Do we want America to survive? I do!

The Mayor's Office

The Los Angeles Times reported that an affair between Los Angeles Mayor Antonio Villaraigosa and a Spanish language newscaster, Mirthala Salinas, ended a couple months ago. Salinas worked at the local Telemundo station KVEA-TV, and was a fill-in anchor on evening newscasts in June when she announced the news of Villaraigosa's separation from his wife, Corina.

Information from an article in "The Tribune", Tribune wire services, San Luis Obispo County, California, November 25, 2007.

My thoughts – Another affair of another politician! **When will they stop?**

Knick Knack

Anti-Americanism has deepened since 2002. It has worsened among America's European Allies and is very bad in the Muslim world. In African countries, "New Europe" and the Far East there is still a favorable view.

Information from an article by Tribune wire services, published in "The Tribune", San Luis Obispo County, California, June 28, 2007.

246

The Gap Between Voters and Nonvoters in California

The gulf between those who vote and those who don't is becoming wider than ever.

Voters: Are older
More likely to be white
Wealthier
Better educated
Tend to own their own homes

Nonvoters: Younger
More likely to be nonwhite
Poorer
Less educated
Renters

Voters are more conservative than nonvoters especially on issues involving taxes and spending.

Of the 12 million adults who are not registered to vote, 5 million are not citizens.

Voters: 72% are white
14% Latino
6% Asian
5% Black

Nonvoters: 63% Latino
24% White
8% Asian
3% Black

Among California Frequent Voters: 62% are older than 45
77% are homeowners
53% are college graduates
56% have household incomes of $60,000 or more

Among those not registered to vote: 76% are younger than 45
66% are renters
27% are college graduates
18% have household incomes of $60,000 or more

Voters – 49% say they would prefer a larger government even if it means paying higher taxes. 44% favor a smaller government and lower taxes. 247

Nonvoters: - 2 out of 3 prefer more services and higher taxes.

On proposition 13, California's landmark law of 1978 limiting the annual increase in property taxes – **Voters** – 56% to 33% believe Proposition 13 turned out to be good thing for the state. **Nonvoters** – 47% to 29% believe the limit has been bad for California, less likely to favor "Term Limits", more likely to support increased spending on health and human services, public colleges and universities, more of the education budget spent on kindergarten-through-12th grade schools that serve the poor. More in favor of school construction bonds and tax increases to pay for transportation.

By 2040 whites are expected to be just a third of California's adults but experts believe they will remain a majority of the state's voters for at least 25 years.

For the foreseeable future, California's growing population of nonvoters will continue to depend on the kindness of strangers and will continue to be disappointed in the results.

> Information from an article by Daniel Weintraub who writes for the Sacramento Bee, published in "The Tribune", San Luis Obispo County, California, September 16, 2006.

> My thoughts – He who votes carries the power. Too bad nonvoters will be disappointed in the results. They have a choice to vote or not to vote! If they know nothing of the issues, I'm glad they don't vote.

Voters Beware

Presidential hopeful Rudy Giuliani, New York's former Mayor, told 200 people in San Diego that he believed illegal immigration must be stopped but at the same time the American economy depends on an influx of workers from abroad.

Also in a speech before a well-appointed crowd at Del Mar he only briefly touched on illegal immigration. New York was a sanctuary city when he was Mayor.

> Article published in "The Tribune", San Luis Obispo County, California August 23, 2007, by Tribune Wire Services.

> My thoughts – We need a strong President who will protect and secure our borders! I don't believe Rudy is the one. We need a strong President who will stop all illegal immigration, close our borders, build a fence to protect the United States and it's citizens. Beware of Rudy!

248

Reverend Jeremiah Wright

He was the pastor of the church in Chicago that Barack Obama and his wife attended for 20 years. He married the Obamas and baptized their two girls.

In a sermon he spoke very badly about the United States and said the government tried to give Aids to black people. He damned the United States. He thinks America deserves what it got on 9/11 because of America's bad deeds.

He drives 2 Mercedes Benz. They are both worth about $142,000.

A 10,000 sq. ft. house is being built on a golf course in an all white area for Reverend Wright and his wife. He has a $10 Million line of credit.

> Heard on the Bill O'Reilly cable TV channel program, The Factor, at 5 & 8 PM P.S.T., May 1, 2008.

> My thoughts – In case you don't know, Reverend Wright is black. For some reason he is giving Barack Obama, the black Candidate running for the office of the United States President problems because of what he is saying. Many people do not want to hear or believe what he says about America. They cannot understand how Obama could attend the church for 20 years and not hear the bad messages the Reverend gave in his sermons.

Knick Knack

Bill O'Reilly asked Hillary Clinton if she became President of the United States would she crackdown on Sanctuary Cities. "I won't crack down on Sanctuary Cities", Hillary Clinton replied to Bill O'Reilly.

> Heard on The O'Reilly Factor" May 1, 2008, Bill's first interview with Hillary Clinton.

> My thoughts – A sanctuary city is proclaimed, illegally, by the Mayor to be a safe city for illegal aliens, which means they won't be arrested by immigration officials. A Sanctuary City is protecting illegal aliens who have broken the law by coming into America. So Hillary would not be enforcing the laws of the United States Government, which she took an oath to uphold!

Knick-Knack

Republican Mitt Romney said he would likely donate his salary to charity if elected president, a financial freedom he described as a byproduct of a successful business career."

> Article published in "The Tribune," San Luis Obispo County, California, May 30, 2007.

> My thoughts – I hope he handpicks 4 students to receive this money to use for college education. The money goes in their college trust fund. No overhead expenses need to be paid to a charity.

You Won't See John Kerry in The 08 Race

John F. Kerry isn't going to run for the United States Presidency in 2008, he said as he choked back tears on the Senate floor. He is running for a fifth sixth year Senate term next year in 2008 and his mission is to end an unpopular war in Iraq.

He found himself shunned by much of his party after joking shortly before the November elections that poor students would "get stuck in Iraq", a comment Kerry called a "botched joke", but that revived memories of his 2004 verbal missteps.

> Information from Rick Klein, "The Boston Globe", published in "The Tribune", San Luis Obispo County, California, January 25, 2007.

> My thoughts – I would title this article "The Best Decision of His Life", not to run for President again. **We need term limits for Congress** – 30 years is too long to be a Senator or Congressman, **2 terms is sufficient**.

I BELIEVE

You cannot help the poor, by destroying the rich.

You cannot strengthen the weak, by weakening the strong.

You cannot bring about prosperity, by discouraging thrift.

You cannot lift the wage earner up, by pulling the wage payer down.

You cannot further the brotherhood of man, by inciting class hatred.

You cannot build character and courage, by taking away man's initiative and independence.

You cannot help man permanently; by doing for them what they could and should do for themselves.

Received as an e-mail November 1, 2008. I have been unable to identify the original author.

Carolyn Cavolt
November 1, 2008

Remember The Holocaust

Berlin----Germany's justice minister, Brigette Zypries, said that Germany's commitment to combating racism and xenophobia and keeping the memory of the Holocaust alive was both an enduring historical obligation and a present day political necessity.

Germany wants to use its European Union presidency to push through legislation that would make denying the Holocaust punishable by stiff prison sentences in all 27 of the union's member states.

> Information from "World Roundup", Tribune Wire Services, January 14, 2007
> Published in "The Tribune, San Luis Obispo County, California

> My thoughts – It can't be denied!

"The Media Miss by a Mile"

Washington – Hillary Clinton was treated as inevitable and Mike Huckabee as invisible for most of 2007. After the Iowa Caucuses in which Huckabee came in first and Hillary didn't, those judgments are looking shortsighted! "Huckabee was regarded as an asterisk who didn't even warrant a mention on "CBS Evening News". He, a former Arkansas governor, was good for comic relief, the wise-cracking, bass-playing, weight losing preacher man was not portrayed to win in Iowa or anyplace else."

They treated Barack Obama as a "rock star then lately as a dull candidate who had little chance to catch up." After Iowa and his win over Clinton, her bubble burst, that was perhaps inflated by a year's worth of press.

Of the Republicans Huckabee had raised $2.3 million in the first 9 months of the year. Romney had raised or "donated to his campaign", $44 million thus relegating Huckabee to the media's second tier. Huckabee did all interviews because he wanted the free press. Romney was drawing coverage for his large fundraising skills thus by this standard Huckabee was a sidebar. "The media's chief benchmark is money."

Information from an article by Howard Kurtz, "The Washington Times,' in "The Tribune", San Luis Obispo County, California, January 6, 2008.

My thoughts – The media has always given liberal Democrats lots of coverage. Most of the media is liberal. So naturally they will give more coverage to the people they like.

REALLY

STUPID

A Mother Drives Teenagers to a Fight

Long Beach, California ------ The mother, 31-year-old Eva Daley, drove 7 members of a gang to a Long Beach park on June 26, 2007 so they could attack Jose Cano, age 13, a rival gang member. She and a 16-year-old boy will be on trial for the stabbing death of Cano. Also charged are Daley's son and 5 other gang members. Prosecutors say she also helped plot the attack and could face the death penalty.

Information from an Associated Press article in "The Tribune", San Luis Obispo County, California, March 30, 2008.

My comments – Remember when you were growing up, can you imagine your mother doing this! Obviously there are many women that shouldn't be mothers! They seem to think nothing of drowning their 5 children or throwing them into the ocean to drown. We need to use our resources here in America to stop this kind of behavior immediately!

Kiss My _____

Orangeburg, South Carolina -------
A woman in South Carolina signed a court document with instructions to the judge to kiss the body part (the defendant) sits on.

The defendant got 90 extra days.

Information from an article in "The Tribune", San Luis Obispo County, California, January 7, 2008, by the Associated Press.

My thoughts – 90 extra days! – for writing kiss my butt! Circuit Judge Diane Goodstein wasn't laughing.

Knick – Knack

The total cost for illegal aliens in the United States is $338.3 Billion a year that American taxpayers must pay.

My thoughts – **And still people complain about the treatment of illegal aliens!**

254

Wrong Knee!

Whoops!!! St Joseph Hospital in Orange County (Southern) California acknowledged it – wrong knee!

A patient had an operation done on the right knee instead of the left! St Joseph's chief medical officer says the hospital has begun a top-to-bottom training program on operating room procedures.

> Information from an Associated Press article in "The Tribune", March 2, 2008, San Luis Obispo County, California.

> My thoughts – Did anyone believe that this kind of mistake was still happening? I thought hospitals were marking the spot! "Operate on the Left Knee", written in ink on the knee with "Do Not Operate" written on the other knee! Maybe the patient should write on his own body parts.

Knick Knack

Hillary Clinton while in Congress as a Senator of New York **voted 7 times against** nuclear power.

> Heard on the Bill O'Reilly TV show. "The Factor" April 30, 2008.

> My thoughts – Bill O'Reilly flew from New York to South Bend, Indiana to interview Hillary Clinton for his TV show "The Factor". We desperately need nuclear power! She is wrong to vote against it.

Would You Believe This?

A dog walker dug potholes in a park trail because mountain bikers were interfering with "his enjoyment of walking his dog". He was caught in the act. He is Warren John Wilson, 52, of Fullerton, (Southern) California. When reached by telephone he said he did not dig any holes. He has been charged with a felony.

> Information from an article in "The Tribune", Tribune wire services, January 6, 2008, San Luis Obispo County, California.

255

Bribing Lawmakers

Anchorage, Alaska-----Former VECO Corporation CEO Bill Allen, 70, testified September 13, 2007 in the Federal corruption trial of another former lawmaker, Pete Kott. Allen and a former company vice president, Rick Smith, have pleaded guilty to bribing lawmakers and await sentencing.

On the stand, September 13, 2007 Allen said he bribed Ben Stevens, (the son of U. S. Senator Ted Stevens) and former Senate President, Pete Kott and Vic Kohring. Ben Stevens is under federal investigation but has not been charged.

Bill Allen is the former head of one of Alaska's largest oil field service companies, VECO Corporation.

> Information from an article in "The Tribune", San Luis Obispo County, California, Associated Press, September 14, 2007.

Drunken Driving

Abbotsford, Wisconsin – Police cited a legless man and his friend with drunken driving. The disabled man was at the wheel while his friend worked the pedals. This is the 3rd. such arrest for the legless man and the 2nd. such arrest for his friend.

Harvey J. Miller, 43, was steering the truck and Edwin H. Marzinske, 55, operated the pedals. They were pulled over August 18, 2007 according to a police report.

> Article by Tribune Wires Services in "The Tribune", San Luis Obispo County, California, August 30, 2007.

> My thoughts – 2 drunken men, one without legs, the other without brains driving a truck. What can be said? What should the penalty be for drunken driving in this case? The Bill Gates Foundation could supply both of them with a journey to the Betty Ford Treatment Center for alcoholism and supply Mr. Miller with 2 new legs.

Dangerous Reading?

The 25th annual **"Banned Books Week"** is September 23-30, 2006. The American Library Association says each book below has been pulled from some libraries or schools.

You'll be surprised by the list. Why were Garfield and a dictionary deemed dangerous? Visit parade.com

1. The Adventures of Captain Underpants
2. The Adventures of Huckleberry Finn
3. Anne Frank: The Diary of a Young Girl
4. The Catcher in the Rye
5. Garfield: His Nine Lives
6. The Handmaid's Tale
7. Harry Potter (entire series)
8. Little Red Riding Hood
9. Merriam – Webster's Collegiate Dictionary
10. To Kill a Mockingbird

Information from an article in Parade, September 10, 2006, "Hot List" Published in "The Tribune", San Luis Obispo County, California.

Smelly Ads

Los Angeles, California – The Los Angeles Times is now into scent marketing. Newspapers are struggling to keep advertisers. On September 9, 2007 the Los Angeles Times is running a full-page ad that when scratched will release a frosted cake scent.

An executive of a scent-marketing company says, "scent has the longest memory and is the most powerful emotional motivator, and that's what advertising is all about."

Information from an article by Alana Semuels, Los Angeles Times, September 5, 2007, in "The Tribune", San Luis Obispo County, California.

My thoughts – It sounds stupid to me.

Atlanta, Georgia

A homeowner in **Marietta, Georgia**, Chris G. Carlos, used 440,000 gallons of water in September 2007 or about 14,700 gallons a day. The average consumption in the United States is about 150 gallons a day per person.

This number was released by county officials in the wealthy suburbs northeast of Atlanta, Georgia just a day after Governor Sonny Perdue asked God to forgive Georgia for being wasteful with its water.

> Information from a Tribune wire services article in "The Tribune", San Luis Obispo County, California, November 15, 2007.

Thornton, Indiana

Adam F. Cooper, 19, became trapped in the vent shaft of a grocery store when he tried to rob it. The authorities used vegetable oil to free him. Earlier, Cooper had been on a team which cleaned the store's vents. He was being held on $10,000 bail on charges of burglary and criminal mischief.

> Information from an article entitled "Did You Hear?" in "The Tribune", San Luis Obispo County, California, November 17, 2007.

> My thoughts – I wonder where Thornton is. I lived in Indiana almost 25 years. Someone needs to give Adam a helping hand. Where's Eve?

Knick Knack

Tehran, Iran (Formerly Persia). The government announced that gasoline rationing would begin. Angry drivers set fire to 2 gas stations.

> Information from Tribune wire services, article published in "The Tribune", San Luis Obispo County, California, June 28, 2007.

SCHOOLS

&

LEARNING

The 2008 Edition of "The Best 366 Colleges"

These rankings are contained in the 2008 edition of "The Best 366 Colleges" which is based on a survey of 120,00 college students at those schools, most during the 2006-07 school year.

Top 10 Party Schools:
1. West Virginia University
2. University of Mississippi
3. University of Texas, Austin
4. University of Florida
5. University of Georgia
6. Penn State University
7. University of New Hampshire
8. Indiana University, Bloomington
9. Ohio University, Athens
10. University California Santa Barbara (UCSB)

Top 10 "Stone cold Sober" Schools:
1. Brigham Young University
2. Wheaton College, Illinois
3. Thomas Aquinas College, California
4. College of the Ozarks, Missouri
5. Grove City College, Pennsylvania
6. U. S. Coast Guard Academy
7. U. S. Air Force Academy
8. U. S. Naval Academy
9. City University of New York, Queens College
10. Webb Institute, New York

The book has 62 categories in all, including:
1. Best Campus Food, Virginia Tech
2. Most Beautiful Campus, Sweet Briar, Virginia
3. Dorms Like Palaces, Smith College, Massachusetts
4. Birkenstock-wearing, Tree-Hugging, Clove-Smoking Vegetarians, Hampshire College, Massachusetts

Taken from an Associated Press Article in "The Tribune", San Luis Obispo County, California, August 23, 2007.

My thoughts – What's left to say?

"It costs so little to teach a child to love, and so much to teach him to hate."

Father Flanagan - Girls and Boys Town   260

The live-in Manny

In Hollywood, having a male nanny, a manny is the rage.

Adam Good, age 25, is one. He is not Gay. His fiancée is in the Peace Corps in Uganda. He loves being with kids; he likes his job.

His duties in his present job:
1. Grocery shopping
2. Laundry
3. Picks up dry cleaning
4. Takes digital photos and videos of the two children
5. Writes up funny things they say
6. e-mails notes to their parents through out the day
7. Cooks dinner
8. Plays dress-up with his two current charges, girl age 4 and boy age 3
9. He picks up the two children from pre-school
10. He has CD's in his car to amuse the children and bottles of bubbles, the Snow White book, and the ABC song.

Nationwide, men make up less than 3% of pre-school teachers and 9% of elementary school teachers.

The children's parents are married and live in Alexandria, VA. Good works 30 hours a week, he is a live-in manny, has health care benefits and the children's mother does his taxes.

Information from an article in The Washington Post, by Bridgit Schulte published in "The Tribune", San Luis Obispo County, California, July 29, 2006.

My Thoughts – How many days does he work? 5 – 6 hour days? Salary? Who takes over after he puts in his hours? Does he cook dinner for the family or only for the children?

Knick – Knack

Teach your children not to stare at people in wheelchairs or who use walkers or a cane. Teach them to smile at the person and say Hi!

American College Students Abroad

American students studying abroad rose to 205,983 in 2005. International enrollment in the United States higher education remained steady last year at about 565,000. American college students are becoming more adventuresome as they study abroad showing less interest in English speaking destinations and more in such alternatives as China, India, Argentina and Brazil. Britain remained the most popular study destination last year (2005) followed by Italy, Spain and France.

Information from an article by Tribune Wire services New York, November 13, 2006, published in "The Tribune", San Luis Obispo, California.

My thoughts - I propose to the Bill Gates Foundation:

Bill Gates-Why don't you and your foundation choose 3,000 American students each year from sixth grade up to college to become proficient in studies of political science, history, government, pay their schooling fees so they can become the next politicians who are intelligent, ethical and love their country. They must not all be liberals, we also need conservatives. You made your money in America so help America! America needs you.

Note-A liberal is a person who wants to take your hard-earned money and give it to someone else!

Knick – Knack

On October 20, 2008 Bill O'Reilly said on "The Factor" that the former CEO of Merrill Lynch, Stanley O'Neal walked away with a golden parachute of $161.5 Million!!!

My thoughts – By the way there is no discrimination here, Stanley O'Neal is black. Do you think he will try to find another job? I doubt it, as he can live anywhere or do anything that he wants to do. I'm curious; I wonder what he did to earn all that money? What could anyone do to earn that much money from a failed company!

Knick – Knack

The left-wing media is out to elect Barack Obama, said Bill O'Reilly on his TV program 10-20-08.

262

Not Quite Finished

40,000 Seniors from the class of 2006 failed to pass the California High School Exit Exam before graduation in June. Many schools offered prep classes and extra help; they wanted the Seniors to keep taking the test until they could pass and graduate. Only 819 students, after five months after graduation have earned winning marks and the chance for their high school diploma.

> Information by Mercury News and in "Monday Morning Memorandum by California Assemblyman Ray Haynes, November 6, 2006.

> My thoughts – **Something's wrong!** Why don't more Seniors want to keep studying to pass the Exit Exam and get their diploma? They don't believe education is important?

> Maybe if the Gates Foundation offered each of them $1,500 when they passed the test that would be the impetus. Of course the 819 who have already passed would be offered the $1,500 also. Then what do the students who passed the first time get? Maybe $2,000?

> Getting them all to pass would help the taxpayers because the students would get better jobs.

Knick – Knack

Senior Editor of the High School Yearbook in Conifer, Colorado-A Mountain Town, Hannah Fredrickson, the editor, said she regrets not balancing the yearbook pictures of teenagers smoking pot and drinking beer with pictures of nondrug users. She is sorry about not warning the principal, but she thinks people need to know what is going on.

> Information from an article published in "The Tribune," San Luis Obispo County, California, May 28, 2007, Tribune wire services.

> My thoughts – **She is one brave Senior Editor, good for her!** She is right! People need to know what is happening at the high school. Parents need to know!

Knick – Knack

On May 27, 1937 the Golden Gate Bridge connecting San Francisco and Marin County opened to Pedestrian traffic. Vehicular traffic crossed the next day.

100 Milliseconds

Princeton University researchers asked 200 people to make judgments about 66 faces with only a glance.

That's less time than it takes to form a rational thought. Impressions made after just 100 milliseconds largely matched those made without time limits.

In 100 milliseconds they formed an impression of another person. They decide whether he or she is attractive, trustworthy, competent and likeable.

This research was published last month in the journal "Psychological Science."

Information from "Style Roundup", by Tribune wire services, published in "The Tribune", San Luis Obispo County, California, September 1, 2006.

My thoughts – I could do it with one trait-attractive – but not with all four. With dogs I could form an impression for 2 traits-attractive and likeable. Call me slow.

Smart youth dress well.
They know if not
they will be under valued
by some of their own
and by older others.

CGC 7-20-08

How Many Times Must You Read an Article?

Do you read articles in the newspapers and discover that you must read it several times to make sense out of it? Or discover it doesn't make sense!

Sometimes authors want to impress their contemporaries with obscure words and lengthy unusual sentences.

This does not help the reader who is trying to get information and knowledge with one reading. One reading should be sufficient.

Carolyn Gerdink Cavolt
November 1, 2008

SENIORS

Your Final Address List

Leave a list of names, addresses, and telephone numbers of the people you want notified when you die. Give it to one or two responsible family members who will carry out your instructions. Update it when a friend dies or moves.

Put it in a very colorful folder or large distinctive envelope that can't be lost or misplaced. If the person you want notified has a daughter or best friend be sure you include that name, address and phone number in case the person is in a rest home.

We lost a friend, didn't hear from her anymore, our mail was returned, and the phone number was no longer in service. We did not have the name or address of either of her married daughters. We did not think of something like this happening. So we have assumed she died. She was someone we had known for many, many years. We had many great times together with her and with her husband when he was alive.

My Space for Seniors, eons.com

The new social networking web-site for Americans 50 and older is modeled on sites such as teen-focused MySpace and Facebook, but with a difference: Members receive alerts when friends or colleagues bite the dust.

The site's online obituary database alerts members when someone from their hometown, company or alma mater dies. Useful tips on planning one's funeral including music suggestions and "notable obits" from entertainment, sports and science.

The free site offers brain-builder puzzles,
> reviews of movies,
> dream travel destinations,
> a hobbies message board,
> tips on investing
> a lifestyle calculator to help members improve longevity.
> Of course if that doesn't work, don't fret. Your friends will hear about it in no time.

Information from an article by McClatchy Tribune, Published in The Tribune, San Luis Obispo County, California, November 4, 2006.

My Thoughts – What a marvelous idea! Just like having a private secretary!

A Roller Coaster Life

A 61-year-old Whittier, Southern California, resident has spent his days at Knott's Berry Farm in Buena Park, California riding the gravity defying, Xcelerator roller coaster. On 1-20-07 he boarded the coaster for the 20,000 time, a park record!

"It feels almost the same as the first time, only I know what to expect," said Richard Krieger, who has been on the ride an average of 12 times a day for the past 4 ½ years. He is semi-retired from various odd jobs.

> Information from Associated Press, an article published in "the Tribune", San Luis Obispo County, California, January 22, 2007.

> My thoughts – Why? Why is he riding the roller coaster? Does he want to get in a world records book? What is the cost of the ride?

Tokyo, Japan

"I don't want to die", Tomoji Tanabe told reporters. He was receiving a certificate from Guinness World Records at a ceremony in Japan verifying him as the world's oldest male.

He's 111; he keeps a daily dairy, drinks milk, no alcohol or smoking. Tanabe was born September 18, 1895.

> Information from an article published in "The Tribune", San Luis Obispo County, California, June 19, 2007, Tribune Wire Services.

> My thoughts – Good for him! He doesn't want to die so he is still enjoying life!

Knick – Knack

Heard on Lou Dobbs television program, October 9, 2008, **Acorn** submitted 5,000 new voter registration cards in October 2008, 2,100 are **fraudulent!**

The Disappearing Pension Plan

Just 33% of workers at large and medium-sized companies today enjoy traditional pension plans (monthly benefits based on salary and years of service) compared to 84% in 1980.

The number is still shrinking.

IBM and General Motors have frozen their plans, while "new economy" Microsoft and Google never offered such pensions.

Many workers seem unaware, 61% said they expect employer-paid benefits, but many don't actually have such a pension at work.

Experts warn at least 40% of retirees won't have enough to live on unless they have a high increase in savings through a 401 (K) or an IRA.

"Fidelity Investments" says a 65 year-old couple will likely need $200,000 just to pay their share of medical bills in retirement.

> Information from an article in "Parade" Intelligence Report by Lyric Wallwork Winik – Hot Topics in "The Tribune", San Luis Obispo County, California, September 3, 2006.

> My thoughts – **Americans have lost again.** Retirement will be very difficult for many people.

Knick – Knack

About 500 Californians celebrate their 60th birthdays every day.

The 2000 Census counted 4.7 million Californians 60 years and older.

By 2010 this number will be 6.4 million.

> Information from Dan Walters, writer for the Sacramento Bee, in "The Tribune", San Luis Obispo County, California, May 4, 2008.

> My thoughts – So don't feel alone. Everyone is getting older. Is there an idea for a business here?

<u>YOU</u>

You wake up early
You wonder – is this the day?
How do you feel?
Feel like livin' another day?
You think of all your friends
Still livin' out there
That is a comforting thought
All those couples your age
Still sleepin' walkin' talkin'
Thank God for them!
I'll stay another day!

Carolyn Cavolt
May 6. 2008

For Children, Grandchildren and Other People

For children, grandchildren and other people who care about their parents, grandparents and older relatives – "Do unto others as you would have them do unto you." You, also, will get old and older!

1. Call at least once a week – even a 5 to 10 minute conversation is good.
2. A visit at least once a month if at all possible. If out of state try once a year.
3. Remember birthdays, anniversaries and holidays.
4. e-mails and letters are good.

Remember your parents clothed, fed, and educated you because they loved you and they took their responsibilities seriously.

Carolyn Gerdink Cavolt

Where has all the family gone?
Where are they?
Why are the phones silent?
Why no e-mail?
Why doesn't the postman come?
Why doesn't the doorbell ring?
Where art thou – oh family?

CGC July 20, 2008

Time Passes By

Understand Older People's Needs and Wishes.
Even if you don't feel old today
You'll be there too someday if you're lucky!
Babies cry
Teenagers act badly
Most older people don't like to whine.
Consider what you'd like with 25 to 50 years added to your age.
Perhaps you'd want attention, thoughtfulness, invitations, phone calls and visits.
Older people want to feel appreciated.
These older people could be friends, acquaintances or your parents!
They could also be forgotten old people in rest homes.

       Carolyn Gerdink Cavolt
       November 1, 2008

Havana, Cuba

Vilma Espin Guillois died June 18, 2007; she was the wife of acting President Rual Castro and one of the Communist nation's most politically powerful women. She was 77. Authorities did not state her illness. She was said to suffer from severe circulatory problems. She was a fellow guerilla fighter who was with the Castro brothers, Fidel and Rual, at the start of their revolutionary battle a half-century ago.

       Information from an article published in "The Tribune", San Luis Obispo
       County, California, June 19, 2007.

This journey is unfulfilled.
The time sped by too fast.
I can't leave now.
I don't want to leave now.
I want to stay
To finish what I must.

       CGC July 20, 2008

270

TAXES

A Poem

Tax his land,
Tax his bed,
Tax his table,
At which he's fed.

Tax his tractor,
Tax his mule,
Teach him taxes,
Are the rule.

Tax his cow,
Tax his goat,
Tax his pants,
Tax his coat.

Tax his ties,
Tax his shirt,
Tax his work,
Tax his dirt,
Tax his tobacco,
Tax his drink,
Tax him if he
Tries to think.

Tax his cigars,
Tax his beer,
 If he cries, then
Tax his tears.

Tax his car,
Tax his gas,
Find other ways
To tax his ass.

Tax all he has
Then let him know
That you won't be done
Till he has no dough.

When he screams and hollers,
Then tax him some more,
Tax him till
He's good and sore.

272

Then tax his coffin,
Tax his grave,
Tax the sod in
Which he's laid.

Put these words
Upon his tomb,
'Taxes drove me to my doom...'

When he's gone,
Do not relax,
Its time to apply
The inheritance tax.

Accounts Receivable Tax
Building Permit Tax
CDL License Tax
Cigarette Tax
Corporate Income Tax
Dog License Tax
Excise Tax
Federal Income Tax
Federal Unemployment Tax
Fishing License Tax
Food License Tax
Fuel Permit Tax
Gasoline Tax
Gross Receipt Tax
Hunting License Tax
Inventory Tax
Liquor Tax
Luxury Tax
Marriage License Tax
Medicare Tax
Personal Property Tax
Property Tax
Real Estate Tax
Service Charge Tax
Social Security Tax
Road Us age Tax
Sales Tax
Recreational Vehicle Tax
School Tax
Income Tax
Unemployment Tax

Telephone Federal Excise Tax
Telephone Federal Universal Service Fee Tax
Telephone Federal, State and Local Surcharge Tax
Telephone Minimum Usage Surcharge Tax
Telephone Recurring and Non-Recurring Charges Tax
Telephone Provincial and Local Tax
Telephone Usage Charge Tax
Utility Taxes
Vehicle License Registration Tax
Vehicle Sales Tax
Watercraft Registration Tax
Well Permit Tax
Workers Compensation Tax

Not one of these existed 100 years ago, and our nation was the most prosperous in the world. We had absolutely no national debt, had the largest middle class in the world, and Mom stayed home to raise the kids.

What the hell happened? Can you spell "politicians!" And I still have to "press 1" for English.

This poem was sent as an e-mail to us in January 2008. Author unknown.

Knick – Knack

On October 24, 2008 Bill O'Reilly said the California Teachers Association (CTA) donated $1 Million to defeat Proposition 8.

My thoughts – That money belongs to the teachers, what right does CTA have to give it to defeat a proposition? Proposition 8 provides that only marriage between a man and a woman is valid or recognized in California.

Knick – Knack

American taxpayers pay $338.3 BILLION Dollars each year to pay for illegal aliens to live in America!

Is this okay with you?

Did you give your permission?

Do you approve of this plan?

What will you do to stop it?

Will you complain to your Congressperson?

Would you like to get all the free benefits that illegal aliens get?

Knick – Knack

Planned Parenthood's budget for one year was $1 Billion. Planned Parenthood also receives $350 million a year from taxpayers. One third of all abortions are of black babies.

Heard on news, April 25, 2008.

My thoughts – Why do they get $350 Million from taxpayers? Where do they get $1 Billion? Why are so many black babies aborted? Sounds as if there should be an investigation! Bill Gates Foundation, will you finance this investigation?

TERRORISM

Beware!

Carrying coins in your pocket? They may have tiny radio frequency transmitters hidden inside. Can they trace your movements?

The Defense Department is warning its American Contractor employees about a new espionage threat straight out of Hollywood. The mysterious coins were found planted on U.S. Contractors with classified security clearances on at least three separate occasions between October 2005 and January 2006 as the contractors traveled through Canada. The U.S. report doesn't suggest who might be tracking American Defense contractors or why.

> Article in "Nation Roundup," Washington, DC, Associated Press, Published in "The Tribune", San Luis Obispo County, California, January 11, 2007.
> CIA's own hollow coin-https://www.cia.gov/cia/information/artifacts/dollar.htm

> My thoughts – Be aware!

Fakes

In a sampling of 300,00 Christian Dior products and 150,000 Louis Vuitton items sold on eBay, 90% were found to be fakes, according to those two manufacturers, who are suing to protect their merchandise and copyrights.

Many buyers who buy luxury items at bargain prices on the web believe they are getting the real thing. People who buy $10 "Designer Bags" on the street know they are fakes.

Also some fakes are made by drug cartels and other crime organizations, thus you may be supporting very bad guys. For tips on how to spot a fake, visit "Parade.com", you'll also find links to the eBay Pay Pal sites that explain your recourse if a purchase turns out to be counterfeit.

> Information from "Parade", "Intelligence Report" by Lyric Wallwork Winik, January 14, 2007, in "The Tribune, San Luis Obispo County, California.

> My thoughts – Now we know, don't support drug cartels by buying fake bags.

Elite Teams Roam the Streets

An elite team of federal scientists are on the streets in the on-going fight against nuclear terrorism. Most Americans do not know this. They hit the streets about every 3 days. This has been happening since the attacks of September 11, 2001.

There are:

A. More than 2 dozen specialized teams.
B. They respond to threats of nuclear terrorism.
C. 2,000 scientists and bomb experts take part.
D. Spending has doubled.
E. A key report known as nuclear forensics is due in February 2008.
F. State sponsors of an attempted nuclear attack could be identified and the United States would be able to retaliate.
G. Scientists fly over cities in special helicopters and airplanes.
H. They are at major sporting events.
I. They have special backpacks that can identify plutonium or highly enriched uranium.
J. These unarmed weapons designers are the last hope of stopping a catastrophic attack if all else fails.
K. They would defuse a bomb.
L. Since 9-11, 26 rapid-response units have been created.
M. If a device is located, 2 other specialized teams would rush to the scene. One from a base in Albuquerque, New Mexico, where a fueled jetliner is on 24-hour alert. Another FBI team would depart from rural Virginia.
N. The teams would attempt to disable the bomb, and then transfer the weapon to the Nevada desert into a G tunnel, a 5,000-foot deep shaft where FBI agents would disassemble the device behind steel blast doors and log the evidence.
O. About 1,000 nuclear weapons scientists and another 500 to 1,000 professionals participate in the effort, but not full time. Terrorists are trying to plant a nuclear device in the United States.

Information from an article by Ralph Vartabedian, the Los Angels Times in "The Tribune", San Luis Obispo County, California, January 6, 2008.

My thoughts – This is great information. It certainly makes one feel less afraid.

278

Santa Ana, California

An **Orange County** Superior Court judge approved a preliminary injunction, November 16, 2007, against more than 220 alleged members of 2 rival gangs, including one in the historic mission town of San Juan Capistrano.

Judge Daniel J. Didier said the terror cannot continue! The injunctions mean that alleged members of the Varrio Viejo and Varrio Chico gangs will be arrested if they are seen associating with one another, wearing gang clothing or making gang hand signs.

> Information from an Associated Press article in "The Tribune", San Luis Obispo County, California, November 17, 2007.

> My thoughts – **Congratulations to the courageous judge!** Why do we have to tolerate gang members in the United States? Why can't we banish evil gangs? Are they illegals? Can they be deported? We need many more gang task force officers to rid our country of gangs. We are not a free country if there are gangs roaming our streets. Help America first! Gangs are the enemies of all of us.

Knick – Knack

The ACLU (American Civil Liberties Union) launched a campaign with the Democratic Congress to demonize the "watch list" of 400,000 people as a Gestapo-like tool of the FBI. The FBI responded.

America is teeming with **20,000 terrorists** says FBI official, Leonard Boyle. Most are foreigners while 5 to 6% are United States citizens or legal residents. Since 9/11 the Justice Department has put more than 440 active terrorists behind bars.

> Information is from "Investor's Business Daily, posted July 25, 2008, IBD editorials.com

TOP

TEN

Is America Still # 1?

The United States remains the most powerful nation in the world. Americans make up less than 5% of the world's population yet leads the world in:

1. Nobel Prize winners – 296.
2. The number of billionaires – 371,worth a reported $1.1 Trillion.
3. The number of Gold Medals – 36, the number of total medals – 102, earned in the most recent summer Olympics.
4. The most roads – 3.98 Million miles.
5. The most airports – 14,858.
6. The most railway tracks – 140,805 miles.
7. More armed forces stationed abroad – 460,000 in 144 countries.
8. The most advanced weapons and equipment in the world.
9. The U.S. spends almost as much on the military as all other nations combined.
10. More deliverable nuclear weapons than anyone else.
11. More Gold reserves $157.88 Billion.
12. Largest national debt - $8.6 Trillion.
13. The largest trade deficit and the largest federal foreign debt - $2.1 Trillion.
14. We spend more money per person on health care a year ($5,700) than any country but we rank 30th in life expectancy for women and 28th for men.
15. We lead the world in the prevalence of obesity.
16. A greater rate of incarceration – 737 per 100,00 people or 2.2 million.
17. Internet users – 205,327,000.
18. The largest gross domestic product - $13.3 Trillion.
19. The U.S. leads all nations in the consumption of oil, using a quarter of the worlds supply.
20. But the U.S. is first in the production of nuclear and geothermal energy.

Information from "Parade", A David Wallechinsky article. He periodically reports on the state of the nation for "Parade." Published January 14, 2007 in "The Tribune", San Luis Obispo County, California.

My thoughts – But how much longer will we remain # 1?

The National Toy Hall of Fame

The National Toy Hall of Fame is in Rochester, New York. Longevity is a key criterion for betting into the all-star lineup. Each toy must not only be widely recognized and foster learning, creativity or discovery through play, but also endure in popularity over multiple generations.

The Easy-Bake Oven and Lionel model trains are the first inductees that need electricity to entertain the tykes. The first Easy-Bake oven showed up in stores in 1964. Lionel trains have been around since 1900.

Her are 36 inductees in the National Toy Hall of Fame:

The All-Star Lineup

1. Easy-Bake Oven
2. Lionel model trains
3. G.I. Joe
4. Crayola Crayons
5. Jacks
6. Monopoly
7. Scrabble
8. Erector Set
9. Etch a Sketch
10. Candyland
11. Silly Putty
12. Jigsaw Puzzle
13. Radio Flyer Wagon
14. Bicycle
15. Duncan Yoyo
16. Alphabet Blocks
17. Slinky
18. Play-Doh
19. Teddy Bear
20. Jump Rope
21. Rocking Horse
22. View-Master
23. Barbie
24. Marbles
25. Lincoln Logs
26. Jack-in-the-B
27. Checkers
28. Mr. Potato Head
29. Roller Skates
30. Cardboard Box
31. Frisbee
32. Lego
33. Tonka Truck
34. Hula Hoop
35. Tinkertoy
36. Raggety Ann

Information from an article by Associated Press, November 11, 2006, published in "The Tribune", San Luis Obispo County, California.

My thoughts – How many of these have you and your children owned and played with? I would say all but 3. Ahhh memories!

Top 10 United States Hot Spots

The top United States Attractions, according to traveler popularity and TripAdvisor:
1. Orlando, Florida (Various places, Sea World is one)
2. Cirque de Soleil, Las Vegas, Nevada
3. Hana Highway, Maui, Hawaii
4. Grand Canyon, Arizona
5. Central Park, New York City, NY
6. Alcatraz, San Francisco, California
7. Top of the Rock Observation Deck, New York City, NY
8. Monterey Bay Aquarium, Monterey, California
9. Bellagio Fountains, Las Vegas, Nevada
10. San Diego Zoo, San Diego, California

Article in "Travel Roundup" in "The Tribune", San Luis Obispo County, California, August 19, 2007.

My thoughts – I've been to all except 2, 7 and 9. We did attend Barbra Streisand's Concert in Las Vegas at the MGM Grand in the early 1990's. The grandchildren really liked the visits to the Monterey Bay Aquarium when we lived in Pebble Beach, California.

Top 10 "On The Boardwalk"

The top 10 American boardwalks:
1. Atlantic City, New Jersey
2. Coney Island, New York
3. Kemah, Texas
4. Mission Beach (San Diego), California
5. Ocean City, Maryland
6. Ocean City, New Jersey
7. Rehoboth Beach, Delaware
8. Santa Cruz, California
9. Venice, California
10. Virginia Beach, Virginia

From "Travel Roundup" in "The Tribune", San Luis Obispo County, California, September 9, 2007, according to www.Shermanstravel.com

My thoughts – I've been to 1, 4, 8, 9, 10, and lived in Venice, California for a short time.

The 10 Best Sports Films

Here is the author's (Tim Wilkin's) choice of the 10 best sports movies ever made. His list is from movies he has seen so that eliminates "Chariots of Fire."

2. "Miracle"

3. "Invincible"

and probably many more.

The best:
1. "Hoosiers" 1986
2. "Eight Men Out" 1988
3. 4. "Cinderella Man" 2005
5. "Caddyshack" 1980
6. "Slapshot" 1977
7. "Rocky"1976
8. "Bill Durham" 1980
9. "Raging Bull" 1980
10. "The Longest Yard" 1974
11. "Seabiscuit" 2003

Article by Tim Wilkin, Albany Times Union, Published in The Tribune, San Luis Obispo County, December 30, 2006.

My thoughts – I agree, "Hoosiers is # 1. I've seen it at least ½ dozen times. I grew up in Indiana.

VEHICLES

How to Select an Auto Repair Shop

1. Verify a repair dealer's license. Go to the Bureau of Automotive Repair web site, www.autorepair.ca.gov and check the license status and possible disciplinary actions.
2. Test a repair shop with a minor maintenance job such as oil change to determine if you're pleased with the work and service.
3. You have the right to have parts that are replaced returned to you, but you must request the parts before the work is done.
4. Select a repair shop before you need one.
5. A state license should be posted in plain view of consumers and a sign should tell consumers their legal rights regarding auto repair.
6. Look for other cars in the shop like yours. Different repair shops will specialize in fixing different makes and models of vehicles, which means they are likely to have specialized experience, training and equipment.
7. A good repair shop should have a neat and well-organized service floor, modern equipment and clearly posted policies regarding labor rates. The shop should also inform you about guarantees and methods of payment.
8. The technicians working on your car and other personnel should be courteous, helpful and willing to answer all your questions.
9. Look for technicians who have professional certifications such as Automotive Service Excellence or other advanced training certificates.
10. Read the owner's manual for your car to find out what the service intervals are and to understand what the gauges and warning lights mean before you take your car in for maintenance or repairs.

Article source: California Bureau of Automotive Repair. Published December 14, 2006 in "The Tribune", San Luis Obispo County, California.

The Good Old Days

25 M.P.G. was the mileage the original Model T Ford achieved in 1908.

Model year 2006 cars and light trucks average 21 M.P.G.
Source: Ford EPA   © CTW Features

Published in The Tribune, San Luis Obispo, California, October 19, 2006, Cars.com.section

My Thoughts – You've come a long way baby for speed, more weight and more comfort and only 4 miles difference for M.P.G.

Hit and Run in San Francisco

Omeed A Popal, 29, of Fremont, California, was arrested after police boxed in his smashed-up black Honda Pilot following a bloody 20-minute spree through San Francisco in which witnesses said Popal intentionally tried to hit pedestrians and bicyclists.

Murder charges will be filed against the man who went on a hit-and-run rampage, using his SUV to kill one pedestrian and injure at least a dozen.

The rampage appeared to have started across San Francisco Bay in Fremont, where investigators believe he hit and killed a 54 year-old man, Stephen Jay Wilson, as he walked home.

> Information from an article, "Northern California – San Francisco", published in "The Tribune", San Luis Obispo County, California August 31, 2006.

> My thoughts – **Is anywhere safe?** Stay alert when you're walking on the sidewalk. Watch the on-coming cars. Pedestrians and bicyclists BEWARE!

Pronounce Porsche, the Car

It's not "porsh."
The word is pronounced with 2 syllables.
It's a family name of Austrian/German origin.
There is no silent e in German.
There is a difference of opinion about the acceptable pronunciation of the 2nd syllable.
Purists say to be accurate, one must say "POREshay" because that's how Germans pronounce an end-of-word e.
In America, it is perfectly acceptable to say "PORE-sha."
If you are in Germany and say "PORE-sha", the reaction will be cold, just don't say "porsh."

> Information from an article by Sharon Peters "Q & A", published in "The Tribune", San Luis Obispo County, California, October 5, 2006.

VICK,

MICHAEL

The Michael Vick Dog Fighting Case

1. Michael Vick is the Atlanta Falcons quarterback.
2. Vick's 3 co-defendants and Vick have been indicted on dog fighting charges in July 2007.
3. The Atlanta Falcons owner is Arthur Blank.
4. Collins Spencer III is a spokesman for Vick's defense team (attorneys).
5. Vick's hometown is Newport News, Virginia.
6. Quanis Phillips of Atlanta is a co-defendant. He agreed to testify against Vick.
7. Purnell Peace of Virginia Beach is a co-defendant and agreed to testify against Vick.
8. Tony Taylor of Hampton, Virginia is a co-defendant and struck a similar deal in July 2007.
9. These 3 defendants have reached plea deals.
10. Vick's co-defendants, Phillips and Peace have said Vick bankrolled gambling on dogfights at Vick's property in rural Surrey County.
11. Vick's dog fighting property is in rural Surrey County, not far from his hometown of Newport News.
12. One of the co-defendants said Vick helped drown or hang dogs that didn't do well, which was Phillips or Peace.

Information from an article of August 20, 2007 titled Richmond, Virginia, in "The Tribune", San Luis Obispo County, California.

My thoughts – These people are villains to do what they have been reported to do to dogs. Dogs are God's gift to humans. They are pets. I get sick when I think of how these people made over 50 or 60 dogs and perhaps many more suffer throughout their lifetimes. How could people be so evil??? I do not want people like this living in the United States! But here they will forever be watched so they cannot make animals suffer again.

Michael Vick's Trial

Sussex, Virginia – Michael Vick's trial has been rescheduled for June 27, 2008; the original date was April 2, 2008. This trial is on state dog fighting charges. The date was suggested by Commonwealth Attorney Gerald Poindexter and Vick's lawyers, who did not attend the hearing.

Information from an Associated Press article in "The Tribune" San Luis Obispo County, California, March 26, 2008.

Whoopi, Rosie and "The View"

New York ------Whoopi Goldberg has replaced Rosie O'Donnell on Barbara Walters' "The View". Whoopi used her first time (9-04-07) to defend Michael Vick. She said that "from where he comes from" IN THE South, dog fighting isn't that unusual. Vick grew up in Newport News, Virginia. He has pleaded guilty to federal dog fighting charges, admitted that he gave money for a dog-fighting ring that operated on his Virginia property and he helped kill 6 or 8 pit bulls.

Co-host Joy Behar asked her "How about dog torture and dog murdering?" as she looked horrified at Whoopi Goldberg. Goldberg replied, for many people, dogs are sport and it took awhile for Vick to realize that he was up against serious charges.

Vick has been suspended indefinitely by the National Football League and will be sentenced on the dog fighting charges in December.

> Information from an article in "The Tribune", San Luis Obispo County, California, September 5, 2007 by Associated Press.

> My thoughts – Whoopi Goldberg has lost me as a viewer when she sympathizes with Michael Vick. I believe he is a disgrace to any team if he ever plays football again. He is a dog torturer if he is proven guilty. I have absolutely no respect for him or anyone like him if he is found guilty. I hope we never see his face again in a newspaper or on TV.

The Brutality of an NFL Player

Michael Vick should go to prison for at least 5 years. I hope he never returns to the football field – ever!

He should have to do 500 hours of community service, at least half spent at animal shelters, under supervision.

He should speak at 100 schools against brutality against animals. He should never be allowed to own an animal.

He should donate at least one million dollars to the animal shelters in Virginia.

> By Carolyn Cavolt, August 2007.

WARS

War in Iraq - $5 to $7 Trillion?

The invasion of Iraq began in March 2003. The Bush administration said the war would be self-financing and rebuilding the nation would cost less than $2 billion!

A new estimate from Nobel Prize-winning economist, Joseph Stiglitz in his new book "The Three Trillion Dollar War" written with Harvard University professor Linda Bilmes, say the wars in Iraq and Afghanistan are very underestimated. "When other factors are added - such as:

      I. Interest on debt

      II. Future borrowing for war expenses

      III. Continued military presence in Iraq

      IV. Lifetime health care and counseling for veterans

They believe that the wars' cost range from **$5 Trillion to $7 Trillion!**

The Bush administration doesn't like these estimates by Stiglitz who is a former chief economist of the World Bank.

      Information from an article by Kevin G. Hall, McClatchy Newspapers in "The Tribune", San Luis Obispo County, California February 28, 2008.

      My thoughts – How could the Bush administration get the total cost so wrong? Theirs was the most underestimated cost of anything I've ever heard about! So what do the citizens do now? Why must we tolerate such stupidity?

Iraq War Toll

Total United States deaths: 4,186

Other Coalition deaths: 306

United States soldiers wounded: 30, 702

Iraqi civilian deaths: 88,610 – 96,719
      Source: www.iraqbodycount.net

      The Associated Press, in "The Tribune", San Luis Obispo County, California, October 25, 2008.

A warning

Indian Wells, Southern California. Senator John Mc Cain warned Republican activists that a United States failure in Iraq would eventually pull America into a "wider and more difficult war" in the troubled region.

"To concede defeat as many leading Democrats now advocate would strengthen al-Qaida, empower Iran and other hostile powers in the Middle East, unleash a full scale civil war in Iraq.... and destabilize the entire region," the Republican presidential candidate said at a Republican convention.

"The consequences would threaten us for years." he added. "It would eventually draw us into a wider and more difficult war that would impose even greater sacrifices on us."

> Information from an article in "The Tribune", San Luis Obispo County, California, September 9, 2007.

> My thoughts – I think he is probably correct. What a mess!

360 in Guantanamo

The Pentagon this weekend, July 17, 2007, sent 16 long-held Guantanamo captives to Saudi Arabia to thin the detainee population.

The Pentagon reported the Guantanamo captive population at approximately 360, which includes 50 Saudis, down from a high of 136 Saudi Citizens. The Afghanis have the largest concentration of captives.

> Information from an article published in "The Tribune", San Luis Obispo County, California, Tuesday, July 17, 2007, Tribune Wire Services.

> My thoughts – 16 less prisoners that we support.

$648 Billion has been spent on the Iraq War.

> Heard on Radio – July 2008

A Select Few

More than a quarter of the youth, age 17 to 24 are qualified for military recruitment in The United States.

Qualified, eligible and available to recruit 15%
Qualified enrolled in college 11%
Medical/physical 39%
Drugs/alcohol 17%
Criminal record 9%
 Dependents 6%
Low aptitude 3%

Source: House Armed Services Committee.

From an article in "The Tribune", San Luis Obispo County, California, Associated Press, August 10, 2007.

World War II Dead By Service

Service	Number Serving	Killed	Percent
Merchant Marine	243,000	9,521	3.9
Marine Corps	669,108	19, 733	2.9
Army	11,268,000	234, 834	2.1
Navy	4,183,466	36,958	.9
Coast Guard	242,093	574	.2
Total	16,576,667	295,790	1.8

Published in an article in "The Tribune," San Luis Obispo County, California, May 28, 2007 Source: www.usmm.org/casualty

Note: The Air Force was part of the Army until 1947.

Sweden Takes Iraqi Refugees

Stockholm, Sweden --------This country of 9.1 million people took in 18,600 Iraqi refugees in 2007. The United States admitted 1,608 Iraqis in 2007. An Iraqi refugee pays more than $15,000 each to people – traffickers to take them to Sweden.

Sweden played no part in the invasion of Iraq by the United States. The United States has pledged to take in 12,000 Iraqi refugees in 2008. The United States gave more than $122 million to Iraq's neighbors to aid refugees.

Sweden's sympathetic attitude and the country's liberal asylum policy is changing. Sweden's migration minister criticized the United States for not doing more. The United Nations estimates 4 million Iraqis have been displaced since 2003 when the United States invaded Iraq. 2 million Iraqis have settled in Syria and Jordon.

A spokeswoman for the United States Department of Homeland Security said the United States had no refugee program out of Iraq until 2007. She said 20% of Iraqi applicants are denied entry for security, medical or other reasons.

Information from an article by Shelley Emling, Cox News Services, February 10, 2008 in "The Tribune", San Luis Obispo County, California.

My thoughts – I hope the United States never goes to war again. Many Iraqis were saved from the brutality of Saddam Hussein and his 2 sons but many thousands have been killed in the war.

WHERE

TO

GO

The Ahwahnee Hotel, Yosemite National Park

On July 16, 1927, the Ahwahnee Hotel opened, a 6-story concrete, stone and steel structure. It has the grandeur of the Yosemite Valley. For 80 years the hotel has given guests a touch of luxury. The picture shows the 3-story dining room with huge wooden beams and floor to ceiling windows. Guests can sit in front of the massive stone fireplace.

During the early 1900s, Stephen Mather, the first director of the National Park Service, ordered a first-class hotel be built in Yosemite National Park to attract people of influence and MONEY. He thought the park service needed influential friends.

Rates begin at $400.00 per night, 559-253-5635; yosemitepark.com.

Information from "Westways", Southern California Lifestyle Magazine, July/August 2007, AAA.com/travel or call AAA Travel office 888-874-7222.

My thoughts – We ate lunch here several years ago, definitely beautiful! I believe Queen Elizabeth was here in the 90s.

Ahwahnee Hotel Dining Room-From Ahwahnee Hotel Photo Gallery

Best Places to Live and Play and Seek Adventure

National Geographic Adventure Magazine, September 2007 issue, includes the following list.

Best wilderness towns-they offer access to forests, canyons, swamps, grasslands, prairies and other wild places.
1. Homer, Alaska
2. Cody, Wyoming
3. Flagstaff, Arizona
4. Valdosta, Georgia
5. Medora, North Dakota
6. Rochester, Minnesota
7. Alexandria, Louisiana
8. Valentine, Nebraska
9. St. George, Utah

Best Small Towns
1. Spearfish, South Dakota
2. Bloomington, Indiana
3. Iowa City, Iowa
4. Northampton, Massachusetts
5. Lynchburg, Pennsylvania
6. Marietta, Ohio
7. Fayetteville, West Virginia
8. Bowling Green, Kentucky
9. Chatsworth, New Jersey
10. Hot Springs, Arkansas
11. Smyrna, Delaware

Best Mountain Towns
1. Bishop, California
2. Gunnison, Colorado
3. Missoula, Montana
4. Hanover, New Hampshire
5. Wenatchee, Washington
6. Hood River, Oregon
7. Boone, North Dakota
8. Jim Thorpe, Pennsylvania
9. Montpelier, Vermont
10. New Paltz, New York

Best Waterfront Towns

1. Waimea, Hawaii
2. Fond du Lac, Wisconsin
3. Newport, Rhode Island
4. Rockland, Maine
5. Mystic, Connecticut
6. Grand Rapids, Michigan
7. Annapolis, Maryland
8. Beaufort, South Carolina
9. Lewiston, Idaho

Article in "The Tribune", San Luis Obispo County, California, "Travel Roundup" August 19, 2007.

My thoughts – Okay, they're listed, go find them.

WORDS

Speaking Differently

1 in 5 people older than 5 spoke a language other than English at home, in 2006, with Spanish being the most common. Hablas espanol?

43% of California residents spoke another language at home; in Los Angeles the number was 53%.

Information from an article in "The Tribune", San Luis Obispo County, California, September 16, 2007 by the New York Times.

How to Improve Your Speech

Heidi Klum, the "Victoria Secret" long-time model and married to Seal, the singer, uses "you know" so many times in her spoken words it is a total turn-off.

Please, Heidi, enroll with a speech teacher. I heard her speak on "Showbiz Tonight", December 9, 2007.

"You know" should be banished from all conversation. If you can't speak without using the annoying "you know" in every sentence – stop talking!

Carolyn Cavolt - January 8, 2008.

You!

Walk in another's path before you speak
You believe you are smart
You know the other person
Give that person a chance
Before you attack with hurtful words!

Carolyn Cavolt – April 2008

Subprime

The American Dialect Society knows how risky home mortgages are these days. "Subprime" was chosen as 2007's Word of the Year by the Society! Runners-up were "Facebook", "Green", Googleganger" and "Waterboarding". Subprime is an adjective that means "a risky or less than ideal loan, mortgage or investment." About 80 members (wordsmiths) spent 2 days deciding.

Information from an Associated Press article in "The Tribune", San Luis Obispo County, California, January 6, 2008.

My thoughts – Subprime is a word that caused problems for millions of people. About 2 million are losing their homes.